Citizen Views of Democracy

in Latin America

Pitt Latin American Series

Billie R. DeWalt, *General Editor*

G. Reid Andrews, Catherine Conaghan,

and Jorge I. Domínguez, *Associate Editors*

Citizen Views of Democracy in Latin America

Edited by Roderic Ai Camp

University of Pittsburgh Press

The survey research for this book was made possible through a generous grant from the William and Flora Hewlett Foundation, and additional support from the Roger Thayer Stone Center for Latin American Studies and the Department of Political Science, Tulane University.

LIBRARY OF CONGRESS CATALOGING-IN-PUBLICATION DATA

Citizen views of democracy in Latin America / edited by Roderic Ai Camp.

    p. cm. — (Pitt Latin American series)

    Includes bibliographical references and index.

    ISBN 0-8229-4154-6 (cloth) — ISBN 0-8229-5756-6 (paper)

    1. Democracy—Mexico—Public opinion. 2. Democracy—Chile—Public opinion. 3. Democracy—Costa Rica—Public opinion. 4. Public opinion—Mexico. 5. Public opinion—Chile. 6. Public opinion—Costa Rica. I. Camp, Roderic Ai. II. Series.

JL1281 .D465 2001

320.98—dc21   2001000363

To the memory of John D. Martz,
colleague and friend

Contents

Part I

Introduction

Chapter 1

Democracy through Latin American Lenses
An Appraisal

Roderic Ai Camp

A decade ago, when I served as a consultant to the Ford Foundation's Bilateral Commission on Mexico, I came to the realization that scholars and the U.S. policy community had little, if any, understanding of the Mexican meaning of democracy. Indeed, I believe that fundamental differences exist between how North Americans view and operationalize the concept of democracy and how Mexicans and other Latin Americans view the same term. When the Bilateral Commission completed its report, the *only* dissenting note in the final document was on this very issue, and the report concluded that "the governments of Mexico and the United States conceived of democracy in different ways, and this is a source of bilateral problems."[1]

Remarkably, the term *democracy,* and how the average Latin American citizen understands it, has not been carefully explored since that report was issued.[2] The failure to do so has potentially tremendous consequences for relations between the United States and Latin America and directly affects individual characteristics of the evolution of democratization and political liberalization in the region.

But how do we determine what democracy is? What does it consist of? It is a fairly straightforward process to determine whether a political model contains certain structural features thought to be associated with democracy, such as competitive elections, the exchange of power between two or more political parties, a division of powers, and so on. Scholars do differ, however, on which features most characteristically define democracy and on the extent, qualitatively speaking, to which they are actually present in any individual society. They disagree even more strongly about preconditions for democracy. For decades, authors have explored numerous variables as possible explanations for the growth of democracy—including structural conditions, such as the level of economic development, or culturally linked characteristics, such as the level of interpersonal trust or support for revolutionary change.[3]

THE PROJECT

How does one go about getting inside the mind of the average Latin American citizen? I believe that, despite many limitations, the most efficacious method for assessing citizen values today is to design a survey research tool—in this case, a questionnaire on democracy, to be administered to a representative sample of respondents from selected countries in the region. The Hewlett Foundation, with additional support from the Roger Thayer Stone Center for Latin American Studies and the Department of Political Science at Tulane University, generously funded this effort in 1998–99. I asked a working group of scholars and experts in survey research in Latin America, as well as country specialists, to meet in early 1998 to formulate a detailed questionnaire.[4]

Because we were interested in measuring changes in citizen views over time, we incorporated into our own survey some questions compiled by Matthew Kenney from earlier polls done in Mexico and Latin America.[5] Specifically, we were interested in possible comparisons with results from the massive, pioneering World Values Survey, a detailed multicountry project administered in 1981, 1990, and 1995; and the Latin American Barometer surveys conducted in the 1990s.

Given the resources available and the desire to capture the broadest possible citizen views of democracy in the region, we chose three countries to survey: Costa Rica, Mexico, and Chile. These three countries were selected for specific reasons.

For decades, Costa Rica has been considered by scholars to be the most "democratic" country in the region, as measured by traditional Western views of democratic institutions and by the fact that genuine competitive elections have characterized its polity for half a century.[6] Recent evidence from the Latin American Barometer poll suggests that Costa Rica stands apart from the remainder of Latin America, with general values more similar to those of Spain—a view that both Mitchell Seligson and Mary Clark support in this volume. Costa Rica, within the Latin American context, might even be thought of as providing a "democratic" political norm.

At the time of the survey in midsummer 1998, Costa Rica continued to enjoy a working democracy. Unlike in Chile or Mexico, political power is more evenly divided among its three branches of government (judicial, legislative, and executive). In recent years, the separation of powers has led to a certain level of disgruntlement with the decision-making process, similar to the gridlock between Congress and the presidency in the second term of the Clinton administration. The most important political change that Costa Ricans witnessed during 1998 was the implementation of new local electoral laws. For the first time, the citizens elected mayors rather than appointing city managers to administer local governments. This change in institutional structure at the local level undoubtedly highlighted Costa Ricans' traditional emphasis on pluralism in government and electoral politics.

Two major parties dominate the national political scene in Costa Rica: the Partido Liberación Nacional (National Liberation Party, or PLN) and the Partido Unidad Social Cristiana (United Social Christian Party, or PUSC). The PUSC, a party that combines a heritage of social reform with neoliberal economic policies, controlled the executive branch at the time of the poll.

Mexico, on the other hand, can be viewed as a country moving, somewhat hesitantly, from an authoritarian to a democratic model.[7] Moreover, its proximity to the United States makes it an interesting case for examining the level of cultural influences from its prominent neighbor. Of the three countries, it has made the fewest strides institutionally toward democracy. In the summer of 1998, Mexico had recently emerged from a severe economic recession that began abruptly in early 1995. Politically, it was at one of its most divided points in recent history.

The dominant party, the Institutional Revolutionary Party (PRI), in 1997 lost control of the lower chamber of congress to a coalition of opposition parties whose members came primarily from the National Action Party (PAN) and the Party of the Democratic Revolution (PRD). Mexicans, therefore, were experiencing firsthand the typical conflicts that occur when executive and legislative branches are controlled by opposing parties. Mexicans were also anticipating considerable future political changes, as the three leading parties contemplated additional electoral reforms—including implementing new primaries for electing presidential candidates within their own organizations, in anticipation of the presidential nomination process in 1999 and the actual race in 2000.

Finally, Chile was included because it was thought to have made the transition to a democratic political model prior to 1973, but suffered through two decades of extreme political repression and authoritarianism after a violent military coup d'état. Yet in spite of these intense authoritarian experiences, it appears to have achieved a rapid democratic transition in the 1990s. In its general cultural variables, however, it continues to rank at the extreme authoritarian end of Latin American cases.

Chile provides an excellent test case of the challenge between democratic and authoritarian influences, of a generation sharing two extreme political experiences, and of the degree to which democratic or authoritarian preferences might persist in an altered political environment. At the time of the survey, Chile was characterized by an electorate in which the centrists, ideologically speaking, accounted for nearly half the population, compared to only a fourth in 1973, at the time of the military coup.

The Chileans were governed in 1998 by Eduardo Frei, a Christian Democrat whose family boasts a long political history in Chile; he was their second elected president since General Augusto Pinochet was rejected in 1988. Nevertheless, the armed forces remained deeply entrenched in the governing process and, through conservative allies, were continuing to thwart constitutional reforms. The legacies of militarism and authoritarianism remain institutionalized and visible despite Chile's significant democratic achievements immediately prior to 1998. The electorate also remains polarized on important issues, including whether or not Pinochet himself should be tried in Spain for alleged crimes against humanity.

After we commissioned a pilot survey of the three countries in March 1998 by MORI International, of Princeton, New Jersey, and presented our initial findings at the David Rockefeller Center for Latin American Studies at Harvard University in May, a final survey instrument emerged. The questionnaire consisted of 43 questions, administered to 3,396 respondents in the three countries in July 1998 (see appendix 2). MORI International made the final results of the survey available in September 1998, and an international group of scholars met at Tulane University in January 1999 to analyze the data.

The results of the Tulane conference and a subsequent one at the University of California, San Diego, in November 1999 are presented here, heavily revised. In mid-March 1999, I commissioned MORI International to include seven of the basic questions focusing on conceptualizing democracy in a *Wall Street Journal* survey of Hispanics and non-Hispanics in the United States. Those data provide the first-ever comparable responses on conceptualizing democracy among non-Hispanic Americans, Hispanic Americans, and Latin Americans.

All of the data from the 1998 Hewlett survey are available to the reader on a CD-ROM included with this book. The contributors to this project believe that the data should be disseminated to the widest possible audience, and that the material should be available in a clear, easy-to-use format. Anyone familiar with a computer can easily use the graphics program on the CD-ROM. This program, designed by the Roper Center at the University of Connecticut, allows the reader to cross-tabulate any of the variables in the survey in a variety of traditional graphic presentations, including pie charts and bar graphs.

Each reader can explore many relationships between or among the 43 variables in the three countries, of which only selected variables have been analyzed in the following chapters. To our knowledge, this is the first time that survey data on Latin America generally, not to mention on democratic values in Latin America, have been made available directly to readers in CD-ROM format. Readers with more sophisticated statistical skills may also obtain the raw data set from Global Quality Research, Princeton, New Jersey.

CITIZEN VIEWS OF DEMOCRACY: SOME THEORETICAL ISSUES

This book addresses three interrelated questions. First, is it possible to offer some hypotheses about why certain variables, individually or in combination, are most influential in explaining citizen views of democracy in Latin America? The second task, based on the assumption that citizens within and from different societies offer heterogeneous definitions of democracy, is to identify how these citizens actually conceptualize democracy. For example, do they equate democracy with liberty, or is social justice uppermost in their perceptions? In short, what are the most important conceptualizations that emerge from Latin American definitions of democracy? Third, does how a person conceptualizes democracy have any consequences for their other perceptions, and do these consequences have potential effects on social, political, and economic behavior?

In addressing these three questions, it is impossible to avoid a significant, complex theoretical debate in the democratization literature: the interaction between culture and democratic behavior. The reason is simply that values and attitudes are integral to the most widely used definitions of culture. Since we have chosen to explore citizen attitudes through a survey research methodology that poses questions about Latin Americans' values, we have naturally entered the realm of political culture.[8]

Culture typically consists of those attitudes, values, beliefs, ideals, and experiences that predominate in a given society.[9] Political culture consists of the same components but focuses on how those values are translated into people's views of politics, their assessment of political systems, and their own role in the polity.[10] At least three relevant questions about culture and its relationship to democratic governance come to mind.

The major, controversial question about the relationship between culture and politics is how culture generally and political culture specifically affect attitudes toward democracy, and whether these attitudes in turn encourage and sustain democratic behavior broadly in a society. Ronald Inglehart's work provides empirical support for this argument. The reverse proposition is equally challenging: To what degree does the existence and practice of democracy actually contribute to certain cultural values and attitudes? Mitchell Seligson and Edward Muller, who found evidence of this relationship, cogently summarize the debate:

> If Inglehart's causal inferences are valid, explanations of democratization that emphasize political culture attitudes must be given primacy over explanations that emphasize the importance of macro socioeconomic conditions. The problem is that the possibility of an effect of years of continuous democracy on civic culture is ignored. A proponent of the alternative hypothesis that democracy causes civic culture attitudes could reasonably argue that the supposed "effect" of civic culture on democracy is really an effect of democracy on civic culture.[11]

Finally, if a relationship does exist between culture and the democratic model, can culture explain the specific characteristics of democracy in one society compared to another?

These three questions have provoked controversy in the social sciences for decades.[12] The controversy emerged from the argument that the existence of a civic culture characterized by citizen values conducive to democracy fostered democratic institutions and political pluralism.[13] For example, some scholars have argued that the degree to which citizens were involved in family decision-making as children directly affects their support for authoritarian or nonauthoritarian political models as adults. In other words, citizens learn behavioral norms from other experiences that are translated into their adult political behavior.

This potential relationship between experiences and values depends on a general process referred to as socialization. Socialization takes place through many agents and experiences that determine how certain values are learned.[14] Students of socialization typically have identified such important agents as family, school, and friends. Indirectly, one of the fundamental issues explored in this book is how these values are learned. However, the difficulty in examining the relationship between culture and democratic political beliefs is that culture is so all-encompassing that it is challenging, if not impossible, to determine any causal relationships between specific cultural variables and democratic attitudes.[15] To illustrate this dilemma, one only has to ask the question, Do democratic institutions produce citizens with democratic values, or do citizens with democratic values, who are a product of general cultural values, produce democratic institutions?[16]

Briefly, what can we say about the question of democracy? Some scholars, including Kenneth Bollen and Paul Cammack, warn against conceptualizing democracy as the achievement of certain political principles and confusing political with social definitions of democracy.[17] Yet it may well be that individual citizens of their own volition define democracy in nonpolitical terms. At the outset, it should be made clear that neither the United States, nor any other long-standing Western-style democracy, can lay exclusive claim to defining the meaning of "democracy."

Most of the recent theory on conceptualizing the definition of a functioning democracy is offered by scholars from postindustrial societies. A perusal of the traditional literature reveals a consensus on such classic components as respect for the rule of law, civil liberties, accountability of the governors, competitive elections, etc. But theorists who have come at the question from a Third World or Latin American perspective add some significant components not found in the North American literature.[18] The analyst who comes closest to the Latin American conception of this ambiguous term is Valerie Bunce, who, in addition to the usual list of democratic principles that most theorists include, incorporates the dispersion of economic resources as a fundamental ingredient.[19]

Unlike most of the recent research on democratization, our data do not primarily measure scholars' assessments, regardless of the variables evaluated, of whether a country is more or less democratic or whether democracy has existed longer in country X compared to country Y. Instead, much of the research presented here allows citizens to speak for themselves, rather than selecting some variables that a priori are thought to measure the presence of democracy. It focuses on citizens' views of what kind of democracy exists in their society, whether they believe that a democratic model is actually functioning in their country, and what their expectations are from democracy.

The data from our survey clearly support the view that most Latin Americans do not conceptualize democracy in the same way as do North American theorists or citizens. Furthermore, the vast majority of Latin Americans do not have the same expectations *from* democracy as do their North American counterparts. It seems probable, given their responses, that some type of relationship exists between how citizens conceptualize democracy and what they expect from democracy as a functioning political model. Finally, what most distinguishes the Latin American version of democracy from that of the United States is its emphasis on social and economic equality and progress.

The findings from these survey data have major implications for understanding the potential success and permanence of the wave of political liberalization that has swept through the region since the late 1980s, part of a well-documented, generalized global trend.[20] Obtaining a deeper and more thorough understanding of what democracy means to the average citizen in the three Latin American countries we surveyed sheds considerable light on the difficulties of fully implementing democratization beyond establishing simple electoral structures.

The present survey data may also explain more fully the degree to which democracy's success in Latin America relies on structural conditions and institutions (for example, the separation of powers) or on deeply held values, and whether important citizen values contradict or facilitate democratic goals. These findings not only will be valuable for assessing and understanding political developments within individual countries and the region as a whole, but may have significant implications in informing the U.S. foreign policy community's understanding of Latin American democratization. For example, one of the most important issues in the present bilateral relationship between Mexico and the United States is the pace, direction, and content of Mexico's political liberalization.

The conceptualization of democracy also has implications for economic development and the acceptance of certain types of economic behavior, as Kenneth Coleman suggests in his essay. Many analysts identify a strong linkage between economic and political liberalization.[21] However, this linkage encounters a conundrum similar to that of the democracy–culture connection: the direction of the causal relationship. If a relationship does indeed exist, then strongly held democratic values, depending on what those values might be, may offer important insights into a culture's receptivity to certain economic behaviors and its desire to practice them.[22]

It can be hypothesized that the issue of social inequality, one of the major stumbling blocks to a more equitable and successful pattern of economic growth in Latin America, is linked to values that have some explanatory power for understanding political—specifically, democratic—behavior. According to Marta Lagos, Latin American citizens from eight countries (including Chile and Mexico), given unsatisfactory economic conditions (from their point of view), are demanding that democracy perform more efficiently in accelerating economic growth. Indeed, her research unquestionably suggests that the implementation of democratic institutions in the region has raised citizens' economic expectations.[23]

The purpose of this book is not to suggest that cultural values, in this case values related to democracy, explain political behavior. There are many variables that lead to differing political processes and behavior, of which culture—specifically, political culture—is just one. Furthermore, this volume does not in any way settle the theoretical or empirical debates about the relationship between culture and democracy.

This project suggests first and foremost that although many Latin American citizens remain desirous of democracy and have erected formal democratic institutions, they may actually conceive of democracy in entirely different ways from each other and, even more likely, from their U.S. counterparts. Moreover, their conceptualizations may affect other political attitudes and behaviors, and possibly the efficacy of traditional Western democratic institutions. Ronald Inglehart and Marita Carballo unquestionably established that Latin America—culturally speaking, from a perspective of specific, basic values—is a region apart from other groups of societies, including such clusters as South Asia, Northern Europe, Africa, Eastern Europe, and even Catholic Europe.[24]

It is probable that some type of linkage exists between how citizens define democracy and their practice of and support for democratic institutions over the long run; some of the authors in this volume consider this potential relationship. Others explore the possible existence of a relationship between democratic values and selected economic policy preferences in the region. Finally, this book proposes to identify what variables, if any, are the most important ones that might be linked to Latin American conceptualizations of democracy—thus, it is hoped, contributing to future theory and explorations of the issues raised.

The first cross-country survey research that argued that an empirical connection existed between political culture and political behavior was Gabriel A. Almond and Sidney Verba's now-classic *The Civic Culture*, which examined five countries in 1959, including Mexico. The authors specifically searched for a causal link between cultural attitudes and a proclivity for democratic behavior. The difficulties of establishing such a linkage have been fully explored by theorists such as Arend Lijphart.[25]

Almond and Verba's survey instrument contained serious methodological limitations and weaknesses, but it demonstrated that Mexican citizens could not be characterized as either completely authoritarian or democratic in their underlying values but instead offered a mixture of beliefs that were thought to both support and contradict democratic practices. Unfortunately, comparable data are not available for Chile and Costa Rica from this period. Today, four decades after that survey was completed, what values and experiences do the citizens in these three countries share, and how do they conceive of their respective "civic" cultures?

In his analysis of democracy and mass belief systems in Latin America, Alejandro Moreno provides a balanced and well-reasoned argument. He has focused specifically on issues related to how Latin Americans view democracy, how they view themselves as democrats, and the consequences of their "democratic" views. One of the most interesting aspects he focuses on in his contribution to this volume is the level of support for democracy among, respectively, "democrats" and "authoritarians."

One of the variables he discovers that exerts a marked influence on democratic attitudes is class, which he conceptualizes with the available survey data as consisting of distinctions in occupation, income, and education. "The higher the income level and the higher the education level, the more pro-democratic the individual is. Moreover, the gap between the highest and the lowest income levels is significantly greater than the gap between the highest and the lowest education levels. In other words, income seems more important than education in explaining the variance in support for democracy. Occupation is a variable that reflects the effects of both income and education." Moreno further argues that these conclusions call into question previous evidence in studies of Latin American political culture that have minimized the impact of class as a variable in citizens' support for democratic values and institutions.

When Moreno breaks down citizens' responses by the degree to which they support democratic versus antidemocratic values, he discovers significant differences in their political expectations. For example, 26 percent of Costa Ricans professing democratic preferences view elections as the main task of democracy. But among Costa Ricans who prefer an authoritarian alternative, only 11 percent consider elections to be democracy's primary task. Similar response patterns, although not as extreme, occur in both Chile and Mexico.

The country that best represents the potential linkage between culture and its political model (in this case democracy), regardless of the direction of the relationship, is Costa Rica. As Mary Clark argues in her essay, Costa Rica stands out not only as the region's oldest democracy, but as a country in which the political system rests on a unique political culture.[26]

Costa Ricans' support for democratic institutions, in spite of substantially lower levels of satisfaction with the way they are functioning, is reflected in the universality of their preference for democracy. Fully 80 percent (84 percent if those who did not answer are excluded) of Costa Ricans preferred democracy to any other form of government. When this preference was measured by such standard background variables as gender, age, education, income, residence, and ethnicity, the variation in response was quite small, suggesting remarkable uniformity in support.

The lowest preference for democracy was among small-town Costa Ricans, of whom only 73 percent preferred democracy. The strongest support was among black Costa Ricans, of whom 88 percent preferred this political model. As Clark concludes, "Considering that about half the citizens of this Central American nation continue to live in the countryside and that black people are a distinct ethnic and cultural minority in

Costa Rica, these findings bode particularly well for the breadth of support for and satisfaction with democracy there."

According to Clark, one of the most impressive findings of the Hewlett survey among Costa Ricans is their level of participation in such social institutions as the family, schools, and the workplace. What is extraordinary is that 51 percent said their parents often or always allowed the children to participate in family decisions. Clark concluded that high scores on measures of social participation "seem to indicate that Costa Ricans' upbringing prepares them for citizenship in a democratic society."

Such familial participation levels have been thought to be supportive of participatory principles in a wider, sociopolitical arena. In fact, family participation was one of the original variables tested in *The Civic Culture*. However, instead of providing strong support for the view that a crucial socializing experience such as family decision-making helps to explain a proclivity toward democratic political practices, our research raises major questions about the theoretical linkage between culture and democracy, a theme that Gabriel Almond himself revisited in 1980.[27]

Given the longevity and depth of the democratic experience in the United States, it would be expected that citizens should recall high levels of participation in family decision-making, which was indeed the case in the 1959 *Civic Culture* survey. Remarkably, however, in the March 1999 collaborative *Wall Street Journal* poll, only 38 percent of non-Hispanic U.S. respondents recalled similar experiences. How is it possible that Costa Ricans participated at significantly higher levels in family decisions than North Americans, and what does this say about the culture–democracy linkage?

Some possible answers emerge. If a relationship between cultural values generally and democracy specifically does exist, then pluralism in family decision-making may be important to *building* democratic political behavior but not necessarily to *sustaining* it. Second, if a functioning democracy produces participatory behavior in other social institutions of society, including the family, then perhaps democracy's newness produces a stronger, more immediate influence; the *Civic Culture* survey was done only a decade after the establishment of democratic institutions in Costa Rica, but more than a century and a half after their beginning in the United States. Third, substantial differences in family structure may exist between the two cultures, and therefore the responses to the question may not be comparable. Some empirical evidence exists, however, that suggests that Mexican children raised in an authoritarian family environment are more supportive of authoritarian political behavior compared to children who do not share those experiences.[28]

A second important contradiction emerges in the Costa Rican data. Interpersonal trust has long been considered to be an important indicator of the potential for citizens to function in a democratic polity.[29] Indeed, Ronald Inglehart, who helped design our survey, found interpersonal trust to be an important variable linked to stable democracies in broad, multicountry studies.[30] Contrary to expectations, Clark discovered that Costa Ricans are highly distrustful of others; yet despite low levels of trust, they prefer compromise and negotiation to conflict. Seligson also initially found no relationship between trust and a preference for democracy, contradicting Robert Putnam's recent important work on Italy.[31] However, when Seligson conducted a multivariate analysis of the data and removed the nationality variable, he discovered that interpersonal trust does become an important, statistically significant variable among several other influential variables.

It is very difficult to explain this contradiction. Again, it may be that high levels of political trust are more significant in initiating and sustaining a democratic process in the beginning phases. On the other hand, it may be that the question used in the survey to measure trust is far too narrow. Timothy Power and Mary Clark demonstrate that a sense of civic responsibility—or what Putnam labeled social capital, a combination of several variables—provides a more accurate appraisal of citizens' trust.[32]

The issue of interpersonal trust is raised dramatically, but with contrasting findings, in the data on Mexico. According to Matthew Kenney's analysis, one of the most salient changes that has taken place in citizen values over time is a rise in interpersonal trust. In the 1998 Hewlett data, 44 percent of Mexicans believed that other individuals could be trusted, a figure comparable to that for the United States and Canada in the 1990s. In 1991, only 31 percent of Mexicans thought people could be trusted. A decade earlier, in 1980, only 17 percent of Mexico's citizens expressed such an opinion.

These figures over 20 years indicate a strong and steady increase in interpersonal trust. As Kenney suggests, it is difficult to attribute this trend to specific causal variables, at least any available to us from the present survey data. What he did discover, not surprisingly, is that Mexicans who are most satisfied with democracy are nearly twice as likely to trust in others.

What explains this pattern in Mexico? As Mexicans move from an authoritarian to a democratic polity, they have become more trusting, in spite of numerous tensions. One explanation, in addition to those mentioned previously, is that during the initial stages of such a transition, increasing trust is a response to increased accountability. Kenney's own argument is that perhaps "Mexicans are coming to realize that they can no longer expect the state to solve the country's problems and that they must instead turn to one another." There is some anecdotal evidence to support this view. In response to the devastating earthquake in Mexico City in 1985, residents ignored government incompetence and instead spontaneously organized rescue efforts to save family, neighbors, and strangers alike.[33] As a result of this collaboration, the earthquake produced a flowering of politically oriented groups and nongovernmental organizations.[34]

Joseph Klesner also discovers that the level of interpersonal trust among Mexicans and Chileans appears to be linked to whether authoritarian or democratic models of government are preferred. For example, citizens who are distrustful or depoliticized tend to be more inclined to be dissatisfied with democracy and to prefer nondemocratic regimes. As Klesner concludes, "[s]ome segments of the population of each country remain antidemocratic in profound ways. . . . they can produce strains in democratic practice and test the tolerance of those who are profoundly democratic in their values. This is a challenge that both Chile and Mexico will face in the years to come."

Klesner believes, however, that specific characteristics of the recent authoritarian regimes in Mexico and Chile shaped citizens' attitudes within the evolving context of greater pluralism in their respective polities. He suggests that Mexicans and Chileans had distinct experiences in the 1970s and 1980s and that the Chileans' experiences contributed to a situation in which, in response to severe repression under the Pinochet dictatorship and extreme ideological divisions, they display high levels of distrust in their fellow citizens and emerged in the 1990s as "depoliticized." This response is illustrated by the fact that many Chileans express little sympathy for any political party, nor do they vote. Mexicans, on the other hand, are characterized by Klesner as demonstrating higher levels of trust, corresponding to findings in the essays by Kenney and by Frederick Turner and Carlos Elordi; but Mexicans lack confidence in the political institutions—parties, the government, and congress—that have ignored or abused their interests.

A LATIN AMERICAN DEMOCRACY?

The second issue on which we hoped to shed some light is how Latin Americans actually conceptualize democracy. The findings on this issue are more straightforward than those on the linkage between culture and democracy; nevertheless, they are equally remarkable. The data suggest three fundamental findings. First, among Latin Americans there is no consensus on what democracy means. Second, only Costa Ricans see democracy in largely political terms, very similar in content to the view professed by North Americans. Third, the Mexicans and Chileans, who are likely to be more representative of Latin Americans from other countries, view democracy in social and economic, not political, terms.

The Costa Rican response to defining democracy rests on one basic value: liberty. Over half of the respondents chose to define democracy as liberty (see table 1). Only a fifth of Mexicans view democracy as liberty, the same percentage as those who view it as equality. Indeed, sizeable remaining percentages of Mexicans identify democracy as voting, progress, form of government, or respect. Chileans respond to the question in figures closely approximating those for Mexicans. As some of the contributors to this volume illustrate in their essays, Costa Ricans' conceptualization of democracy sets them apart.

It is interesting that Costa Ricans' responses in conceptualizing democracy are very similar to those of Americans, much closer than to Chilean or Mexican attitudes. Costa Ricans also prefer democracy over other forms of government in much higher percentages than Chileans or Mexicans. For several of the contributors, the fundamental question becomes why the Costa Ricans favor democracy so much more strongly than do Chileans or Mexicans.

To explain what he describes as "Costa Rican exceptionalism," Mitchell Seligson examines some important variables that democratic theorists traditionally have thought to be associated with democracy. He first analyzes selected variables individually. He explores level of social tolerance, for example, and discovers that it does not offer much insight into why Costa Ricans strongly support a democratic polity. When he moves on to accountability, he does find a potential linkage with Costa Rican democratic preferences, but the Hewlett survey lacks sufficient additional questions to test this relationship fully.

To provide a more sophisticated analysis of what might explain the respective importance of different variables for Costa Rican exceptionalism, Seligson resorts to multivariate analysis of the data in which a preference for democracy is the dependent variable, while he sorts through independent variables collectively to determine if a significant relationship exists. His statistical analysis leads to several important conclusions. In the first place, one's nationality becomes extremely influential in determining a preference for democracy. As Seligson argues, "the overwhelming explanatory factor is being a Costa Rican, versus being a Chilean or a Mexican." This finding is limited in value, however, because the important question remains, What variables produce these national differences?

The data from the March 1999 *Wall Street Journal* poll, in combination with the July 1998 Hewlett survey results, illustrate the differences in citizens' expectations from

TABLE 1 *Citizen Views of Democracy in Latin America and the United States*
(percent)

Question: In one word, could you tell me what democracy means to you?	Chile	Costa Rica	Mexico	United States
Liberty/Freedom	25	54	21	68
Equality	18	6	21	5
Voting/Elections	10	3	12	2
Form of Government	12	6	14	2
Welfare/Progress	8	7	14	1
Respect/Rule of Law	10	3	13	1
Don't Know/No Answer	8	13	3	12
Other	8	7	2	9

Sample: N=3,396, Latin American columns, *N*=1,659, United States column.

democracy among the four countries (see table 2). Not only do Costa Ricans, Chileans, and Mexicans have different conceptions *of* democracy, but they also have different expectations *from* democracy. It is apparent that how they define democracy, attributing greater importance to equality, influences what they expect from democracy. In fact, citizens in all three Latin American countries might be said to expect greater equality in economic terms, given their emphasis on progress. While most Latin Americans define their democratic expectations in the socioeconomic terms of equality and progress (which together account for 37 to 54 percent of the responses), only 18 percent of Americans share such expectations.

Americans, on the other hand, define their expectations overwhelmingly in political terms, half (48 percent) desirous of liberty/freedom. The difference between the United States and Latin America is again supported by the fact that only 34 percent of Hispanics in the United States identified liberty as their most important expectation, exactly midway between the figure for non-Hispanic Americans and the average for the

TABLE 2 *What Latin American and U.S. Citizens Expect from Democracy*
(percent)

In one word, could you tell me what you expect from democracy?	United States	Mexico	Costa Rica	Chile
Liberty/freedom	48	16	27	15
Equality	15	30	14	27
Progress	3	24	23	25
Voting/elections	2	10	2	6
Culture of law/respect	4	14	7	15
Other	15	4	9	7
No answer/Didn't know	14	3	18	4

Sample: N = 3,396, Latin American columns; *N* = 1,659, U.S. column.

three Latin American countries (19 percent). As might be expected, Costa Ricans come closest to the U.S. response, having much higher expectations of liberty and much lower expectations of equality than do Chileans and Mexicans.

As the data in table 2 suggest, differing perceptions of democracy do have consequences for the public's expectations and attitudes about government. One of the contributors to this volume, Kenneth Coleman, focuses on how such beliefs affect Latin American attitudes toward public ownership, a central issue in the neoliberal economic transformation of the region in the 1990s.

It should not be surprising that U.S. and Latin American citizens would differ in their views on whether certain services should be provided by the public or the private sector. Given the antigovernment rhetoric prevalent in the United States, especially in the last two decades, Americans could be expected to be more likely to favor private ownership of most services. Coleman found this to be the case, but his more important discovery is that substantial differences existed among the three Latin American countries, and that age and religious beliefs influenced these economic policy concerns.

With respect to variables more directly related to democracy, Coleman finds that "[t]hose who believe that 'democracy is working well' are likely to endorse the private provision of services—perhaps because the neoliberal thrust of public policy in the 1990s is toward privatization." Most importantly, perhaps, Coleman concludes that "[w]ith respect to the relationship between democracy and markets, there appear potentially to be two Latin American political cultures." He discovers, for example, that Mexicans have evolved views on this issue that seem closer to those found in the United States, and he speculates that geographic proximity—a variable considered below in my analysis of socializing agents—may have played a role. Among his more significant findings is that little correspondence exists between democratic systems and support for a market economy when measured by views on public versus private ownership, suggesting that this relationship, from the point of view of the citizenry, is at best tenuous.

SOCIALIZATION

One of the most important underlying issues related to specific political orientations, democratic or nondemocratic, is how those orientations are learned and what agents determine their composition. In fact, we do not know very much about adult socialization or what sources contribute most significantly to altering the views and attitudes of individuals beyond their childhood and adolescent years, the period most scholars consider to have the greatest impact.[35] The most comprehensive examination of adult behavior over time is Theodore Newcomb's classic multidecade survey, which

TABLE 3 *Hispanic Conceptualizations of Democracy Based on Time Spent in the United States* (percent)

In one word, could you tell me what democracy means to you?	Latin American	Years Lived in the United States			Non-Hispanic
		1–5	6–10	10+	
Liberty/freedom	32	42	48	54	68

Sample: N = 3,396, Latin American column; *N* = 1,659, U.S. columns (an oversample of 502 Americans of Hispanic origin were interviewed).

concluded that existing attitudes may be maintained by creating environments that block new information, or supportive environments that reinforce an individual's initial point of view.[36] Some of the agents known to be important in molding values include geographic origins, family, influential events, occupation, and education.

The data from both of the surveys demonstrate for the first time, with great clarity, the impact of adult socialization on the conceptualization of democracy. If respondents to the question about defining democracy in our *Wall Street Journal* poll are controlled according to the number of years they have resided in the United States, a linear trend moving from the Latin American conception (Chileans, Mexicans, and Costa Ricans) to the Hispanic conception (Latin Americans living in the United States) to the American conception is apparent (see table 3).

About half of the Hispanics in the United States chose to define democracy as liberty, followed by only 8 percent favoring equality. Since the Chilean response in the 1998 Hewlett survey closely approximates that of the Mexicans, this might well suggest that Latin Americans who migrate to the United States, after residing there for even relatively short periods of time, begin to shed their specific national biases toward the meaning of democracy and reconceptualize it to correspond with interpretations shared by the majority of non-Hispanic Americans.

This pattern corresponds to the results of a socialization study of elite Americans, whose author concluded that "[a]lmost no attitudes were related to the number of generations an elite respondent's family had been in the United States. . . . The socialization process occurs very quickly, within one generation."[37] The Hewlett data also might suggest that experiential processes, such as living, working, and being educated in the United States, affect basic adult political socialization, including conceptualizing democracy.

Mexico is one of the most interesting countries from which to draw data on socialization. Considering Mexico's physical proximity to the United States, the foremost representative of democratic political institutions internationally (whether that status is deserved or not), it would be fascinating to explore interactions between the two distinct political cultures. It is apparent from my own research that since the 1970s, elite Mexicans from all fields have been socialized by international influences from North America both within Mexico and in the United States. Among the most important of those agents are higher education and being raised in northern Mexico, in close proximity to the U.S. border.[38]

Frederick Turner and Carlos Elordi attempt this comparative task here, using all three World Values Surveys to answer the question, Do Mexico and the United States represent two distinct political cultures? The authors, citing previous studies of Mexican and U.S. political cultures, note that Mexico has never been a totally "authoritarian" culture.[39] Indeed, they argue that an early study by John Booth and Mitchell Seligson suggested that Mexicans held some democratic values, but that these values did not appear to influence the country's semiauthoritarian governmental structures.[40] It could also be the case, however, that even if a causal relationship were to exist, democratic values would not necessarily have the same causal impact on the evolution of government structures as in the United States, since Mexicans conceptualize democracy quite differently from Americans. Moreover, an argument could be made that history, day-to-day practices, and existing governmental structures, all of which reinforce culture, leaned strongly in favor of an authoritarian orientation, strengthening that posture vis-à-vis shared democratic attitudes.

The authors discover that the political values in the two countries, gauged by traditional measures, are distinct. For example, they find much stronger support for military rule or for an authoritarian leader in Mexico than is the case in the United States. Both of these variables suggest more authoritarian leanings on the part of the citizenry. On the other hand, they find dramatic similarities among other responses, similarities they did not expect to encounter. For example, "[b]etween half and three-quarters of the population of both nations supports gradual reform as opposed to either radical reform or defense of the status quo, and this orientation is fundamental to the initiation and maintenance of democratic institutions." The survey also found that in 1998, the level of satisfaction with the functioning of democracy was only somewhat higher in the United States than in Mexico.

There is no question that different historical experiences influence citizen views. But it is equally true that turbulent political times can produce formative socializing patterns within a society, both across a generation and between generations. In his analysis of citizen views in Chile, Louis Goodman stresses the importance of the extreme political changes that have occurred since 1973, when Chile's democratically elected socialist government was overthrown in a violent coup d'état, followed by a repressive military government. Chile has been characterized by an extremely divided polity for 150 years, and Goodman suggests that during the country's democratic history, the centrist party typically formed alliances with the left or right to hold the system together.[41]

This historical context and Chile's intense recent political experience with alternatives on the extreme right and left have produced, in Goodman's view, a divided citizenry. He argues that the survey data support the interpretation that many of Chile's voters are alienated and remain fearful that politicians will plunge the political system back into the dark experiences of the 1970s. He believes Chilean political fears are a recent phenomenon, attributing them to "the extreme trauma experienced by Chileans of all political persuasions during the turbulent Allende years and then during the extremely repressive government headed by Augusto Pinochet."

In Latin America, one of the most influential background variables, about which very little is known cross-nationally, is race. In the Hewlett project, the individual interviewer was asked to categorize respondents on the basis of skin color, which would correspond to citizens of European, dark mestizo, and light mestizo origin. Admittedly, as our contributors point out, the interviewer relied on subjective judgments when making these distinctions, and indigenous people were not interviewed. Mary Clark makes brief reference to this variable in her analysis of Costa Rica, but Miguel Basáñez and Pablo Parás explore it as the central focus of their chapter.

Keeping the aforementioned limitations in mind, race as a determinant of political and economic attitudes across Latin America may be one of the most influential variables. A typical background variable, income—which Moreno shows to be influential across the region—is less significant than racial heritage. For example, when the authors examined level of satisfaction with democracy according to a respondent's racial mixture, controlling for income, they discovered extreme variations in citizen support. The most marked differences were among Costa Ricans and Chileans.

A CONTRARIAN APPROACH TO DEMOCRACY AND CULTURE

To approach a project as comprehensive as this while attempting to maintain a degree of intellectual integrity, it is helpful to be challenged by a doubting Thomas. To this end, I asked Alan Knight, the distinguished English historian of Latin America, to take his knowledge of Mexico and appraise our efforts as social scientists with his skeptical historian's eye. My request placed him in a difficult position among his fellow collaborators, but he raises many penetrating, critical questions about culture and value surveys with humor and grace.

One of the most important points Knight makes is that a strong tendency exists among social scientists (and often historians) to reach broad conclusions about a country's citizenry and to skip over penetrating, local differences. In short, Knight is highly suspicious of characterizing countries as having a meaningful, broad, national culture. His criticisms are well-founded. Survey research is inherently limited in this regard because only so many distinctions can be made within a single demographic variable in order to quantitatively cross-tabulate that variable with another. For example, national surveys rarely have adequate data to compare societal views city by city, let alone state by state.

To illustrate, researchers in both the United States and Latin America have long considered religious affiliation as an essential background variable, highly useful in denoting differing political attitudes and behavior. Yet recent research in the United States suggests that an individual's specific, local religious community produces far more influential consequences on religious and secular behavior and beliefs than whether the respondent is Catholic, Protestant, Evangelical Protestant, or some other denomination.[42] The findings by Basáñez and Parás also demonstrate that on some values, more than one Chile or Mexico exists.

Knight also offers a healthy dose of skepticism about survey research methodology, which one would expect from any good historian. He notes, for example, that a survey that proposes to compare three countries might well run into linguistic differences in posing specific questions. He even argues that the questions themselves may not measure what they are designed to measure.

The Hewlett working group, which included experts in polling methodology and language usage in the three countries, addressed these very issues and spent much time eliminating certain problems, including the use of different words to ask the same question. Naturally, differing interpretations exist. We cannot reasonably conclude that we eliminated all potential problems, but this is why survey researchers are so willing to share their methodological shortcomings and experiences with their colleagues.

Generally, what Knight has accomplished, and what I hope is in many respects unique to this collection, is to identify the sorts of critical questions readers themselves from differing disciplinary backgrounds and interests might conceivably raise—questions that will provoke meaningful discussion about concepts of culture, values, and democracy, about the methodology and reliability of survey research in general, and about the substance of our findings.

CONCLUSION

It is apparent from this brief overview that the contributors have discovered numerous relationships and characteristics within each country, about each individual country, among all three countries, and between Latin America and the United States. In pursuit of the book's goals, they have also generated a number of provocative and promising new relationships, many of which demand in-depth interpretations on the part of country analysts or deserve future research. Some of the most fruitful research along these lines is likely to be comparisons with other countries, and especially comparisons between Hispanics and non-Hispanics in the United States. If one considers that seven million Mexicans residing in the United States technically could participate in some manner in Mexico's presidential elections and in the future might even be allowed to cast absentee ballots while remaining in the United States, then the impact of their newly acquired democratic views and expectations on their partisan choices is well worth contemplating.

Plenty of evidence exists in this volume to suggest the importance of further efforts at understanding citizens' conceptualizations of democracy, even to the extent of developing differing definitions for distinct societies. It is also apparent that the importance of social inequality, social injustice, and poverty to many Latin Americans molds their views of democracy, or perhaps of any political model. If this is indeed the case, then scholars need to search for other, more powerful variables in explaining political values, such as the degree of inequality Latin Americans perceive in their societies and the intensity with which they hold those perceptions, as well as how those political values are altered over time.

The research presented here does not clarify the linkage between culture and democracy, does not establish a causal relationship between culture and democracy, and does not prove the direction of such a linkage. It does suggest important differences within and between cultures that do seem attributable to differing values and experiences. Whatever the origins of citizens' conceptualizations of democracy or other political models, how they define democracy offers significant new insights into Latin American politics.

Part II

Is There a Latin American Democracy?

New Theory about the Region

Chapter 2

Democracy and Mass Belief Systems in Latin America

Alejandro Moreno

Support for democracy is seen as a cultural matter. In this chapter I argue that support for democracy is also a matter of information, cognition, and belief systems. The way people think about democracy is based on cognitive and informational skills and resources. The concept of democracy varies depending on society's belief systems, and mass belief systems depend on individual characteristics such as education, informational background, cognitive skills, degrees of political "sophistication," and so on.

To a greater or lesser extent, the concept of "democracy" is a component of a society's belief system. Its centrality, meaning, and attributes vary significantly among individuals. Education and information shape the way people conceptualize democracy, from abstract views based on elite-defined ideas to more concrete views based on daily-life facts.

Based on survey data gathered in the 1990s, this chapter focuses on the varied ways in which individuals and societies support and conceptualize democracy. The chapter starts by looking at cross-national and individual variations in a wide range of societies included in the 1995–97 World Values Surveys. Then the discussion moves on to a more specific analysis of three Latin American nations—Chile, Costa Rica, and Mexico—where the Hewlett survey conducted for this book took place. Before getting into the data analysis, the next section describes the questions and the theoretical propositions that guide this chapter.

DEMOCRACY, POLITICAL CULTURE, AND MASS BELIEF SYSTEMS

Do people support democracy? Are people satisfied with democratic institutions? Who are democrats? Who aren't? How many are there? Does it really matter? These are some of the scholarly questions about democratic culture that have been asked for years. Attempts to answer them have come from different theoretical perspectives, employing different methodologies and data. In the process, each general question provides a number of more detailed and particular ones. In this chapter, I deal with two main topics.

First, I focus on support for democracy and on the determinants of that support. Modernization theorists argued that economic development was conducive to democratic politics because it produces social mobilization. Understood as the individual's propensity to abandon traditional values and adopt modern ones, social mobilization tends to increase political participation and expand the attitudes and beliefs of society that are favorable to democracy. In other words, "economic development is conducive to democracy not only because it mobilizes mass publics, but also because it tends to give rise to supportive cultural orientations."[1]

Gabriel Almond and Sidney Verba's classic work *The Civic Culture*, published in 1963, provided an image of a "democrat" as someone relatively well informed, aware of and relatively proud of the country's institutions, with a general sense of interpersonal trust, and ready to participate in politics or engage in political action.[2] Nowadays, the civic culture type may fit a wide range of individuals, both democrats and nondemocrats. Moreover, there is evidence about the decline in some of the particular aspects emphasized by Almond and Verba. For example, empirical evidence has shown a decline of deference among the mass publics in advanced industrial democracies,[3] and some scholars have even talked about the rise of an "uncivic culture."[4]

The question is whether people support democracy based on how they conceive it or based on what they expect from it. As Giuseppe Di Palma has put it, "an incentive to transfer loyalties to democracy stems, especially nowadays, from a better appreciation of democracy's original meaning as a system of coexistence in diversity."[5] However, not all people think of democracy in those terms. Instead, democracy may just be a type of government indistinguishable from other types.

A second topic of inquiry is precisely the mass meaning of democracy. What is it? How do citizens view it? According to Robert Dahl, democracy should be a system with relatively high levels of "contestation" and "participation" in which certain political rights are guaranteed—including freedom of expression and association and the rights to vote and get electoral support.[6] Democracy should also be a system where citizens have access to alternative sources of information, where free and fair elections are held regularly, and where government institutions are held accountable. Do Latin American mass publics view democracy in those terms? The most likely answer is that only a few of them do and not in all those terms.

This chapter presents evidence that Latin American mass publics view democracy in different ways, depending on their age, education, levels of information, values, and ideology and on the contexts in which they live. This thing called "democracy" is part of individual belief systems that vary in complexity. As mentioned earlier, some citizens are likely to conceptualize democracy in abstract terms with a philosophical or academic basis, ranging from a minimal electoral definition that includes free and fair elections with universal vote to the extension of political rights to traditional and new minorities. However, many citizens view democracy in more concrete terms. Some may generally think of democracy just as a type of government and have expectations about it that may not be exclusive to democratic rule, such as fighting crime or redistributing wealth. These differences do not make the citizens' views about democracy right or wrong, but they can tell us why they may or may not support it.

The findings reported in this chapter indicate that Latin Americans are not as pro-democratic as one might think, and that there are strong individual variations in support for democracy based on class and values. The mass meaning of democracy can be as ideal as it can be instrumental among Latin Americans, and it varies depending upon levels of education and information.

The main task of this chapter is to demonstrate that the meaning that citizens attribute to democracy varies according to individual belief systems, and that the latter vary depending upon individuals' levels of information, education, ideologies, and values. In other words, "democracy" is a component of mass belief systems. Therefore, understanding both the mass meaning of democracy and mass support for democracy should focus on the configuration of mass belief systems in society.

The concept of mass belief systems that I use throughout this chapter draws from Philip Converse's seminal 1964 article.[7] The empirical evidence used here is more limited than Converse's; he used panel data to assess the stability and centrality of attitudes in Americans' belief systems, as well as open-ended questions that gave him a more detailed measure of individual political ideologies. Nonetheless, my main argument rests on similar notions.

Converse defined a belief system as a "configuration of ideas and attitudes in which the elements are bound together by some form of constraint or functional interdependence."[8] In his research, Converse found fundamental differences in the nature of belief systems held by political elites and those of the mass publics. Generally, elites held more abstract and more highly organized elements in their belief systems than the masses. Among the mass publics, education and political information were closely and positively related, and higher scores on such measures were also related to a wider range of elements and a higher centrality in the individual's belief system. As Converse put it, as one moves downward on a scale of political information, the use of political concepts was more vague, less organized, and even less central to the individual. That is, political sophisticates understood and viewed politics more clearly—in the terms established by political elites—while the less sophisticated individuals tended to be less ideological and to express less constrained ideas, and their views reflected a "close-to-home" type of reasoning guided by daily-life facts.

In this volume, Alan Knight argues that individuals may be more familiar with some objects than others and therefore express a more reliable opinion or statement about them. For example, individuals may give a more crystallized answer to a poll in regard to police than to democracy, simply because they may have more personal experience with the former than the latter. I would say that Knight's assertion is basically right, and that it becomes more likely as we take educational and informational differences into account. Converse demonstrated that there are significant differences in how individuals think of politics depending on their level of political sophistication. By no means did Converse argue that some views were more adequate or better than others, but simply that they were different.

Following Converse's findings, which have been continuously tested by public opinion scholars,[9] I focus on how differences in education and information lead individuals to have different concepts of democracy. Some segments of the public emphasize more general features of a democratic rule and other segments emphasize more of its particularly defining features. Moreover, parts of the public see democracy in terms that are not even part of a standard definition of democracy. For example, many Latin Americans consider that the fundamental task of democracy is fighting crime. One may argue, as shown by Mary Clark in this volume for the Costa Rican case, that as one moves downward on the educational scale, individuals may not distinguish conceptually between a type of regime and a government. In other words, fighting crime may be a task of government, but it does not matter if it is a democratic government or a non-democratic one. However, one may in fact view the protection of minorities as a task of democracy. The evidence I give in this chapter shows that each task may be emphasized by different individuals: fighting crime by less informed and less educated citizens, and protecting minorities by more informed and more educated ones.

The following sections develop each of the questions stated above, starting with support for democracy.

SUPPORT FOR DEMOCRACY:
A CROSS-NATIONAL COMPARISON

Support for democracy varies from country to country. Since Almond and Verba, scholars have looked at the level of support for a democratic regime as a way not only to identify different political cultures but also to explain democratic stability. The causality between a civic culture and democracy is controversial;[10] but the idea that political culture and democratic stability are strongly linked has been relatively widely accepted.[11] The chances for democracy to be stable are greater if democracy is viewed and taken as "the only game in town." Observers tend to agree on this even though democratic outcomes may be uncertain.[12] In addition, academic research suggests that support for democracy and broad civic orientations may contribute not only to democratic stability, but also to democratic "effectiveness"[13] and democratic consolidation.[14]

How much support for democracy is there among Latin Americans? How does it compare with support for democracy in other regions and countries? The answer to both questions depends on how we measure "support for democracy." Empirical attempts to measure it in Latin America have been based on opinion surveys that ask respondents whether they agree or disagree with statements such as "Democracy is preferable to any other kind of government."[15] If we just take the percentage of people that say "democracy is the best system" or "democracy is preferred to any other system," we may be looking at the issue just partially. We may also raise the question of whether support for democracy is observed when democracy is performing badly. Mass legitimacy of democracy may sustain democratic institutions even in "difficult times."[16] Moreover, support for democracy in a given society may depend not only on a majority that views democracy as the best system, but also on lack of significant support for alternative political systems.[17] Therefore, although still limited, a more complete measure of support for democracy may include gauging preferences for a democratic system, fears and concerns about a democratic system, and support for alternative political regimes.

Figure 1 displays a measure of support for democracy based on those three elements. The measure is an index of democratic and nondemocratic attitudes based on

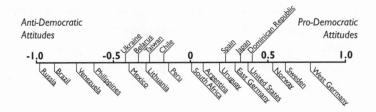

Fig. 1. *Support for democracy: National average scores on democratic-attitudes index. The nations' placement on the democratic-attitudes index is given by the average score on the first principal component calculated with data from 48 societies (N = 45,011). Only selected countries are shown.* Source: 1995–97 World Values Survey.

data from 48 societies gathered in the mid-1990s.[18] The index includes seven variables from the World Values Survey that tap three main issues: Two variables measure general support for democracy as a political system. Three variables measure support for democracy based on attitudes toward its ability to perform well economically, its efficiency, and its ability to maintain order. It is necessary to say that the variable that taps economic performance is not a measure of how the current government is handling the economy or whether the current economy is doing well or poorly. Rather, it taps a general attitude toward the ability or inability of democracy to cope with economic situations.[19] Finally, two more variables measure support for nondemocratic forms of government. Question wording for each of these variables can be consulted in the appendix to this chapter.

The average scores of different societies on the attitudinal index in figure 1 indicate several aspects of support for democracy. First, there is an important cross-national variation. The scores for selected countries show West Germany and Scandinavian societies—Sweden and Norway—at the highest levels of support for democracy. Almost four decades ago, Almond and Verba measured German political culture and saw it as basically less civic than that of the United States or Britain.[20] That may not be the case today. Figure 1 shows that Germans from the western and eastern samples together expressed even more support for democracy than Americans did in the mid-1990s. On the opposite side, Russia has the lowest level of support for democracy.

Second, support for democracy is high in most stable democracies and relatively high in newly consolidated democracies, but not as high in societies that were undergoing a process of democratic transition or consolidation at the time of the survey. The mass public in Spain's consolidated democracy, for example, expresses a high level of support for democracy, which, although lower than that of the United States or Japan, can be included in the average-score "vicinity" of those two countries. In Latin America and the Caribbean, the Dominican Republic, Uruguay, and Argentina express relatively high average levels of support for democracy.[21] However, the average level of support for democracy among the Latin American and Caribbean nations is considerably lower than that in Scandinavian societies.

Although the placements for each nation in figure 1 represent national sample averages on the democratic-attitudes index, each mean placement has its own variance, meaning that in each nation some individuals may be much more supportive of democracy than others. In an earlier work, I demonstrated that the polarization of democratic and authoritarian attitudes has a strong effect on party support and even shapes political cleavages in many new democracies.[22]

Finally, although the Latin American cases mentioned above might be considered predominantly pro-democratic, support for democracy in Latin America may not be as high as one might think. Marta Lagos has already called our attention to this.[23] According to Latinobarómetro data reported by her, support for democracy may be as high as 80 percent in Costa Rica and Uruguay and as low as 42 percent in Honduras.[24] The composite index shown in figure 1 indicates that the average scores on the attitudinal index are rather low among several Latin American publics, thereby confirming the fact that support for democracy in Latin America is comparatively low. Chileans, Peruvians, and Mexicans express a level of support for democracy similar to that in other transitional societies such as Taiwan and some former Soviet republics such as Lithuania, Belarus, and Ukraine. This set of scores is below the average support for democracy for all 48 societies used in the pooled analysis. Support for democracy among Venezuelans is even lower, which suggests that the political and economic crises in Venezuela during the 1990s have undermined mass public support for a democratic system. The average score in support for democracy in Brazil is the lowest among the Latin American samples and is almost as low as the Russian score.

It is probably useful to say that the mean national placements on the democratic-attitudes index do not reflect the position of a nation as a whole, but simply where the nation stands on average in comparison to other nations. As Alan Knight argues convincingly in his chapter in this volume, cross-national differences are not persuasive or even plausible when we talk about categorical differences such as the political cultures of Mexicans, Chileans, French, or Germans. However, there are in fact variations in terms of the underlying characteristics that define a Mexican, Chilean, French, or German environment, based on economic development, institutions, procedures, and even the number of years that the society has been democratic. Moreover, each nation shows clear variation among individuals in support for democracy, which means that some Mexicans may be more supportive of democracy than some Spaniards, even though the national average in support for democracy is higher in Spain than in Mexico.

In sum, figure 1 shows an important cross-national variation in support for democracy based on average scores on a seven-item attitudinal index. Variations in support for democracy can be observed not only between nations, but between individuals as well.

Individual Support for Democracy: Gender, Age, and Class

This section addresses the question of who are democrats in terms of their supportive views toward democracy. The individual differences examined here are based on gender, age, and class. The next section examines individual differences based on values.

As mentioned earlier, economic development is strongly associated with democracy. If structural conditions such as the level of economic development may cause variation in support for a democratic political system at the societal level, we may also expect that different structural conditions may cause variation in support for democracy at the individual level. Class is an important factor to be considered. The evidence shown here indicates that class, based on separate measures of income, education, and occupation, is significantly linked to supportive or opposing views toward democracy regardless of the context. In the 45 societies examined as a whole, age and gender make little difference.

The theoretical expectations are that women may be more or less supportive of democracy than men depending on a number of variables, including the structural and cultural contexts. As women in different settings may have less access to channels of political participation and work opportunities than men do, they may be more likely to express greater demands for democratization. However, the opposite effect may also be true, in the sense that limited access to political participation and paid work places women in traditional roles, and their expectations about a democratic system may be lower than men's. The evidence shown later indicates that there are not significant differences in support for democracy by gender in a wide range of nations taken together.

Younger age cohorts may be expected to be more supportive of democracy, for two reasons. First of all, they are likely to express value priorities different from the ones of their elders—priorities that may be more supportive of democracy, as will be seen in the next section. Second, younger cohorts of individuals may be more supportive of democracy simply because they have been more exposed to it, not only in advanced industrial societies, but also in an increasing number of democracies in the world.

Income, education, and occupation provide individuals with the resources, abilities, and experiences that may affect their expectations and views about democracy. Democracy provides rights and opportunities to the individual, but it also involves competition and choices. Affluent, skillful, and independent individuals may be more likely to support democracy than less affluent, unskillful, and dependent ones. In other words, the greater the income and education levels, the more likely an individual is to support democracy. Also, those in some particular types of occupation, related to both income and education—such as managers, professionals, and upper-level white-collar workers—may be more likely to cope successfully with competition than agricultural workers or blue-collar manual workers. Herbert Kitschelt has already called our attention to these differences by studying their effects on party competition.[25]

Figure 2 *(see page 36)* shows the attitudinal index of figure 1, but displays the average placement for different social categories. The figure shows very important differences in democratic attitudes by class, but not by gender. Men and women from all societies included in the analysis are, on average, equally supportive of (or opposed to) democracy. The similar placement of men and women in an analysis that includes 48 societies indicates that, although we may observe gender differences in particular countries, in the aggregate, taking the contextual settings as constant, gender differences may cancel each other out. In sum, the data do not show any significant differences in support for democracy by gender. Although younger cohorts are more supportive of democracy in some countries, the average obtained from the pooled analysis does not show any significant differences by age. Given the lack of significant differences by age, this variable is not shown in figure 2, so that the information included can be observed more clearly. Nonetheless, the analysis in the last part of this chapter shows that differences in age actually lead to different concepts of democracy among Latin Americans.

In contrast, the differences in democratic attitudes by class are remarkable. The higher the income level and the higher the education level, the more pro-democratic the individual is. Moreover, the gap between the highest and the lowest income levels is significantly greater than the gap between the highest and the lowest education levels. In other words, income seems more important than education in explaining the variance in support for democracy.

Occupation is a variable that reflects the effects of both income and education. In addition, occupation reflects work experience and expectations. Professionals are the most pro-democratic of all occupational categories. Managerial and white-collar, non-

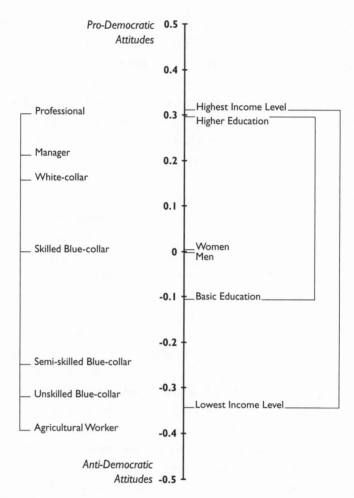

Fig. 2. Support for democracy: Gender and class differences. The categories' placement on the democratic-attitudes index is given by the average score on the first principal component calculated with data from 48 societies (N = 45,011). Only selected categories are shown. Source: 1995–97 World Values Survey.

manual occupations are also predominantly pro-democratic. Among blue-collar workers, the level of support is generally lower than among nonmanual occupations. However, there are significant differences among blue-collar workers based on skills and expertise: the higher the level of expertise or capabilities, the higher the level of support for democracy. Skilled blue-collar workers are significantly more pro-democratic than semiskilled ones, and the latter are slightly less antidemocratic than unskilled workers. Agricultural workers are the least supportive of democracy among all occupational categories used in the analysis. This reflects the urban-rural division in explaining variations in support for democracy, with urban dwellers being generally more supportive.

The results presented here indicate that there are strong differences in support for democracy based on class differences, that is, depending upon education, income, and occupation. These findings suggest that there should be a reexamination of previous evidence, in the sense that studies of Latin American political culture have minimized—perhaps more on the basis of empirical limitations, rather than theoretical unawareness—the impact of class in attitudinal support for democratic values and institutions. Jorge Domínguez and James McCann argue, for example, that

authoritarianism may have weakened between the 1960s and the 1980s [in Mexico], perhaps to the point where majority support would exist for democratic values. Education remained an important source of explanation for variance in support for or opposition to authoritarian values; gender seemed to matter as well. Some studies suggest that economic stakes and instrumental motivations may explain the range of variation in support for authoritarian values. Religiosity did not seem to explain authoritarian propensities. There was no consensus on whether social class was a helpful explanation for such variance.[26]

John Booth and Mitchell Seligson's study on democratic political culture in Costa Rica, Mexico, and Nicaragua also pays attention to differences in support for democratic values by gender, age, education, and the urban-rural divide, but it virtually ignores class.[27] In contrast, Edgardo Catterberg noticed sharp differences in support for democratic values according to socioeconomic levels in Argentina.[28] His findings indicate that the higher the individual's socioeconomic status, the more democratic his attitudes. The results shown in this section call for a greater attention to class as a determinant of democratic attitudes and values in Latin America.

In sum, figure 2 shows that individual class differences are related to support for a democratic system. The pooled data analysis from 48 societies does not indicate that there is a significant gender gap or significant differences based on age in regard to support for democracy. However, there are important differences based on education, income, and occupation. More educated and more affluent individuals are more supportive of democracy. Also, nonmanual and relatively independent occupations and work experiences tend to reflect more democratic values.

Individual Support for Democracy: Value Orientations

Support for democracy also varies significantly at the individual level depending on the individual's value orientations. In this section I examine the differences in support for democracy by value type using Ronald Inglehart's 12-item Materialist-Postmaterialist index.[29] The index measures individual value orientations that reflect physical and physiological priorities (Materialist), values that emphasize self-expression and the quality of life (Postmaterialist), or a combination of both (Mixed). The expected relationship is that Postmaterialist individuals tend to be more supportive of democracy because their value priorities emphasize freedom and participation. On the other hand, Materialist individuals are expected to be relatively less supportive of democracy because they emphasize aspects such as order, economic stability, and physical security, even at the expense of freedom and participation.

Figure 3 shows that Postmaterialists are in fact more supportive of democracy than Materialists are. This is true not only for particular countries, but also for the whole set of 48 societies taken together. The cross-national variations observed in figure 1 are also evident in figure 3, together with the variations along the value dimension. In all the countries shown, from Sweden and West Germany to Mexico and Brazil, the general trend is that as we move toward the Postmaterialist side of the horizontal axis, the score on the democratic-attitudes index increases. In every society, within-country differences show that Postmaterialists are more pro-democratic than Materialists are. The differences between countries show, however, that Swedish Materialists, for example, may be even more pro-democratic on average than Brazilian or Mexican Postmaterialists. Russian Materialists are the least pro-democratic individuals among the categories shown in the figure. However, Russian Postmaterialists are, on average, as pro-democratic as Mexican Postmaterialists, or even slightly more so. The most Postmaterialist category for Russia was not displayed in figure 3 because it had very few cases. This indicates that Postmaterialists are in fact a scarce type in Russia.

Within-country variations between Materialists and Postmaterialists do not show any particular case of extreme polarization, such as we will see later in the chapter in regard to ideological differences.

In sum, value orientations are strongly linked with democratic attitudes. Postmaterialist values tend to be more supportive of democracy than Materialist values are. This is the case for virtually every society examined in this chapter. If we take zero as the mean value of the democratic-attitudes scale, it is evident that Postmaterialists from all 48 societies taken together score above zero (which means they are more supportive of democracy) and Materialists score below zero (which means they are less supportive of democracy).

In this chapter I have analyzed support for democracy in Latin America compared with other countries, as well as who is more supportive of democracy according to individual differences based on class and value orientations. The next section focuses on

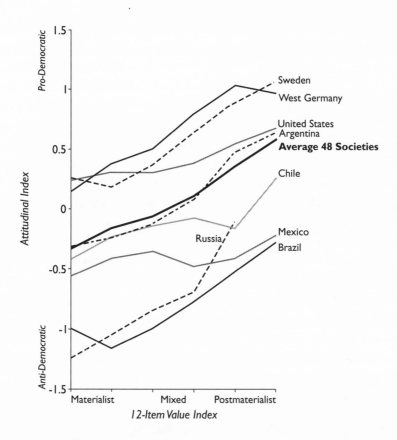

Fig. 3. Support for democracy: Value differences. The categories' placement on the democratic-attitudes index is given by the average score on the first principal component calculated with data from 48 societies (N = 45,011). Only selected countries are shown. Source: 1995–97 World Values Survey.

the meaning of democracy in Latin America. It centers, first, on individual preferences for freedom or order based on ideological self-placement; and, second, on the tasks that individuals attribute to democracy according to their attitudinal and value differences.

THE MEANING OF DEMOCRACY

Why should Latin Americans support democracy? What does "democracy" mean to them? What do they expect from it?

Democracy may be associated with ideal goals or with instrumental procedures. As mentioned earlier in the chapter, democracy may have different meanings among the mass publics, and these meanings may differ from those attributed to democracy by political or intellectual elites. The idea of democracy may be a part of mass belief systems and may or may not reflect elite-defined meanings. The extent to which it reflects such meanings may depend upon the intensity and centrality that individuals grant to the concept.

The results from the 1998 Hewlett survey indicate that Costa Ricans, Chileans, and Mexicans view democracy predominantly in terms of general ideal goals, such as freedom and equality. Freedom is overwhelmingly mentioned by Costa Ricans, while Chileans and Mexicans mention both freedom and equality. Lower percentages associate "voting and elections," "a form of government," "welfare and progress," and "respect and the rule of law" with democracy. If taken separately, ideal goals such as freedom and equality define the idea of democracy among Latin Americans. However, if taken together, instrumental concepts of democracy, such as elections, government, and the rule of law, are as important as ideal concepts. Latin Americans are both ideal and instrumental when trying to define democracy. Of course, there are individual differences in the conception of democracy as well. The following sections focus on two aspects. First, I examine the cross-national variations in preference for freedom or order, as well as individual variations based on ideological orientations. Second, I explore what Latin Americans think the main task of democracy is, and how attitudes and values relate to such expectations.

Freedom and Order: Cross-National and Ideological Differences

Freedom and order are sometimes viewed in terms of a trade-off. Too much freedom may imply little order; too much order may imply little freedom. At the extreme, these two aspects are two sides of the same coin: if you can see one entire side, you cannot see the other side. In political terms, freedom and order are associated with, respectively, democracy and authoritarianism. In this sense, democrats should prefer more freedom than order, while authoritarians may prefer more order than freedom. One way to see who prefers what is by looking at variations in attitudes toward democracy, from which we would expect that democratic attitudes are associated with a greater preference for freedom. This section focuses on ideological differences as determined by the respondents' self-placement on a left-right scale. The purpose is to see how well crystallized the left and right terminology is among the Latin American publics in regard to democracy and the issues of order and freedom. The expected results are that individuals who consider themselves to be on the left are more likely to prefer freedom over order; inversely, individuals who consider themselves to be on the right are more

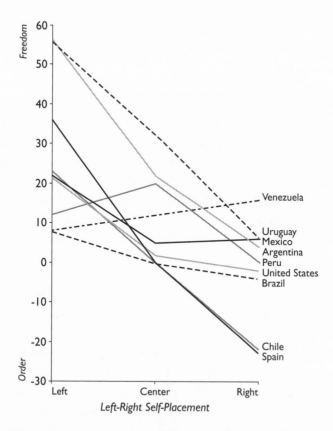

Fig. 4. *Freedom versus order by left-right self-placement. Percentages are taken from the question, "If you had to choose, which would you say is the most important responsibility of government: to maintain order in society, or to respect freedom of the individual?" The percentage shown is "percent freedom" minus "percent order." Source: 1995–97 World Values Survey.*

likely to prefer order over freedom. In other words, the "liberal" leftists are expected to be more pro-democratic than the "conservative" rightists.

Figure 4 shows differences between countries in preferences for freedom over order, and differences within countries in regard to such preferences based on ideological orientations. The percentages shown were calculated by subtracting the percentage that prefers order from the percentage that prefers freedom. Positive percentages indicate that more respondents preferred freedom to order. Negative percentages mean that more respondents preferred order to freedom.

The data show very clearly that individuals who consider themselves to be on the left (leftists) prefer freedom, whereas those on the right prefer order. This is the case throughout Latin America, except in Venezuela, where both leftists and rightists prefer freedom to order, with rightists preferring freedom even slightly more than leftists do. In the United States, Mexico, Brazil, and Peru, the gap in preference by ideological orientation is relatively moderate. However, Argentina, Uruguay, Spain, and Chile have a significant variation in preference for freedom or order depending upon the individual's ideological self-identification. In other words, these countries show a strong polarization between the right, with its emphasis on order, and the left, with its emphasis on freedom. Nonetheless, Argentineans and Uruguayans are polarized on the more pro-democratic side; that is, even the rightists express relatively high support for freedom. However, Spaniards and Chileans are highly polarized with rightists preferring order to freedom. It may be argued that, in general, the left-right terminology tends to reflect preferences for freedom or order among Latin American mass publics.

The Tasks of Democracy: Attitudinal and Value Differences

What do individuals expect from democracy? The 1998 Hewlett survey in Costa Rica, Chile, and Mexico shows that individuals have different expectations about the tasks of democracy. According to the data displayed in table 1, some people view fighting crime as democracy's main goal (in Costa Rica more than in the other two countries). For others, democracy is about elections, in addition to fighting crime (Mexico). For Chileans, democracy is associated with redistributing wealth and protecting minorities as much as with fighting crime. In any case, attitudinal and value differences are associated with these expectations. In terms of values, Materialists emphasize fighting crime over protecting minorities. In Chile and Mexico, authoritarians are more supportive of fighting crime as the main task of democracy than democrats are. In contrast, democrats in Mexico are more supportive of elections as the main goal. (I classified democrats and authoritarians according to their answers to the question of whether democracy or authoritarianism is more desirable as a type of government.)

The relationships shown in table 1 indicate that there are different ways to think about democracy depending on the individual's attitudes and values and the contexts in which he or she lives. Contextual differences even alter the relationships based on values and attitudes. For example, fighting crime is mostly emphasized by democrats in Costa Rica, but by authoritarians in Chile and Mexico. However, Materialists from all three countries tend to stress these aspects more than Postmaterialists do. Emphasis on elections as the main task of democracy is observed among democrats from all three countries, rather than among authoritarians. Redistributing wealth is a goal men-

TABLE 1　*The Main Task of Democracy by Attitude and Value Types: Costa Rica, Chile, and Mexico, 1998* (percent)

Which is the main task of democracy?	Fighting Crime	Elections	Redistribution of Wealth	Protecting Minorities
Costa Rica	38	24	12	25
Attitudes				
Democratic	39	26	12	23
Indifferent	38	17	13	32
Authoritarian	31	11	15	44
Values				
Postmaterialist	32	23	12	33
Mixed	36	26	12	26
Materialist	43	25	12	20
Chile	26	18	28	25
Attitudes				
Democratic	23	21	26	30
Indifferent	23	19	38	20
Authoritarian	42	16	18	25
Values				
Postmaterialist	24	19	28	30
Mixed	27	19	28	27
Materialist	30	20	30	21
Mexico	31	33	17	16
Attitudes				
Democratic	26	36	20	17
Indifferent	37	35	14	15
Authoritarian	38	29	15	18
Values				
Postmaterialist	26	43	14	17
Mixed	31	34	17	18
Materialist	35	31	21	13

Source: 1998 Hewlett survey.

tioned by Mexican Materialists, while protecting minorities is a clear Postmaterialist goal in Costa Rica and Chile.

　Which of these variables is more important in explaining different concepts of democracy? Moreover, what is the role of information in defining such concepts? The next section addresses these questions by showing a multivariate model of different concepts of democracy in Chile, Costa Rica, and Mexico.

DEMOCRACY AND BELIEF SYSTEMS:
A MULTIVARIATE EXPLANATION

What are the strongest determinants of how citizens conceptualize democracy? Table 2 displays some evidence about individual and cross-national differences in the conceptualization of democracy. It shows the four tasks of democracy mentioned in the previous section, plus "liberty," as concepts of democracy.

Each concept is empirically defined as a dummy variable for which I use logistic regression as a tool of analysis. The independent variables are grouped in five general categories. First, I include structural variables: age, education, and whether the respondent is a rural or urban dweller. Second, the model employs information variables: the individual's news exposure and previous political knowledge, which, together with education, define the level of political sophistication. Third, I use political culture variables: interpersonal trust, reported participant socialization, subjective political efficacy, tolerance, and Materialist-Postmaterialist values; these variables are usually thought of as measures of pro-democratic attitudes, so I include them in order to assess whether they are related to the individual's concept of democracy. Fourth, I use ideological variables as a way to see whether some policy or ideological preferences are related to how individuals perceive or view democracy. Finally, I employ dummy variables for nationalities, as a way to control for contextual factors. As the survey includes three nations, I use one of them, Costa Rica, as a base for comparison. The appendix to this chapter shows the way in which each variable was coded.

The analysis shows several aspects. First of all, information variables matter, in some cases even more than cultural variables. Second, individuals' levels of sophistication clearly correspond to different ways of thinking of democracy. Third, age also makes a difference in how individuals see democracy, suggesting that there is an important generation gap in Latin America with respect to the meaning of democracy. As mentioned earlier, age differences are found in the Hewlett survey in regard to the concept of democracy in three Latin American nations, but not in the World Values Survey in regard to support for democracy in 48 nations. Finally, ideological orientations also filter the way individuals understand democracy and what they expect from it. Let me elaborate on each of these points.

Information variables consistently explain why certain individuals emphasize some tasks of democracy instead of others. In most cases, information variables are reinforced by education. Individuals who are more educated and more informed—in terms of news reception—are more likely to emphasize "liberty" as a one-word definition of democracy than the less educated and less informed ones. Taken together or

TABLE 2 *Predictors of the Conceptualization of Democracy:*
Chile, Costa Rica, and Mexico, 1998

	Concept of Democracy as Liberty	The Main Task of Democracy			
		Fight Crime	Elect Rulers	Redistribute Wealth	Protect Minorities
Structural variables					
Age	−0.15*	0.11*	0.25***	−0.11	−0.30***
Education	0.04***	0.02*	−0.05***	0.01	0.03**
Size of town (rural-urban)	−0.04	0.03	−0.05	0.03	−0.03
Information variables					
News reception	0.18**	−0.04	−0.20***	0.16*	0.14*
Political knowledge	0.02	−0.13***	0.06*	0.08*	0.03
Political culture variables					
Interpersonal trust	−0.15	−0.06	−0.04	−0.05	0.15
Socialization (participation)	0.03	0.06**	−0.02	−0.12***	0.04
Political efficacy	0.07**	−0.09***	0.12***	0.01	−0.02
Tolerance	0.03	−0.01	−0.05	0.03	0.03
Materialist-Postmaterialist	0.08	−0.18**	0.06	−0.07	0.2**
Ideological variables					
Left-right self-placement	−0.01	0.07***	−0.06**	−0.02	0.00
Economic left-right	−0.07	−0.02	0.12**	−0.07	−0.06
Country					
Mexico	−1.54***	−0.17	0.38***	0.35**	−0.48***
Chile	−1.23***	−0.51***	−0.34*	0.87***	0.19
Constant	−0.93*	−0.48	−0.62	−1.85***	−1.94***
Model Chi-Square	284.7	90.3	116.3	84.9	52.3
Percent correctly predicted	72%	70%	73%	80%	78%
No. of cases in the analysis	2,482	2,482	2,482	2,482	2,546

Source: 1998 Hewlett survey. Figures for the variables are logistic regression coefficients.

   Note: The country variables are dummy variables with values 1 and 0. Costa Rica is the omitted category. Levels of statistical significance:

   * $p < 0.1$; ** $p < 0.05$; *** $p < 0.01$.

individually, both news reception and political knowledge are consistently significant determinants of the conceptualization of democracy. The lower the level of political knowledge, the more likely the individual will be to say that fighting crime is the main task of democracy. The lower the level of news reception, the more likely the individual will be to identify democracy as a matter of electing rulers. In other words, associating democracy with the election of rulers does not seem to require too much knowledge or information. However, seeing democracy as a system that protects minorities requires relatively high levels of education and information.

Among the political culture variables included in the analysis are interpersonal trust, a reported measure of whether the individual socialized in a participant environment at home and school, a measure of political efficacy, a measure of tolerance, and the Materialist-Postmaterialist index. In the analysis, neither trust nor tolerance makes a difference in how individuals conceptualize democracy. In regard to the other cultural traits, the more the individual had a participant environment, the more likely it is that emphasis will be put on fighting crime, with less emphasis on redistribution of wealth. The higher the sense of political efficacy, the more likely it is that individuals think of democracy as a system of freedom and election of rulers, rather than in terms of fighting crime. Finally, Postmaterialist values significantly explain the role of protecting minorities in a democracy, while Materialists are strongly guided by the goal of fighting crime.

The analysis shows that the youth and the elderly think of democracy differently in Latin America. Age differences are clearly observed across issues: younger individuals are more likely to emphasize liberty and protection of minorities, while older ones are more likely to mention fighting crime and election of rulers. These differences point to a very significant gender gap in the conceptualization of democracy, with the older citizens giving importance to order and a minimal electoral definition and younger citizens giving importance to issues related to diversity and political minorities. The two worldviews are indicative of the way the concept of democracy may change among future generations—from a system having a minimal electoral character to an increasingly inclusive system that expands political rights to new groups in society.

Ideological differences are also illustrative. The left-right self-placement measure shows that right-wing individuals give more importance to fighting crime, while left-wing individuals give more importance to election of rulers. This is no surprise: the left follows an electoral definition of democracy, while the right emphasizes order. However, an interesting finding is that the economic right is more likely to see democracy in electoral terms than the economic left. Ideologically speaking, an electoral democracy is predominantly conceived by individuals with a politically leftist and economically rightist orientation. The data do not go so far as to confirm it, but they do suggest that electoral democracy is more the idea of liberal capitalists than conservatives among the mass publics in Latin America. This finding may follow some of the patterns already observed in industrial societies. Terry Nichols Clark and Ronald Inglehart, for example, argue that the rise of a "new political culture" reflects the transformation of the classic left-right dimension, market individualism, social individualism, new social issues, a questioning of the welfare state, and the rise of broader citizen participation.[30]

Finally, table 2 also shows dummy variables for two of the three countries included in the Hewlett study. With only two exceptions, all the coefficients are statistically significant. The coefficient's sign indicates whether Chileans or Mexicans place more or less emphasis—depending on whether the sign is positive or negative, respectively—on the tasks and the concept of democracy in relation to Costa Ricans. For example, both Mexicans and Chileans place less importance on liberty as a defining feature of democracy than Costa Ricans do. Chileans place less importance on fighting crime and the election of rulers than Costa Ricans do, but more importance on wealth redistribution. Mexicans place more emphasis on the election of rulers and the redistribution of wealth than Costa Ricans do, but significantly less emphasis on minority protection. This aspect clearly suggests that Mexicans are much less concerned about their minorities than Chileans or Costa Ricans are.

CONCLUSION

Democracy is conceptualized differently at the individual and societal levels in Latin America. Democracy is an element in the belief systems of Latin American mass publics, and its meaning and centrality vary depending upon individuals' levels of information and sophistication. Values also matter, but not all of the value orientations identified as part of a democratic political culture make a difference in how democracy is conceptualized.

This chapter shows evidence of significant class differences in support for democracy. In addition, age is a strong determinant of how individuals think of democracy, with older citizens providing a minimal electoral definition of democracy and younger ones providing a definition that is more inclusive and protective of minorities. However, age did not account for differences in support for democracy in a wide number of countries taken together. The results presented here suggest that the concept of democracy varies significantly on a scale of political sophistication measured in educational, cognitive, and informational terms: as we move downward on such a scale, the concept of democracy becomes more tied to aspects of daily life, such as fighting crime.

APPENDIX SURVEYS AND VARIABLES

The empirical evidence for this chapter draws from the Hewlett Foundation–sponsored survey conducted in Chile, Costa Rica, and Mexico in 1998 (H98) and from the third wave of the World Values Surveys conducted in 48 societies from 1995 to 1997 (WVS95).

The variables and indexes used in the analysis are listed in alphabetical order according to their analytical name. Each variable or index name is followed by the survey's short name and then by the question wording (my translations from the Spanish of the Hewlett questionnaire) or by a description.

Concept of democracy (H98)

In one word, could you tell me what democracy means to you?

1 Liberty; 2 Equality; 3 Voting and elections; 4 A form of government; 5 Welfare and progress; 6 Respect and the rule of law; 7 Don't know; 8 Other.

(The analysis in table 2 uses a dummy variable in which 1 = Liberty and 0 = Otherwise.)

Democratic-attitudes index, pro-democratic and antidemocratic (WVS95)

This is an index constructed using principal component factor analysis that included the following variables:

I am going to describe various types of political systems and ask what you think about each as a way of governing this country. For each one, would you say it is a very good, fairly good, fairly bad, or very bad way of governing this country?

Having a strong leader who does not have to bother with parliament and elections.
Having the army rule.
Having a democratic political system.

I am going to read off some things that people sometimes say about a democratic political system. Could you please tell me if you agree strongly, agree, disagree, or disagree strongly, after I read each one of them?

In democracy, the economic system runs badly.
Democracies are indecisive and have too much squabbling.
Democracies aren't good at maintaining order.
Democracy may have problems, but it's better than any other form of government.

Economic left-right (H98)

This is a five-category index of economic left-right attitudes, where 1 = left and 5 = right, constructed with the following variables:

Please tell me which of the following should be government-owned and which should be privately owned.
Airlines; Schools; Water; Television
(Recoded as: 1 Government ownership; 2 Both; 3 Private ownership)

Which of the following phrases do you agree with? The government should be responsible for the individual's welfare or each individual should be responsible for his or her own welfare.
(Recoded as: 1 Government responsible; 2 Both; 3 Individual responsible)

Freedom versus order (WVS95)

If you had to choose, which would you say is the most important responsibility of government: to maintain order in society, or to respect individual freedom?

Interpersonal trust (H98)

In general, would you say that most people can be trusted or that you can't really trust people?
(Used as a dummy variable where 1 = Trust and 0 = Otherwise)

Left-right self-placement (H98 and WVS95)

In political matters, people generally talk about "left" and "right." On a 10-point scale where 1 is "left" and 10 is "right," where would you place your own views?

Materialist-Postmaterialist four-item index (H98)

This is the four-item index developed by Ronald Inglehart *(Culture Shift in Advanced Industrial Society* [Princeton: Princeton University Press, 1990]; *Modernization and Postmodernization: Cultural, Economic, and Political Change in 43 Societies [Princeton: Princeton University Press, 1997]).* The index is constructed using the following variable:

If you had to choose, which one of the things on this card would you say is most important? And which would be the next most important?

1 Maintaining order in the country; 2 Giving people more say in important government decisions; 3 Fighting inflation; 4 Protecting freedom of expression.

(The individual is categorized as "Materialist" if the first and second responses are a combination of categories 1 and 3; "Postmaterialist" if the responses are a combination of categories 2 and 4; and "Mixed" if the responses are a combination of categories 1 and 2, 1 and 4, 2 and 3, or 3 and 4.)

Materialist-Postmaterialist 12-item index (WVS95)

This is a 12-item index developed by Inglehart *(Culture Shift in Advanced Industrial Society; Modernization and Postmodernization).* The index is constructed with the following items in a question format similar to that of the four-item index:

Categories from questions 1 and 2: 1 A high level of economic growth; 2 Making sure this country has strong defense forces; 3 Seeing that people have more say about how things are done at their jobs and in their communities; 4 Trying to make our cities and countryside more beautiful.

Categories from questions 3 and 4: 1 Maintaining order in the country; 2 Giving people more say in important government decisions; 3 Fighting inflation; 4 Protecting freedom of expression.

Categories from questions 5 and 6: 1 A stable economy; 2 Progress toward a less impersonal and more humane society; 3 Progress toward a society in which ideas count more than money; 4 The fight against crime.

News exposure (H98)

How often do you follow the news?

(Recoded as: 1 Almost never; 2 two or three times a month; 3 Once a week; 4 two or three times per week; 5 Every day)

Political efficacy (H98)

Would you personally be willing to demand government accountability?

(Recoded as: 1 Definitely not; 2 Maybe not; 3 It depends; 4 Maybe yes; 5 Definitely yes)

Political knowledge (H98)

This is an index constructed with a question about knowledge of basic political facts:

As you have probably heard, the law establishes the separation of the three branches of government. Could you tell me the name of each of the three branches?

(The options were: Executive, Legislative, and Judiciary.)

(Recoded as: 1 Don't know; 2 Wrong response; 3 Incomplete response; 4 Correct response.)

Socialization (participation) (H98)

This is an index of the individual's socialization, focusing on whether it occurred in an environment that emphasized participation at home and school.

Based on what you may remember, how often did children participate with parents in your family's decisions?

Based on what you may remember, how often did students participate with teachers in class decisions?

(Both variables recoded as: 1 Never or almost never; 2 Only sometimes/little; 3 Almost always/a lot; 4 Always.)

The index is a seven-category variable where 1 = Low level of participation and 7 = High level of participation.

Task of democracy, main (H98)

If you had to choose, which of the following would you say is the main task of democracy?

1 Fighting crime; 2 Electing rulers; 3 Redistributing wealth; 4 Protecting minorities; 5 None; 6 Don't know.

(The analysis in table 2 uses dummy variables for the first four categories, in which 1 = the respective category and 0 = Otherwise.)

Tolerance (H98)

This is an index of tolerance constructed with the following variables:

I am going to read a list of people. Please tell me which of them you would not like to have as neighbors.

Evangelicals; Homosexuals; Foreigners.

(Recoded as dummy variables where 1 = the category of interest and 0 = Otherwise, and then added into a single four-category variable where 1 = fully intolerant and 4 = fully tolerant)

Chapter 3

Does Trust Matter?

Interpersonal Trust and Democratic Values in Chile,
Costa Rica, and Mexico

Timothy J. Power and Mary A. Clark

In the comparative study of politics, few questions have been as enduring as "What causes democracy?" As perhaps our favorite dependent variable, democracy has been poked and prodded repeatedly by each of the major theoretical approaches in comparative politics: structural, institutional, voluntarist, and cultural. The last of these approaches, political culture, figured prominently in the first wave of modern comparative studies in the 1950s and 1960s but came under severe attack in the 1970s and early 1980s, somewhat fading from the scene. Over the past 10 years, however, there has been a resurgence of interest in the relationship between cultural values and democratic sustainability (accompanied, it should be noted, by similarly renewed attention to the relationship between culture and economic development). It is now no longer hyperbole to speak of the analytical revival that Ronald Inglehart announced in the pages of the *American Political Science Review* in 1988: the "renaissance of political culture."[1]

This chapter—albeit in a preliminary fashion—speaks to one of the key questions in the renewed research program of political culture theory: the relationship between democracy and interpersonal trust. In our brief treatment, we perform three tasks. First, we review the literature on interpersonal trust as it applies both to comparative macropolitical theory and to the world region in which we are interested, Latin America. In so doing, we derive several expectations and hypotheses that can be tested comparatively. Second, we temporarily make interpersonal trust the dependent variable, and we attempt to identify its individual-level and group-level correlates. We review cross-national differences in trust levels in the three Latin American societies explored by the Hewlett opinion survey conducted in July 1998. Third, we then reconnect the concept of interpersonal trust to the variable it supposedly affects—political democracy (in this case measured indirectly by citizens' democratic values). Through this final test we attempt to provide an answer, or at least a partial one, to the question posed by the title of this essay: "Does trust matter?"

POLITICAL CULTURE, INTERPERSONAL TRUST, AND DEMOCRACY

Political culture can be described in general terms as the set of attitudes, feelings, and value orientations toward politics that are present in a given society at a given moment. When we aggregate these individual-level attitudes to the level of society, we can begin to speak of "national political cultures," as in general features of Canadian, Brazilian, Japanese political culture, etc. An enduring goal of the research program has been to relate abstract features of national political culture to concrete political outcomes, and such efforts have long attracted the fire of skeptics. Some critics have argued that political culture is nothing more than "a cause in search of an effect," that it is a second-order explanation that should only be used when structural and institutional explanations of political phenomena have been ruled out. The critics argue that political culture is a "permissive" rather than a "direct causal" factor; that it should not be used alone, but rather in conjunction with other, more empirically testable explanations; and that it provides somewhat of a residual category for explaining phenomena that prove immune to more conventional analytical approaches.[2]

Another commonly cited objection to political culture, particularly relevant to the literature on Third World development, is that the concept too easily lends itself to ethnocentrism. In the "wrong hands," cultural variables can be used in judgmental and deterministic ways that would seem to rule out democracy and development for Third World nations.[3] In his thought-provoking contribution to this volume, Alan Knight revisits a number of these criticisms and demonstrates why many scholars retain a healthy skepticism vis-à-vis the more blunt and indiscriminate uses of cultural explanations.

In essence, resistance to cultural approaches remains widespread in comparative politics, even in light of the "renaissance" in recent years. This is not the place to delve into—as Knight does impressively in his chapter—such a fundamental epistemological debate. Our objective is not to evaluate political culture as a general theory of politics, but rather to focus on one aspect of culture: interpersonal trust. From the classic works of the modernization school to the rebirth of political culture in the 1990s, cultural theorists have argued that interpersonal trust is causally related to the sustainability of democracy.[4] In their pathbreaking five-country study, *The Civic Culture,* Gabriel Almond and Sidney Verba noted the apparent correlation between societal trust and confidence in democratic institutions and surmised that trusting publics were a key facet of regime legitimacy. More recently, cross-national work has uncovered a strong empirical relationship between interpersonal trust and the number of years of continuous democracy in a given country. For example, for the 43 societies analyzed in the 1990–93 World Values Survey, the correlation between the number of consecutive years of democracy and the percentage of citizens saying "Most people can be trusted" was a strong .72 (N = 43, p < .0001).[5] Trust and stable democracy, it would appear, go hand in hand.

Correlation does not imply causality, however, and recently a debate has ensued on the precise direction of causation. Does sustained democracy generate societal trust, or does societal trust beget democratic institutions? Edward Muller and Mitchell Seligson, in a study of 27 European and Central American societies, claim that democratic experience causes interpersonal trust.[6] Robert Putnam et al., in their historical comparison of northern and southern Italy, suggest that trust enhances democratic institutions (although this argument is not made as strongly as their related argument about economic development, in which culture-as-causation is more centrally specified).[7] Ronald Inglehart, in contrast, has been very careful not to specify a direction of causation, but rather to emphasize the elective affinity between trust and democracy: "The available evidence cannot determine the causal direction, but it does indicate that culture and political institutions have a strong tendency to go together—with trust and stable democracy being closely linked, as the political culture literature has long claimed."[8]

Even if—as Inglehart laments—the available data cannot determine whether trust causes democracy or democracy causes trust, we still need to assess what is behind the correlation between the two. It is important to ask this question aggressively, given that Knight and others are skeptical about any purported causal connection. *Why* is trust apparently necessary to democracy, and what exactly is the theoretical *content* of this relationship? Two sets of answers have come forth, which we will term the "alternation in power" argument and the "social capital" argument, respectively.

In the first of these, the alternation in power thesis, interpersonal trust is viewed as necessary to achieve the rotations in governing elites that are characteristic of stable democracy. Adam Przeworski has felicitously defined democracy as "a system in which parties lose elections."[9] As Inglehart writes, "Democratic institutions depend on trust that the opposition will accept the rules of the democratic process. One must view one's political opponents as a *loyal* opposition who will not imprison you or execute you if you surrender political power to them, but can be relied on to govern within the laws, and to surrender power if your side wins the next election."[10] Similarly, Larry Diamond argues that "[t]heoretically, trust is a foundation of cooperation. If rival political elites do not trust one another to honor agreements, it will be much more difficult for them to institutionalize the pacts, settlements, understandings, and mutual restraints that stabilize politics and consolidate democracy at the elite level."[11] In the alternation in power argument, trust operates as a sort of filter that affects the degree to which the democratic rules of the game will be respected.

In the second version of the trust-and-democracy thesis, the social capital argument, interpersonal trust has a more indirect role. According to Putnam, "The theory of social capital presumes that, generally speaking, the more we connect with other people, the more we trust them, and vice versa."[12] In this model, interpersonal trust is associated with a tendency toward the proliferation of secondary associations and the resulting empowerment of civil society. As social theorists from de Tocqueville to Putnam have insisted, a vigorous civil society provides fertile ground for democratic government. An enormous literature has suggested that as membership in secondary associations increases within a given society, then "private" forms of political interaction, such as clientelism, are eroded; "public" or "civic" styles of politics, based on republican notions of citizenship, are more likely to take root; virtually all forms of political partic-ipation increase across the board; values of equality and solidarity tend to become more diffused; the ideal of self-government becomes more highly valued; and, perhaps most importantly, citizens are empowered in a way that allows them to hold their leaders more *accountable.*[13] A dense network of secondary associations provides a check on state power; thus, a society of "joiners" is an empowered society. Interpersonal trust, civic engagement, and effective democracy appear to be strongly intercorrelated.

The alternation in power argument and the social capital argument focus on differ-ent sectors of the political community: the former on elites and the latter on mass soci-ety. Although they are both characterized as "cultural" arguments, they could just as easily be seen as *institutional* arguments, with the former emphasizing political institu-tions and the latter privileging social institutions. And although neither thesis is explic-itly addressed by Knight, an "institutional" translation of these "cultural" arguments may satisfy his plea for more specific, disaggregated, behavioral, and empirically based approaches. What the two theses have in common is a strong belief that institutional development is conditioned by interpersonal trust. Diamond writes that "if trust is low and expectations of fellow citizens are pervasively cynical, institutions will be mere formalities, lacking compliance and effectiveness, as most people defect from obedience in the expectation that most everyone else will [do the same]."[14] Much of the current literature on democratic transition and consolidation concurs, insisting that democratic sustainability is all about institution building.[15] Logically, if at the macro level democratization is about institution building, then at the micro level democratization must be about the building of interpersonal trust.

TAKING THE ARGUMENTS TO LATIN AMERICA

Modern social science research on Latin American political culture has until recently been quite fragmentary and underdeveloped. This may be the result of a reaction against two trends effectively skewered by Knight: on the one hand, the impressionistic and deterministic "national character" studies that one finds in every country, whose purveyors wax literary while reeling off nonfalsifiable hypotheses about their compatriots; on the other hand, the perceived ethnocentric biases associated with some of the more prominent advocates of cultural interpretations. Authors such as Glen Dealy and Howard Wiarda, for example, have long argued that the Iberic and organic-statist culture of Latin America is inimical to democracy;[16] more recently, Lawrence Harrison has made the controversial argument that "underdevelopment is a state of mind," and has catalogued Latin cultural characteristics that he views as inimical to economic progress.[17] Given the reaction to these controversies, many scholars who were trained as Latin Americanists in the 1970s and 1980s (including the authors of this chapter) acquired anticulturalist biases as the received wisdom, and those of us familiar with the folkways of U.S.-based Latin American studies can still recognize widespread hostility to political culture throughout the social science disciplines. Until recently, examples of empirically based political culture research were few and far between.[18]

A prominent theme in the literature on Latin American political culture has been the apparently low levels of interpersonal trust, and the pervasiveness of "uncivic" behavior, that seem to characterize the region. Marta Lagos, for example, writes that to understand the kind of democracy that is currently evolving in Latin America, "one must consider not only the formal and institutional bases of politics, but also the nonrational or prerational cultural traits that form such an important part of the region's soul. . . . Silence and appearance—the twin progeny of distrust—have historically been crucial tools for survival."[19] In some of his lesser known but most fascinating work, Guillermo O'Donnell has addressed the issue of deeply embedded forms of social authoritarianism in Latin America. In an autobiographical essay on daily life in Brazil (which, by the way, had the lowest level of interpersonal trust—2.8 percent—of any of the 59 societies in the 1995–97 World Values Survey), O'Donnell suggests that the low level of social trust encourages an exaggerated form of individualism that breeds class hostility and disrespect for the rule of law and generally exposes Brazil to a massive "prisoners' dilemma" that inhibits political and economic development.[20] The most casual visitor to Latin America will detect the syndrome of *incivismo* that Putnam described for southern (but not northern) Italy: a set of individualistic, privatizing, free-riding, and anticivic behaviors that seem to undermine a wide range of institutions: social, economic, and political. It would be easy to trivialize *incivismo* by treating it in a purely anecdotal fashion—reducing it to stories about aggressive driving, cutting in line, failure to pay taxes, and the like—but both O'Donnell and Putnam succeed in connecting *incivismo* and the lack of interpersonal trust to relevant macropolitical trends.

As both Frederick Turner[21] and the essays in this volume attest, newer research on Latin American political culture has become more empirically based, more theoretically sophisticated, and more apt to place Latin America in comparative perspective. The advent of the Latinobarómetro surveys (inspired by the Eurobarometer studies conducted by the European Commission since the 1970s) has made it possible for the first time to compare major aspects of political culture in Latin America—for example, interpersonal trust and support for political democracy—to trends elsewhere in the world. And interpersonal trust in Latin America, as expected, turns out to be low in comparative terms. In the 1990–93 World Values Survey (WVS), the percentage of respondents saying "Most people can be trusted" to the standardized question ("Generally speaking, would you say that you can trust most people or that you can never be too careful when dealing with others?") ranged from 58–66 percent in the Scandinavian countries, to 52 and 50 percent in the United States and Canada, to 37 and 34 percent for Spain and Italy. For the four Latin American countries included in the WVS, the figure for Mexico was 33 percent, for Chile and Argentina 23 percent each, and for Brazil only 7 percent.[22] More recently, when the same question was asked in 11 Latin American countries for the 1996 Latinobarómetro, Uruguay topped the field at 33 percent, 10 points ahead of a three-way tie for second place (Argentina, Colombia, and Paraguay at 23 percent). At the bottom of the list were Peru at 13 percent, and Brazil and Venezuela both with 11 percent. Again, the data demonstrated a strong relationship between levels of interpersonal trust and support for political democracy.[23]

The correlation between interpersonal trust and democracy seems well established. However, most research designs using the WVS, Latinobarómetro, Eurobarometer, etc. compare only national units (i.e., whole societies). This strategy limits the number of cases, with a ceiling of about 18–20 observations in Latin America, and it also does not explore the individual-level correlates of interpersonal trust. Below, we aim to discover whether the relationship between interpersonal trust and democracy holds up at the individual level.

THE DATA AND CASES

The three countries examined in the 1998 Hewlett study represent an appropriate mix of political traditions and democratic development. Costa Rica is the region's longest-surviving competitive regime, having enjoyed continuous democracy since 1948, and is generally regarded as the most consolidated democracy in Latin America. Thus, it can be regarded as a sort of "reference category" for the rest of Latin America, and it is used as such in some of the analyses reported below. Historically speaking, Chile also has impressive democratic credentials, and as recently as the early 1970s enjoyed the same reputation that Costa Rica does today—the "senior democracy" of Latin America. But Chilean democracy was subverted in the 1973 coup, and Chileans endured the brutal authoritarian rule of General Augusto Pinochet until the elections of 1989. Since then, the resumption of Chilean democracy—although truncated in important ways by Pinochet's *leyes de amarre* (laws that restrict the freedom of action of the successor democratic governments)—has generally been perceived as quite successful and has now passed the milestone of its tenth anniversary. The first Socialist president since the 1973 coup, Ricardo Lagos, was inaugurated in 2000.

Mexico, in contrast to the other two cases, has a long history of authoritarian rule, with the PRI (Institutional Revolutionary Party) controlling the national government from 1929 to 2000. In 2000, Mexico is a transitional regime, perhaps best characterized as a semidemocratic state. There was significant progress toward truly free and fair elections in the 1990s, leading to the historic opposition takeover of the Chamber of Deputies in 1997 and the election of the first non-PRI president in modern times, Vicente Fox, in 2000. The Hewlett survey was conducted in 1998 at a very opportune time, as the PRI era was coming to a close; however, the legacy of 75 years of authoritarian rule still cast its shadow over Mexican politics. Comparing Mexico, Chile, and Costa Rica provides an appropriate cross-sectional view of democratic development in Latin America.

PREDICTING TRUST AND *CIVISMO*

The question on interpersonal trust used in the Hewlett study was of a slightly different wording than the WVS/Latinobarómetro question. Respondents were asked, "En términos generales, ¿diría Ud. Que *SI* se puede confiar en la gente o más bien que *NO* se puede confiar en la gente?" For the entire sample of Latin Americans in the three countries, the overall level of social trust stood at 30.4 percent, low by international standards. But the results by country are somewhat surprising: Chile scored the lowest at 20.7 percent, and Costa Rica was not far away at 24.2 percent (fig. 1). The highest level of interpersonal trust was registered in Mexico (44.8 percent), precisely the country with the weakest democratic tradition (and reputationally, at least, this finding also seems to contradict Mexico's image of *incivismo*). In the 1990–93 WVS, Chile had scored 23 percent, very close to its Hewlett score in 1998. But in the 1990–93 WVS, Mexico stood at 33 percent, falling to 21 in the 1996 Latinobarómetro and rising to 45 in the 1998 Hewlett study. The instability of the Mexican results is puzzling and is cause for some concern. Moreover, given Costa Rica's consolidated democracy, its score for social trust should logically have been higher. In Lagos's Index of Democratic Perceptions (a combination of support for democracy, satisfaction with democracy, and willingness to actually defend democracy), Costa Rica ranks as the most democratic Spanish-speaking society in the world, even higher than Spain.[24] Clearly, at the macropolitical level, the levels of social trust registered in the Hewlett survey do not perform according to expectation.

Among the citizens of these three countries, apparently 70 percent do not trust most other people. What sets apart the 30 percent who *do* trust? Pooling the entire sample (which is really only appropriate as a first stab at "Latin American" political culture) and looking at bivariate correlations, we examined the performance of some basic

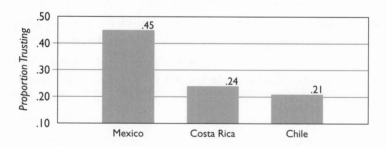

Fig. 1. Interpersonal trust compared

demographic indicators.[25] Interpersonal trust was *negatively* correlated with age (–.05), with city size (–.06), and with the female gender (–.06). Trust was *positively* correlated with income (.06) and with the number of years of education (.11). All of these correlations are very weak, although they are all highly statistically significant (at the .01 level or better) due to the very large sample size. The best bivariate predictor of trust is education.

The Hewlett instrument also offers a way to measure *incivismo,* or anticivic, socially noncooperative behavior seen as indicating low levels of social trust. In the survey, respondents were presented with several scenarios of social interactions and were asked to state whether they thought people who engaged in certain behaviors were very smart *(listo),* somewhat smart, somewhat stupid *(tonto),* or very stupid. The activities included cutting in line, saying nothing if one received extra change, fare-jumping on the metro or bus lines, running a stoplight when no one was looking, and inventing a false excuse. We coded the responses in the following way: 2 for those who said the people in the scenarios were very stupid, 1 for those who said they were stupid, –1 for those who said they were somewhat smart, and –2 for those who said they were very smart. Given the five scenarios, the scores were combined to generate a 21-point index of individual-level *civismo,* ranging from –10 (highly anticivic orientation) to 10 (highly civic orientation).

We note that in their contributions to this volume, Alan Knight and, to a lesser extent, Mitchell Seligson criticize this battery of five questions that we use to operationalize *civismo.* Seligson argues that three of the five scenarios in question are not obviously illegal and thus do not speak to respect for the law. He is quite correct about legality in the narrow sense, but it is not the narrow sense that we are interested in here. Knight protests that the questions tap a "smart/stupid" rather than a normative "right/wrong" orientation toward respect for the rules; in his words, "[r]especting rules is a matter of obeying norms, not displaying intelligence." Although Knight has a valid point, we feel that orientations to the five free-riding behaviors in question speak volumes about the "stickiness" or "enforceability" of social institutions. It seems quite reasonable to us to assume that respondents who see these behaviors as "stupid" would be more likely to intervene in such situations—thus preserving institutions or, in Knight's words, "obeying norms." Thus, we suggest that our *civismo* variable can be viewed as a *proxy* for the propensity to intervene against free-riding or norms-transgressing individuals. This is clearly an indirect measure (as are all proxy variables), and it is clearly fuzzy and unsatisfactory (as is all survey research). However, while acknowledging and accepting the limitations of our methods, we continue to believe that the

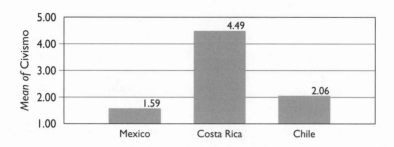

Fig. 2. *Levels of* civismo

five *civismo* questions in the Hewlett survey are innovative and useful lenses with which to focus—albeit fuzzily—the depth of interpersonal trust, the viscosity of social norms, and the density of social capital.

Figure 2 presents mean levels of *civismo* by country. Here, Costa Rica lives up to its reputation as a civic culture, where social norms and respect for the law are deeply embedded. Its mean level of *civismo* (4.49) is more than twice that of Chile or Mexico. Mexico, a country in which 64 percent of citizens believe that their compatriots are generally dishonest and 72 percent believe that Mexicans are generally not law-abiding,[26] turns out to have the lowest mean level of *civismo* (1.59). Pooling the sample again, we find that *civismo* correlates positively with age (.11) and negatively with city size (–.08), education (–.08), and income (–.07). There is no relationship with gender.

The counterintuitive findings that education and income correlate positively with trust but negatively with *civismo* remind us that bivariate correlations are meaningless in causal analysis. Moreover, pooling three very different country samples (without controlling for national factors not captured by other variables) is appropriate only for a very preliminary look at the data. Therefore, we attempted to predict trust and *civismo* using multivariate models and employing country dummy variables to control for presumed national differences. Costa Rica served as the reference category, so only Chile and Mexico were dummied in the analyses. We examined the same family of basic demographic variables: the "usual suspects" of age, gender, urbanization, education, and income.

Using logistic regression, we ran a model in which an affirmative response to the trust question was scored as a 1 and a negative response as a 0. The model correctly predicted some 69 percent of the cases overall, but predicted only 13 percent of the "trusters" in the pooled sample. The independent variables that proved insignificant to predicting trust were age, income, and the Chilean country dummy. The variable of urbanization was marginally significant at the .06 level and had a negative coefficient, meaning that the smaller the size of the community, the greater the level of social trust when one controls for the other variables. In conducting further work on the urbanization variable, we learned that this occurs not so much because people in rural areas are more trusting than others, but because people living in very large cities of more than one million people (such as Mexico City or Santiago) are significantly *less* trusting. We find that trust levels decline precipitously in such large urban centers. (Costa Rica has no city in this category.) The variables that were highly significant predictors of trust were the Mexican country dummy (positive), the number of years of formal education (positive), and a dummy variable for the female gender (negative).

The finding that women have lower levels of interpersonal trust than men (when controlling for age, education, urbanization, income, and nationality) is fascinating indeed. We suspect that this may derive from individual and environmental effects that are linked to women's generally inferior socioeconomic status and to their generally lower life chances in the Latin American context, thus leading them to be understandably mistrustful of others. One might object that our statistical controls for income and education should be capturing some of these effects, but we suspect that these variables do not embrace the full range of the social context in which women are embedded. For example, patterns of power relations at the micro level of society—which we are incapable of measuring with this methodology—may endow men with more personal confidence in their ability to interact with others and may imbue women with less, and this effect could be somehow independent of the objective economic resources held by individuals of either gender. In any case, the jury is still out on this question, and much more research is needed on the relationship between social trust and gender in Latin America.

Our multivariate analyses found consistently that when education and income were used together to predict interpersonal trust, education was always the primary influence. Putnam, using the General Social Survey, found the same relationship in the United States. He also found that "the four years of education between 14 and 18 total years have *ten times more impact* on trust . . . than the first four years of formal education."[27] We did not find such a strong relationship at the upper level of the educational scale, perhaps because of the very small number of respondents (9.2 percent) in the Hewlett survey who had progressed beyond 14 years of formal education. But the impressionistic evidence in figure 3 suggests that a larger survey might indeed have found increasing marginal payoffs for education, especially in Costa Rica and Chile. The relationship seems strongest in Chile. Not only do highly educated Chileans pos-

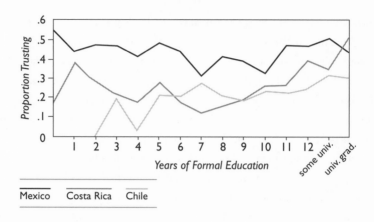

Fig. 3. *Trust and education*

sess the highest rates of interpersonal trust in their country, but the reverse is also true: Chileans of low educational levels are *extremely* distrustful. Of the 188 Chilean respondents with two years or less of education, *not a single person* (0.0 percent) responded affirmatively to the interpersonal trust question, compared to 30.3 percent of Chileans who have attended college (fig. 3). This is one of the most astonishing intranational findings uncovered by the survey.

Our *civismo* variable is a continuous variable with both negative and positive values, so to predict it we employed ordinary least squares regression. Using the same seven independent variables as in the logistic regression for interpersonal trust, we found the goodness-of-fit value again to be quite low, with the model predicting about 6 percent of the total variance in *civismo*. In this model the dummy variables for Chile and Mexico had large and negative coefficients and were highly significant, which occurred because Costa Rica is the reference category and enjoys far higher levels of *civismo* than the two other countries. The only other variable that achieved statistical significance in the model was age: older individuals appear to have deeper civic norms. With the available data, we have no way of knowing whether the age finding represents a "life cycle" effect (in which people routinely acquire deeper civic norms as they age) or a "generational" effect (in which earlier birth cohorts were innately more civic than later birth cohorts, and the cohorts conserve their respective attitudinal characteristics throughout the process of intergenerational population replacement). Finally, in contrast to our findings on trust, here we found that gender is the weakest predictor of *civismo:* there is no difference between men and women when one controls for other factors.

Clearly, the individual-level variance in interpersonal trust and in *civismo* is not easy to explain using standard sociodemographic models. On balance, as Seligson points out in his contribution to this volume, the best predictors seem to be purely national differences: Mexico versus Chile versus Costa Rica. "Costa Rican-ness" in particular is responsible for much of the *civismo* registered in the pooled sample. Costa Rica is also the country where trust and *civismo* are most closely related. The correlation between the two variables is .14 in Costa Rica (p < .0001), but only .05 in Mexico (p < .10), and there is no relationship at all in Chile. Although one would expect social trust and *civismo* to have a reciprocal causal relationship and thus to be highly intercorrelated, we did not find such a connection. The bivariate correlation is only .03 (N = 2,852, p < .10) for the pooled sample of three Latin American societies.

TRUST, *CIVISMO*, AND SUPPORT FOR DEMOCRACY

We can now proceed to see what relationship there is, if any, between interpersonal trust and democratic values at the individual level. The Hewlett survey asked respondents which of the following statements they agreed with most: (1) "Democracy is preferable to any other form of government," (2) "We are indifferent to a democratic or nondemocratic regime," or (3) "In some circumstances, an authoritarian regime can be preferable to a democratic one." Following Seligson, on this question we created a dichotomous variable where 1 equals clear preference for democracy and 0 equals indifference or preference for authoritarianism.

The cross-national differences are again striking. A phenomenal 84 percent of Costa Ricans declare support for democracy, compared to 53 percent of Chileans and 51 percent of Mexicans (fig. 4). These figures correspond very closely to the 1996 Latino-barómetro, in which the same question was asked. In 1996, the corresponding figures were 80 percent for Costa Rica, 54 percent for Chile, and 53 percent for Mexico. This

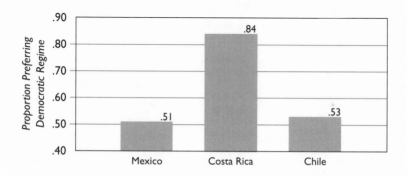

Fig. 4. Support for democracy

generates confidence in the validity of the 1998 Hewlett results and also supports the notion of a uniquely democratic political culture in Costa Rica.

Because the variables for trust and support for democracy are both dichotomous variables, the easiest way to test for bivariate relationships is through simple cross-tabulations with chi-square tests. For the pooled sample, there is no statistically significant relationship between interpersonal trust and democratic support at the individual level. Of self-proclaimed "trusters," some 62.2 percent are self-proclaimed democrats, compared to 60.7 percent of nontrusters. But conducting the same cross-tabulation on the three separate country samples produces an interesting result. Among Mexicans, 52.0 percent of trusters are democrats, compared to an almost identical 51.9 percent of nontrusters (no relationship). Among Costa Ricans, 85.1 percent of trusters are democrats, compared to 83.0 percent of nontrusters (again, no relationship). But among Chileans, we find a strong and statistically significant relationship: 63.1 percent of trusters are democrats, compared to 49.9 percent of nontrusters (p < .0001). At first cut, the hypothesized relationship between interpersonal trust and democratic values seems to hold in only one of the three countries.

What about the hypothesized relationship between *civismo* and support for democracy? The former is a continuous variable, so here we report the correlation coefficients. The overall correlation for the pooled sample is .16 (p < .0001). In Chile, there is no correlation. In Costa Rica, the correlation is .07 (p < .05), and in Mexico, the coefficient rises to .21 (p < .0001). Mexicans, therefore, are responsible for most of the overall relationship in the pooled sample; for some reason, *civismo* is a better predictor of democratic support in Mexico than in the two other countries.

The Mexican riddle is presented in figures 5 and 6. For figure 5, we divided the entire pooled sample of Latin Americans by *civismo* levels, creating three groups of approximately equal size. The first third was composed of individuals who scored from −10 to 0 on *civismo*, the second third had scores from 1 through 5, and the final third had scores from 6 to the maximum 10. The relationship in figure 5 is visually powerful: overall, Latin Americans with strong civic norms are far more likely to support democracy (73 percent) than those with weaker civic orientations (52 percent). However, as figure 6 reveals, the relationship in figure 5 is really concealing the strong effect of Mexico in the pooled sample. Highly civic Mexicans possess democratic attachments that are more than 50 percent higher than those of Mexicans with weak civic orientations. If *incivismo*—the disregard for rule-based or universalistic norms of interpersonal behavior— can be taken as a form of social authoritarianism, then the relationship between social and political authoritarianism seems to be strongest among the Mexican respondents.

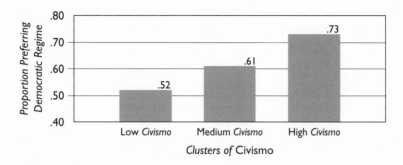

Fig. 5. Civismo *and support for democracy, pooled sample*

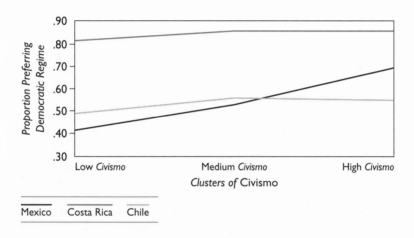

Fig. 6. Civismo *and support for democracy by country*

At the bivariate level, then, we have found some strange results: interpersonal trust strongly predicts democratic support in Chile but not in Mexico, and *civismo* is a good predictor of democratic support in Mexico but not at all in Chile. Again, national differences are paramount. Our next step was to introduce these two variables into multivariate models and control for other factors. We first did so controlling only for national differences; we then repeated the procedure including national differences and the lineup of standard sociodemographic variables discussed earlier.

In a logistic regression using only interpersonal trust and the country dummies to predict support for democracy, we found a fairly weak goodness of fit, with a 60.4 percent rate of correct predictions; the generally weak fit is true of all of our multivariate models reported here. In this model, trust turned out to have a positive and significant effect on support for democracy. The Chilean and Mexican country dummies were strongly predictive in the negative direction, the reference category being democratically minded Costa Rica. We then respecified the model substituting *civismo* for trust, and we obtained virtually the same results. *Civismo* was highly significant and the model's overall goodness of fit improved (to 63.9 percent) when *civismo* took the place of interpersonal trust.

We then proceeded to reintroduce individual-level sociodemographic variables into the models while retaining the country dummies. The country dummies for Chile and Mexico remained strongly predictive and negative. Age and education were significant positive predictors of support for democracy. Urbanization was insignificant in a model using the interpersonal trust variable and was marginally significant in an alternate model using *civismo* instead. Income and gender had no effect in either specification. But, interestingly, both the interpersonal trust and *civismo* variables remained valid and statistically significant predictors of democratic values even net of all the other factors (demographics and country dummies). Similarly to the parsimonious country-based models reported above, we found that when *civismo* was substituted for interpersonal trust, it performed better and improved the overall predictive capacity of the equations (from 63.7 percent concordant predictions using trust to 67.3 percent using *civismo*).

To cross-check these results, we used a different method of measuring the dependent variable, support for democracy. We transformed it into a continuous variable where a value of 1 indicates a preference for democracy as the best system of government, 0 indicates indifference, and −1 indicates a preference for authoritarianism "under certain circumstances." This coding is more sensitive to the intensity of authoritarian preferences. With the dependent variable measured in this way, we were able to reestimate the models using ordinary least squares regression. However, the OLS results turned out to differ only trivially from the logistic regressions discussed above. The only difference was that the trust variable now narrowly missed the .10 test of statistical significance (p < .12). *Civismo*, on the other hand, remained positive and significant at the .0001 level in the OLS model with the other seven independent variables included. The two OLS models explained 7 and 9 percent of the variance in support for democracy, respectively. Again, *civismo* outperformed interpersonal trust in predicting democratic support.

So far we have treated interpersonal trust and *civismo* separately, because each embodies slightly different facets of the trust-and-democracy hypotheses discussed earlier. Interpersonal trust is measured here in an abstract fashion: does the respondent generally trust people, or not? The *civismo* index created out of the Hewlett instrument attempts to gauge to what degree individuals will tolerate abuses of certain social norms: universalism, civicness, transparency, and respect for the law. The former variable taps into abstract notions of social trust, while the latter addresses the potential for achieving self-enforceable norms in a given society. The greater the level of *civismo,* the greater the potential for the society to be a self-regulating entity in which *all* institutions (not merely the quotidian ones cited in the questions) are taken seriously by social actors; this speaks to the argument of Diamond, who notes that a lack of social trust leads to widespread defection from institutions. Although both variables speak to the issue of social trust, which one performs better in predicting support for democracy?

To answer this question, we included *both* variables—interpersonal trust and *civismo*—simultaneously in the expanded logistic and OLS regression models discussed earlier. What we found is that *civismo* consistently dominates interpersonal trust. When we treated support for democracy as a dummy variable and used logistic regression, both independent variables were significant and positive, but *civismo* performed better than trust. When we treated support for democracy as a gradation admitting of both positive and negative values and employed OLS, we found again that *civismo* predominated, with trust now becoming marginally insignificant ($p < .13$).

DISCUSSION AND CONCLUSIONS

In this chapter we have conducted a preliminary review of the 1998 Hewlett data in order to examine a perennial question in political culture: the relationship between interpersonal trust and democracy. Unlike previous studies that examine these variables cross-nationally by aggregating data from whole societies, in this research note we examined the question of trust and democracy at the individual level. Our analysis suggests four tentative conclusions, all of which should be considered preliminary as researchers further investigate the relationship between democratic values and social trust.

The first conclusion that stands out is the obvious inability of our analytical models to explain much of the variance in individual attitudes—whether it be in interpersonal trust, *civismo,* or preference for a democratic over an authoritarian regime. When we resort to standard individual-level sociodemographic variables such as age, income, urbanization, etc., we find that 90 percent or more of the variance is usually left unexplained. This could be due to inherent problems in survey research, such as difficulty in wording questions so as to capture the concepts of interest, etc. Such measurement error tends to work against the hypotheses. As Alan Knight suggests in this volume, this phenomenon could also be due to idiosyncrasies of respondents, such as instability in responses due to lack of information about politics or low ideological constraint; or it could be a combination of all of the aforementioned factors. Whatever the reason for the vast uncharted waters of the survey data set, the researcher must sometimes be content with explaining no more than a tenth of the variance in a given attitudinal variable.

Following on the above, the second conclusion that emerges here—and one that is replicated by other contributors to this volume—is the strong performance of country dummy variables in all of the multivariate analyses. They are meant to capture national differences that are not being picked up by the standard demographic factors. And, very importantly, these national differences—being a Mexican as opposed to a Costa Rican, or a Chilean as opposed to a Mexican—turn out to explain much more of the variance in attitudes than any of the demographic "usual suspects." At first glance, this appears tautological: can culture actually explain culture? The relationship is not tautological if one views it as national-level political culture—the history, traditions, and national myths to which all of us are socialized—explaining individual-level attitudes. The direction of political socialization is from the top down and from the past to the present, whether it occurs within the family or via the state. As Mitchell Seligson argues in his contribution to this volume, the national myth of Costa Rica portrays the country (not wholly inaccurately, it must be said) as a paragon of democracy: a country that enjoyed one of the few truly liberal revolutions in the Third World, a country equipped with an egalitarian society, a democratic and progressive welfare state, a pacifist outlook on life (Costa Rica abolished its army in the 1940s), and open and accountable political institutions. Costa Rica views itself, again correctly, as an "outlier" in Latin America—with a self-conscious attitude that is almost an isthmian answer to de Gaulle's *une certaine différence.* As Seligson shows, the Costa Rican process of political socialization, and particularly the educational system (again, as in France), reinforces these ideas from childhood. Thus, it is not surprising that Costa Ricans loudly proclaim their support for political democracy. Compare this to Chile, which recently had an authoritarian regime that was viewed as economically successful by key sectors of society, and where today between 30 and 40 percent of the electorate continues to view the Pinochet period approvingly. A large proportion of Chileans grew up learning the Pinochet diagnosis of the ills of pre-1973 democracy. Again, national-level attributes are consistently the best predictors of attitudinal differences among the members of these three Latin American publics.

Third, of the sociodemographic "usual suspects," the one variable that does perform consistently well is education. The greater an individual's level of education, the more likely he or she is to trust others, to support norms of civic behavior in interpersonal relations, and to support democracy. Just as Putnam found for the United States, the effect of education consistently overwhelms the effect of income. This finding has important policy implications for democrats throughout Latin America. Policymakers will find it difficult to raise incomes rapidly and consistently, but they do have it in their power to increase educational levels by making education more accessible. Given that increased education tends to increase trust, *civismo,* and support for democracy, policymakers should recognize that long-term regime legitimacy can apparently be generated independently of economic outputs—although both are worthy goals and should be pursued simultaneously.

Finally, our long-awaited response to the question posed in the title of this chapter: trust *does* matter. We have found that even when controlling for major individual-level characteristics and national-identity attributes, our two measures of social trust continue to be positive predictors of support for political democracy. We have already noted some of the differences between our two measures, one of which is based on an abstract question about trusting people and the other of which is based on a series of five questions about reactions to hypothetical free-riding and antisocial behaviors. But perhaps our most interesting finding is that *civismo* consistently outperforms interpersonal trust as a predictor of support for democracy—and that when the two are used together to predict democratic support, *civismo* predominates.

There are two possible interpretations of this finding. One is that the two indicators are measuring the same general phenomenon—social trust—and that *civismo* is simply a more efficient way of tapping interpersonal trust than a general question about whether "most people can be trusted." The second interpretation is that *civismo* is capturing a somewhat different phenomenon: the intolerance of free-riding behavior, or, conversely, the willingness of individuals to enforce universalistic norms of interpersonal behavior. Granted, we are still talking here about attitudes, not concrete actions, which survey research cannot measure. Still, it seems logical that the greater the intolerance of such behavior, the more likely individuals are to intervene and enforce social norms, and the more the wider society can benefit from self-regulating interactions. Taking this one step further, societies that have high levels of interpersonal *civismo* are likely to enjoy a spillover effect in which self-enforcing norms lend credibility to social, economic, and especially political institutions. To put this into the language of game theory, a high level of *civismo* raises the costs of defection and lowers the costs of cooperation.

Civismo, then, fits Putnam's general definition of social capital, which he defines as the trust, norms, and networks that allow people to work together more effectively. Perhaps because the operational definition of *civismo* used in this chapter comes closer to suggesting possible *behaviors* than does the typical question about trusting people, it turns out to be a more sharp-edged predictor of our dependent variable: support for the regime of political democracy. Although it would be a ludicrous overstatement to claim that civic-oriented individuals are democrats and free-riders are authoritarians, the analyses undertaken here suggest that there is at least a grain of truth to this generalization.

If this generalization holds water, then surely sociologists and cultural anthropologists have as much to say about the causes of democracy as do political scientists. But political scientists have also recognized the connection between micro and macro factors. Guillermo O'Donnell was onto something when he described his day driving around São Paulo—a day in which he encountered reckless drivers, healthy people parked in handicapped spaces, and rich families illegally closing off their neighborhoods to traffic—and then connected these free-riding and privatizing behaviors to the macropolitical ills of Brazilian democracy.[28] Like O'Donnell, it may be necessary for us to reformulate the concept of social trust, and to measure it in different ways, before we can understand the precise nature of its connection to political democracy. But the evidence presented here—crude and preliminary as it may be—suggests that the relationship between trust and democracy, so obvious at the cross-national level, is also detectable at the level of individuals.

Part III

Cultural Explanations for Democracy:

Is There a Link? The Role of Traditional Variables

Chapter 4

Costa Rica

Portrait of an Established Democracy

Mary A. Clark

The study of political culture is an important complement to political scientists' focus on institutions, organizations, processes, and policies. Research in this field allows us to understand the way that individuals think about politics and to pinpoint which groups of people hold what beliefs. Given the recent wave of democratizations in Latin America, it seems logical to ask: Do people find official proclamations of democracy to be legitimate, and do they prefer this type of regime to others? Do their attitudes reflect a participatory political culture, tolerance for political and social differences, and a willingness to follow the rules even when this calls for personal restraint?[1] Indeed, a central concern of the literature on political culture is the fit between a country's regime type and its population's beliefs, values, norms, and attitudes about politics, and, more specifically, whether the country's political culture approaches the characteristics thought necessary to support a functioning democracy. If we can locate a mature, stable democracy in which democratic culture is not evident among the masses, there may be something seriously wrong with our theories.

As Latin America's longest-standing and most stable democracy, then, Costa Rica becomes a particularly important place in which to evaluate the extent to which there is a match between regime and culture. Whether one believes that political cultures evolve slowly or shift rapidly according to regime fluctuations, we can reasonably expect Costa Rica's 50-year-old democracy to have produced a corresponding mass culture by now. For the purposes of the Hewlett project in particular, it was hoped that Costa Rica would show this sort of congruity and fulfill the role of "baseline democracy" for the study. In this survey, the Costa Rican public did, for the most part, respond according to our expectations. The majority of mass attitudes about system legitimacy, regime performance, political efficacy, and civic culture match Costa Rica's democratic regime type.

Below I begin by describing Costa Rica's political institutions and the degree to which the Costa Rican public's responses seem to mirror them. Then, because the Hewlett survey offers several measures of civic culture, I examine the degree of "demo-craticness" within Costa Rica's culture. The final section explores two public concerns that came across strongly in the survey: corruption and crime.

THE INSTITUTIONAL BASIS OF
COSTA RICA'S DEMOCRACY

The brief civil war of 1948 ushered in a new political era for Costa Rica. Although the country had enjoyed competitive elections since 1899, the political system had been marred by vote fraud, coup attempts, and a brief dictatorship.[2] Everything changed in 1948 when a charismatic young man named José (Pepe) Figueres led a coalition of forces with conflicting ideologies into a six-week battle against a government alliance that included large coffee growers and the Communist Party. During the 1940s, coop-eration between President Rafael Ángel Calderón Guardia, a member of the oligarchy, and the Communist Party had allowed the latter to push forward its agenda on social security and labor legislation. This alliance irritated many agro-elites almost as much as Calderón's abuses of executive privileges, in and out of office. Wealthy coffee grow-ers represented by the Partido Unión Nacional (National Union Party, or PUN) decided to unite with José Figueres and the Partido Social Demócrata (Social Democratic Party, or PSD) in order to defeat Calderón in the 1948 elections.[3] Joined behind the PUN can-didate, Otilio Ulate, the *anti-calderonista* opposition was pleased when it appeared that he had won the election. But the *calderonistas* claimed that the opposition had stolen the election and used their majority in the Legislative Assembly to overturn it.

With both sides crying fraud, Figueres decided to act on his own. He and an irregu-lar army that was put together with help from the Caribbean Legion fought govern-ment forces and Communist Party volunteers for six weeks until it became clear that Figueres would win.[4] The two sides agreed to a truce, Rafael Calderón left the country, and a junta headed by Figueres ran the country for the next 18 months. Figueres took several steps that would shape Costa Rica's development in the decades to come: he abolished the army, nationalized the banks, and called a constituent assembly to write a new constitution. Yet while members of the PSD dominated the junta, they would not dominate the Constituent Assembly. In fact, conservative delegates from the PUN won a majority of seats in that body. They used their majority to reduce the junta's decree powers, limit Figueres's proposals for state intervention in the economy, and focus on reworking the balance of power among government institutions.

The 1949 constitution lays down Costa Rica's modern political institutions. One of the chief concerns of the Constituent Assembly was to reduce the president's power vis-à-vis other branches of government and thus avoid repetition of past abuses. As a result, the Costa Rican system has probably the weakest executive in Latin America. Costa Rican presidents cannot veto the national budget as determined by the legislature, use a pocket or line-item veto, assume emergency powers without a supporting vote by a two-thirds majority of the legislature, legislate by decree, or stand for reelection.[5] The president does appoint and dismiss cabinet members independently and can also call a special session of the Legislative Assembly to consider only legislation proposed by the executive. But the latter power is constrained by the president's inability to control the procedures used or the amendments attached to legislation during a special session.

All elections are held concurrently every four years. Those elected to the Legislative Assembly, a unicameral body with 57 seats, must sit out one term before standing for office again. Costa Rica's seven provinces are divided into 81 cantons (roughly, counties), each of which has an elected municipal council. At present, each municipal council appoints an executive officer, but voters will elect mayors directly beginning in 2002. In any case, the municipal governments have little real power, as the national government controls most of their financial decisions and provides almost all services.[6]

The Tribunal Supremo Electoral (Supreme Electoral Tribunal, or TSE) oversees all elections. Its magistrates are appointed to six-year terms by the Supreme Court. In Costa Rica, electoral laws and regulations, voter registration, and public campaign funding are reviewed and administered exclusively by the TSE. The tribunal is designed to make elections as fair and honest as possible. In fact, in an important public ceremony held shortly before each election, it takes legal control of the country's police and rural guard. Because of its independent power, the TSE is sometimes said to be the fourth branch of the Costa Rican government.

Costa Rica's judicial branch is unusually independent and, since 1989, enormously powerful. Its 22 members are appointed by the Legislative Assembly to staggered eight-year terms. They are reelected automatically and thus tend to serve lifetime terms. Until 1989, the Supreme Court was divided by legal topics into three chambers. In that year, the Legislative Assembly created a fourth chamber (Sala IV) to handle questions of constitutionality of legislation and government rules and procedures. The advent of the Sala IV greatly enhanced the weight of the judiciary in policymaking by strengthening the Supreme Court's powers of judicial review. Since constitutionality questions do not need to pass through the lower courts before being heard by the Supreme Court, the Sala IV has become a central arbiter of legal disputes; political foes habitually appeal to it in attempts to block policy measures.

The structure of Costa Rica's political institutions decentralizes power and enlivens debate, but it also encourages gridlock. In fact, a common complaint from representatives of multilateral development banks and Costa Rican officials alike is that the country suffers from "too much" democracy, a condition that causes policymaking to be agonizingly slow. Nevertheless, we should not mistake Costa Rican expressions of frustration with any true rejection of pluralism or real effort to subvert the constitutional order.

REGIME LEGITIMACY AND PERFORMANCE

Indeed, Costa Ricans are notably committed to democracy. When asked about their preferences in political regimes, 80 percent of Costa Ricans responded that democracy was preferable to any other form of government.[7] As table 1 shows, the answer to this question was stable across most demographic variables, although rural dwellers, the wealthy, and black citizens demonstrated a somewhat greater preference for democracy. Another recent study using an identical question finds that in Latin America, only Uruguayans, who scored the same 80 percent, ascribe a similar level of legitimacy to democracy.[8] The same study offers an Index of Democratic Perceptions, on which Costa Rica scores higher than any other Latin American country.[9]

Citizens are also fairly satisfied with the quantity of democracy in local and national government. Sixty-six percent of Costa Ricans polled responded that there was much or some democracy in their country, and 69 percent answered the same way when asked about democracy in their own city. Table 1 again shows that rural people, the wealthy, and black citizens gave slightly more positive answers about democracy in their country than did city dwellers, the poor, and other ethnicities. And those over age 50, people with higher incomes, and rural residents felt that there was more democracy in their local areas. The survey also found that 58 percent of Costa Ricans were very or somewhat satisfied with the way democracy was working in their country. Here the most highly educated and wealthiest citizens were considerably less satisfied than others, while blacks and rural inhabitants were more satisfied. Considering that about half the citizens of this Central American nation continue to live in the countryside and that

TABLE 1 *Costa Rican Public Opinion about Democracy*

	"Democracy is preferable to any other form of government." (% agreed with this statement)	"How much democracy would you say there is in this country?" (% great deal/some)	"How much democracy would you say there is in this city?" (% great deal/some)	"Are you satisfied or dissatisfied with the way democracy is functioning in this country?" (% very/somewhat satisfied)
All respondents	80	66	69	58
Sex				
Male	79	65	71	62
Female	81	69	68	54
Age				
<30	76	67	63	62
<50	85	68	68	54
50+	79	65	74	60
Education				
Primary	79	64	69	62
Secondary	82	72	70	54
College	84	70	70	46
Income				
Low	80	65	65	60
Lower-middle	78	69	68	58
Upper-middle	82	67	73	59
High	86	71	73	40
Location				
Large city	79	61	68	55
Medium city	81	65	65	49
Small city	73	66	70	57
Rural area	86	72	76	72
Ethnicity				
White	80	70	72	58
Light dark	81	56	67	54
Deep dark	77	70	60	60
Black	88	85	72	83

N = 1,002

black people are a distinct ethnic and cultural minority in Costa Rica, these findings bode particularly well for the breadth of support for and satisfaction with democracy there.

Costa Ricans have correspondingly high feelings of political efficacy. For example, 75 percent said that "politics" were somewhat or very important, and 66 percent answered affirmatively when asked if they were prepared to do something to demand government accountability. These questions did reveal that some demographic groups felt more engaged than others, particularly those with the highest levels of income and education. The same was true when political competency was measured by asking people to name the three branches of government. The executive, legislative, and judicial branches scored equally well, with about half of the respondents overall able to name them, but those with greater education, more income, and whiter skin performed much better at this task. So there may be room for improvement in ensuring that all social groups feel equally able to have some impact on their government.

POLITICAL PARTIES AND THE ELECTORATE

The ideological leanings and party orientations of the Costa Rican electorate also reflect the country's historical development. A key finding of the Hewlett survey was that the Costa Rican electorate has a strong center-right leaning. As table 2 shows, 67 percent of respondents placed themselves on the center or right of a 10-point left-right political scale, while only 4 percent identified their beliefs as left of center. Nineteen percent of the respondents placed themselves at the extreme right (point 10) of the scale. Table 2 also shows that party identification is not a good predictor of respondents' political ideologies.[10] When party identification is cross-tabulated with the left-right scale, we see that the ideological distribution of the general population is almost replicated within the two main parties and among those making the third most popular choice: no party or not voting at all. The Partido Liberación Nacional (National Liberation Party, or PLN) appears to have a slightly larger center than other groups; those not voting may be a little less right-wing; and the few who chose other parties seem to

TABLE 2 *Political Ideology of All Respondents and by Party Preference* (percent)

		Party Preference[a]			
L-R Scale[b]	All Respondents	PUSC	PLN	Other	None/Don't Vote
Left	4	4	5	1	5
Center	36	32	41	38	37
Right	31	31	32	38	25
Don't Know	29	33	22	20	34
Total	100	100	100	97	101

$N = 1,002$

Notes: a. Based on the question, "If the elections were today, what party would you vote for?" Thirty-three percent chose the PUSC, 29 percent said the PLN, 24 percent replied that they didn't vote or preferred no party, 5 percent named another party, and 8 percent said they didn't know.

b. Respondents were asked to place themselves on a 10-point scale representing their political beliefs where 1 was the farthest left and 10 the farthest right. Here the scale is collapsed into left (1–3), center (4–7), and right (8–10).

TABLE 3 *Public versus Private Responsibility for Individual Welfare*

(percent)

Should the government look after the individual's well-being, or should each individual look after him/herself?	All Respondents	Party Preference	
		PUSC	PLN
Government	41	44	45
Individual	41	37	41
Both	16	17	14
Neither	I	1	0
Don't know	I	1	0
Total	100	100	100

N = 1,002

be a degree more conservative. But each group tells roughly the same story as the general electorate: little support for the left, and large constituencies on the center and right of the scale.

Not surprisingly, the survey results show that supporters of the two main parties are also split on questions about the proper roles of the welfare state and the private sector in the same proportions as the general public. As table 3 illustrates, Costa Rican respondents overall split evenly on who should look after a person's well-being: 41 percent said the state, and 41 percent said the individual. PUSC and PLN supporters were divided by roughly the same percentages. The same held true when people were asked about who should own the airlines, schools, water companies, and television stations. As table 4 indicates, citizens preferred public ownership of the water companies and schools and private holding of the airlines and television stations. Respondents within each party divided their answers in almost exactly the same way. Thus, just as party identification is not a good predictor of political beliefs, neither can we see any clear difference between the two parties' voters according to their ideas about the division of public and private responsibilities.

Costa Ricans' center-right orientation and the ideological diversity found within each major political grouping are largely rooted in the development of the country's party system in the postwar era. Since 1948, Costa Rica has been evolving toward a two-party system. The axis of political competition has always divided the PLN, created in 1951 by José Figueres, and coalitions of anti-PLN forces. In the first postwar elections, held in 1953, Figueres and his party won the presidency and a majority in the Legislative Assembly, beginning almost four decades of near-dominance on the Costa Rican political scene. The PLN won the presidency in seven of the twelve elections held in the postwar era and held more congressional seats than any other party during eight of those administrations.[11]

TABLE 4 *Public versus Private Ownership* (percent)

Which activities should be government owned and which private?	All Respondents	Party Preference	
		PUSC	PLN
Airlines			
Government	34	39	33
Private sector	44	44	43
Both	17	14	19
Don't know	5	3	5
Total	100	100	100
Television			
Government	25	27	25
Private sector	52	53	51
Both	19	17	22
Don't know	4	3	2
Total	100	100	100
Schools			
Government	69	71	72
Private sector	9	10	5
Both	20	17	22
Don't know	2	2	1
Total	100	100	100
Water companies			
Government	64	63	72
Private sector	19	22	13
Both	14	14	14
Don't know	3	2	2
Total	100	101	101

$N = 1,002$

Although the PLN identifies itself as a social democratic party and is a longtime member of the Socialist International, the working class did not play a significant role in its formation, nor can it be counted on for solid electoral support. The PLN has always been an amalgam. During its first three decades of existence, the party appealed to the middle and lower classes (who mainly resided in the countryside), urban professionals, and a nascent group of national industrialists, with redistributionist policies, rapid expansion of the welfare state, improved access to credit through the state banking system, public investment in rural infrastructure, and ample protection for domestic agricultural and manufactured products. The PLN's efforts to reach out to the rural masses, in particular, won it popularity, and that is where the party's major support base still lies.

As Costa Rican society and the economy became more complex, so did the support base of the PLN, making it a true catch-all party. The PLN's rhetoric had always identified it with middle-class peasants, and in the 1970s that discourse expanded to encompass the growing numbers of white-collar urban workers. And as Costa Rica responded to the changing international environment in the 1980s and 1990s, the PLN incorporated new private-sector groups such as bankers and exporters of nontraditional products. The party has also undergone a generational shift. Until midway through the 1980s, three personalities linked to the events of 1948–49 (José Figueres, Daniel Oduber, and Francisco Orlich) ran the PLN. But the election of Oscar Arias Sánchez to the presidency in 1986 signaled the ascendance of a new generation, one too young to have been involved in the civil war. Many of the younger leaders are "new democrats" or technocrats who would streamline the state and embrace internationally oriented businesses.

In the 1950s, the main anti-PLN groups re-formed into a set of conservative parties. These parties, including the prewar PRN (Partido Republicano Nacional, or National Republican Party) and PUN labels, usually came together in fragile coalitions every four years in order to run a single candidate for president. They have elected five presidents since 1948. In the Legislative Assembly, the conservative opposition parties have a weaker record, winning a majority only once, in 1990. Until that time, opposition parties were not well enough established throughout the country's electoral districts to garner sufficient seats for a majority in the Assembly. In 1983, the opposition parties coalesced into a single organization, the Partido Unidad Social Cristiana (United Social Christian Party, or PUSC).

During the 1950s, 1960s, and 1970s, the opposition parties drew most of their supporters from metropolitan San José and from the cantons on either coast where the banana plantations were located (these had been strongholds of the Communist Party).[12] The opposition alliances and later the PUSC have always drawn multiclass support from an unlikely mix of people including the urban and rural proletariat, conservative agricultural and business elites, and hard-core supporters of neoliberal economic policies. In the 1980s and 1990s, the PUSC has made inroads among the urban middle classes. Until recently, the conservative parties only came together on the basis of mutual antipathy toward the PLN. For example, two decades ago a politician named Rodrigo Carazo had a falling-out with the PLN, quit the party, rallied the conservative parties around him, and won the presidency. But the PUSC has held together well, found leadership from younger generations (such as former president Rafael Ángel Calderón Fournier and current president Miguel Ángel Rodríguez), and is perhaps developing its own, independent identity. The PUSC maintains a multiclass appeal because its neoliberal position on economic policy is tempered by a Christian democratic approach to social policy and the issuing of reminders to the electorate that the party's forefather, Rafael Ángel Calderón Guardia, was responsible for the original social reform legislation in Costa Rica.[13]

Neither end of the Costa Rican left-right political continuum is well represented in the electoral process. Although nearly one-fifth of Costa Rican respondents identify with the extreme right, they are not represented by any national political party. But an organization called Movimiento Costa Rica Libre (the Free Costa Rica Movement) was a visible and rabid anticommunist presence in the 1980s and early 1990s.[14] Those on the left are slightly better represented. With the Communist Party banned until the mid-1970s, a variety of left parties have come and gone. The draw of the only one of these to achieve national appeal, Pueblo Unido (United People, or PU), peaked in 1982 when it garnered 3.3 percent of the vote in the presidential race and four seats in the Assembly.[15] Internal divisions eventually doomed the PU, but in 1998, two very small left-leaning parties elected a total of four deputies to the Assembly.[16]

Given the significance of the Communist Party in the 1940s, the poor showing of left parties and the appeal of anticommunism in modern Costa Rica deserve explanation. Recall that the Communist Party had formed an alliance with President Rafael Ángel Calderón Guardia and fought alongside government forces during the 1948 civil war. In the aftermath of the war, José Figueres took care to eliminate any leftist threat to his brand of socialism and to his power over the country. The ruling junta outlawed the Communist Party, jailed its leaders, and dismantled the radical Confederación de Trabajadores de Costa Rica (Confederation of Costa Rican Workers, or CTCR) in order to eliminate the party's social base. To replace the radical unions, the PLN and conservative parties promoted labor organizations with milder social democratic and Christian democratic orientations. In addition, private enterprise sponsored a uniquely Costa Rican labor movement called *solidarismo*.[17] *Solidarismo* is a company union system that strives to maintain harmonious relations between management and workers and eschews confrontation. By the 1980s, *solidarismo* had come to dominate the private sector and make important inroads among public-sector employees. As of 1993, only 14 percent of Costa Rican workers belonged to traditional labor unions.[18]

Thus, after 1948, the forces victorious in the war were able to remake two key institutions—political parties and labor organizations—in ways that made Costa Rica an inhospitable environment for anticapitalist ideologies. The growth of public welfare

services in the subsequent three decades and the fact that the two major party group-
ings supported the state's expansion in these areas also robbed leftist organizations of
the political space and social issues that otherwise might have been fertile ground for
them. By the 1980s, state agencies had extended health, education, sanitation, and pen-
sion services to virtually the entire population. This is no small feat for a Latin American country in which more than half of the population still lives in rural areas.

What factors explain each party's appeal to the right? Given its origins in conservative politics, it is not surprising that the PUSC contains a center-right constituency;
more interesting is that the PLN counts on a similar following and that 18 percent of its
adherents placed themselves at the extreme right (point 10) of the ideological scale. As
discussed above, Costa Rican social democracy arose as an alternative to communism
and radical labor movements and does not embrace the same notions of class conflict
as its Western European counterparts. In addition, personalism still plays a strong role
in Costa Rican politics; John Booth reports that many voters identify with candidates
as opposed to parties, so they may switch parties often and not pay much attention to
policy platforms.[19] It is also possible that the PLN's acceptance of market-oriented economic reform during the last 15 years has either caused or reflected a conservative shift
in its electoral base. The PLN has certainly moved away from its original statist and
redistributionist orientation. In 1995, the party changed its ideological charter to
endorse private-sector participation in public monopolies. And common wisdom has
it that internationally oriented business interests have grown within the party.

What we are left with in the late 1990s is a bipartisan system dominated by two
catch-all parties. Although the PUSC more clearly identifies itself with neoliberal ideas
during the campaign season, both parties take care to honor the gains made by the welfare state in the past and promise to continue the public provision of basic social services. The clearest policy implication of the ideological diversity within the two parties is
that during the last 16 years, neither party has been impressive in implementing market-oriented structural adjustment while in office. As a result, Costa Rica's progress
toward economic reform falls below the regional mean.[20] The Costa Rican system presents enormous institutional barriers to economic reform, so it is too far a leap to say
that past administrations have been unsuccessful purely because of the mixed feelings
about privatization among their supporters. But the ambiguity within both major parties about the proper division of public and private responsibilities could be part of the
explanation.

COSTA RICAN CIVIC CULTURE

Almost everything we know about Costa Rican political culture demonstrates a degree of civicness matching the country's reputation as Latin America's most stable democracy. Of course, it is far more difficult to identify the origins of democratic political culture than the origins of the country's formal institutions. But it seems reasonable to speculate that some combination of the postwar elite accommodations discussed above and attendant socioeconomic factors is responsible for building and reinforcing democratic values.[21]

One of the oldest measures of civic culture is political participation. Gabriel Almond and Sidney Verba believed that political participation was a crucial element of what they called "citizen culture."[22] A recent study by John Booth evaluates data from a 1973 national survey and a 1995 urban survey in Costa Rica that asked about conventional types of political participation such as voting, campaigning, and contacting public officials. Booth finds that the levels and modes of political participation detected in these surveys resembled those found in the United States and other advanced industrialized countries.[23] For instance, the 1995 survey reported that 88 percent of respondents had voted in the last election, 35 percent had contacted a public official, and 26 percent had worked for a political party or candidate.[24]

The 1998 Hewlett survey asked Costa Ricans about their involvement in and attitudes toward political protest activities, especially those outside of formal channels of participation. Both because of the electorate's rejection of leftist parties and ideas and because ample avenues of formal participation exist in Costa Rica, we might predict unconventional participation to be low. As expected, the percentage of Costa Rican respondents who had signed a protest letter, participated in a march, taken part in an illegal strike, occupied a building, or joined a boycott was indeed quite low. Only 14 percent admitted to the first two activities, 8 percent said they had taken part in an illegal strike, and less than 4 percent had occupied a building or joined a boycott.

Besides asking about actual participation, there are a number of ways to gauge how democratic or authoritarian a culture is. For example, we can look at socializing institutions to see if they promote participatory behaviors. The 1998 survey provides data on how much participation Costa Ricans enjoyed in social institutions such as the family, schools, and the workplace. Costa Ricans scored impressively in their participation in family and school matters. Fifty-one percent said that their parents had always or almost always allowed the children to participate in family decisions. And 57 percent answered the same way when asked if their teachers had allowed students to participate in classroom decisions. Not unexpectedly, Costa Rican employees scored less impressively on how much they were allowed to share workplace decisions with managers (only 28 percent always or almost always did). Nevertheless, the high scores on the first two measures of social participation seem to indicate that Costa Ricans' upbringing prepares them for citizenship in a democratic society.

Tolerance for others, especially people of other races, religions, lifestyles, and nationalities, is also often considered a crucial component of democratic, as opposed to authoritarian, personalities.[25] In the 1998 survey, Costa Ricans were asked whether they would be opposed to an immediate family member's marrying a person of a different religion than their own. Only 23 percent said they would somewhat or very much oppose such a union. Respondents were also asked which, if any, kinds of people listed (evangelical Protestants, homosexuals, or foreigners) they would *not* like to have for neighbors. While Costa Ricans demonstrated a marked intolerance for homosexuals, fewer than 14 percent were bothered by evangelicals or foreigners living next door.[26]

Another way to evaluate the social foundations of democracy is to measure citizens' tolerance for anticivic behavior or their respect for the rule of law. The 1998 survey asked Costa Ricans what they thought of a person who cut in line, kept silent if they received extra change from a cashier, neglected to pay bus fare, ran a traffic light at night when streets were empty, or told a white lie. In no case did more than 29 percent of respondents think it was a good idea for a person to do any of these things, a result that indicates that Costa Rica's social norms support the restraint of short-term self-interest required for democratic institutions to work.[27]

Finally, because Costa Rica is an established democracy, it makes sense to ask how Costa Ricans score on some of the indicators of interpersonal trust and life satisfaction that Ronald Inglehart has found to be correlated with stable democracy.[28] Costa Ricans are notoriously distrustful; a full 70 percent of respondents said that people were not reliable. What is more, Costa Ricans are well aware of this trait and often advise foreigners that their countrymen are "muy individualista." Interpersonal trust is thought to be supportive of democracy because it facilitates compromise by reducing fears that political actors will defect from negotiated agreements or use their turn in government to annihilate the opposition.[29] Curiously, despite low trust, Costa Ricans much prefer compromise and negotiation to conflict. Mavis, Richard, and Karen Biesanz note what many others have also observed about public and private life in Costa Rica: the terrific importance of building consensus and avoiding personal offense.[30]

The responses to the survey questions about life satisfaction seem more congruent with Inglehart's findings about culture and established democracy. Costa Ricans are generally happy and enjoy reasonable economic security. A full 61 percent of them say that they are "very happy." And a significantly greater percentage of Costa Ricans consider that their personal financial situation is very good or somewhat good (42 percent) than say it is bad or somewhat bad (26 percent). Twice as many as not thought that their own economic outlook would improve within the next year.

The 1998 survey thus attempts to measure the civicness of the Costa Rican public through several types of question batteries. Most of the answers show that Costa Ricans are participatory, tolerant, civic-minded, and satisfied citizens. With the exceptions of their low interpersonal trust and intolerance of homosexuals, this is about what we would expect in a stable democracy.

FEARS OF THE MASS PUBLIC:
CORRUPTION AND CRIME

In the late 1990s, citizens listed government corruption and crime as the issues their system should be most concerned about. In this concluding section, I will discuss why people might be so worried about these phenomena and whether corruption and crime pose any real threat to Costa Rica's democracy.

The Costa Rican public perceives that government corruption is an enormous problem. Seventy-five percent of respondents said that many or almost all government officials commit acts of corruption (known as *chorizos*). As table 5 shows, there is substantial variation within several categories on this question. Younger people, those with greater incomes, residents of rural areas and small cities, and non-blacks all saw more corruption than others within their demographic groups. Perhaps even more revealing is that, when asked to name the principal obstacle to democracy in Costa Rica, respondents mentioned corruption far and away most often. The answers to this question varied most within the categories of sex, education, location, and ethnicity. Men, better-educated citizens, those living in places other than large cities, and non-blacks were more likely to say that corruption was the main obstacle facing Costa Rican democracy.

Costa Rican beliefs about corruption closely resemble those of the Mexican respondents, which is surprising given that outside observers think of Mexico as having a much greater actual incidence of corruption. In fact, in 1997, a study by a nonprofit group called Transparency International found that there was less corruption in the Costa Rican government than in any other in Latin America.[31] Probably the best explanation for Costa Ricans' concern about corruption is that they are so well informed about every scandal, large and small, that goes on in the government. We know from the Hewlett survey that 82 percent of Costa Ricans get the news every day. Costa Rica's

TABLE 5   *Perceptions of Corruption and Crime*

	"How many government officials are corrupt?" (% who answered many/almost all)	"What is the main obstacle to democracy in this country?" (% who answered corruption)	"What is the main task of democracy?" (% who answered crime)
All respondents	75	46	38
Sex			
Male	76	51	32
Female	72	41	44
Age			
<30	79	47	31
<50	74	47	36
50+	71	44	44
Education			
Primary	72	43	47
Secondary	78	50	27
College	77	54	19
Income			
Low	65	44	48
Lower-middle	79	42	37
Upper-middle	80	52	28
High	80	48	27
Location			
Large city	65	35	39
Medium city	71	53	38
Small city	79	45	29
Rural area	80	42	42
Ethnicity			
White	74	46	38
Light dark	77	45	31
Deep dark	77	47	48
Black	49	39	54

$N = 1,002$

news media are competitive and aggressive, and journalists rarely face political intimidation. During the month this poll was taken, for example (July 1998), the press was
reporting daily on an investigation into corruption in the country's principal social
welfare fund.

While local scandals may be tame compared to those of neighboring countries, Costa Ricans still perceive that corruption is a large problem for their system. One effect
such a perception may have on a country's citizenry is a refusal to become involved in
politics, even through voting, or at least a tendency to prefer smaller parties over the

two main ones. But among those who said that most or all government officials are corrupt and those who chose corruption as the principal obstacle to democracy, party affiliation and nonaffiliation/nonvoting break down almost exactly as they do in the general population. Thus, the survey data provide no evidence that public perceptions of corruption pose a threat to the two-party system.

Exposure to sensationalist news reporting might also partially explain Costa Ricans' extremely high concerns about crime.[32] When asked, "Which of the following is the main task of democracy?" Costa Ricans put combating crime in first place, ranking this response over electing officials, distributing wealth, and protecting minorities. As table 5 shows, older people, women, poor people, those with the least education, and ethnic minorities were most concerned about crime. These are the most vulnerable groups in society and almost the opposites of those most concerned about corruption.

Perhaps when citizens already enjoy a solid democracy, decent social welfare services, and reasonably good economic performance, the need to make improvements in these areas may come to mind less quickly than newer problems. But statistics and personal observations confirm a striking crime wave in Costa Rica, much as we are seeing in many other Latin American countries. Measured in terms of crimes per 100,000 inhabitants, most types of offenses have risen steeply since the 1980s. Between 1987 and 1996, property crimes increased 25 percent; and between 1985 and 1996, violent crime rose 44 percent, homicides 25 percent, and sex offenses 40 percent.[33]

Although there are numerous possible reasons for the increase in crime,[34] our main concern here is what the phenomenon might mean for Costa Rica's democracy. One possible problem is that public opinion might allow the justice system to trample on due process while trying to apprehend and convict criminals. This fear seems well-founded, because 57 percent of Costa Ricans said that the authorities should try to punish delinquents even if that meant not abiding strictly by the law.

The other potential problem is the augmentation of police capabilities that might logically be required to fight crime. Pacifism, the abolition of the military, and incompetent police forces are all part of the democratic heritage Costa Ricans see as differentiating themselves from the militarism of neighboring countries. During the 1980s, Costa Rica accepted some aid from the United States to better equip border guards and form urban SWAT teams, but the country resisted U.S. pressure for greater militarization. Costa Ricans' fear of militarization has kept the police poorly trained and poorly paid. As a result, 58 percent of citizens say they have little or no confidence in the police. Professionalization and the formation of corporate interests have been further discouraged by a spoils system that awards almost all police jobs to supporters of the incoming president. Because the presidency changes hands every four years, this custom has kept the composition of the police forces in constant flux. But to meet concerns about the current crime wave, President José María Figueres (1994–98) proposed to create a permanent, professional police force. This controversial step has not yet been taken, and it is unclear what solution will come out of the clash between the concern about crime and the fear of *militarismo.*

CONCLUSION

For the most part, Costa Ricans responded to the Hewlett survey in the ways we expected from citizens of a mature and stable democracy. They strongly supported democracy as the best form of government and displayed high levels of satisfaction and efficacy within their own regime. Most of the measures of civic culture also reflected a participatory, law-abiding, and secure populace. Intolerance for homosexuals and low interpersonal trust were marked, however, just as they are in most other Latin American countries.[35] Costa Rica seems to share some regional heritage of distrust and homophobia, perhaps rooted in a common Ibero-Catholic culture.

The Costa Rican electorate and political parties also seem to mirror each other. Like the overall population, the two main parties share a center-right orientation and mixed feelings about state paternalism. While anticapitalist ideologies were made unwelcome in Costa Rica after the 1948 war, neither party is anxious to tear down the welfare state, whose gains both lay claim to. Rather than representing separate camps over issues such as privatization, the two parties each contain ideological differences within them. This debate over neoliberalism is of great concern to academics and elites, but during the last few years, the Costa Rican public has been much more worried about corrupt politicians and street crime. Whether these worries are justified or not (above I suggested that perceptions of corruption may be due to sensationalist media coverage, while the crime wave is quite real), the danger for political parties is that the mass public may become disaffected with them if these issues are not made a priority. It now seems more likely that corruption and quality-of-life issues have the power to alienate the public from political leaders, rather than conflict over neoliberalism.

Chapter 5

Costa Rican Exceptionalism
Why the Ticos Are Different

Mitchell A. Seligson

Costa Ricans, who call themselves *ticos*, have long prided themselves on being different from their neighbors in Latin America. As Mary Clark has pointed out in her discussion in this volume, Costa Ricans are justifiably proud of their high standard of living, which in the area of health matches that of the advanced industrial countries despite a per capita income one-tenth as high.[1] Indeed, according to the latest World Bank data, male life expectancy in Costa Rica exceeds that in the United States, and Costa Rica's overall level of human development outranks its level of income to a greater degree than in any other country.[2] Costa Ricans are also proud of their nonviolent tradition and their efforts to bring peace to war-torn countries in Central America.[3] They boast of their system of national parks and nature preserves, which are probably second to none in Latin America. Yet in my many years of conducting research on Costa Rica, the one theme that emerges most frequently in interviews with scholars and lay people alike is pride in Costa Rican democracy. Certainly the objective facts support this pride; Costa Rica consistently scores at the top of Latin America in various rankings of democracy, and violations of human rights are virtually unknown in the country. Moreover, it has had the longest uninterrupted run of democratic rule of any country in Latin America.[4]

The data collected for this project strongly support the view that Costa Ricans are indeed different when it comes to their belief in democracy. In July 1998, 3,396 adults (18 and over) were interviewed in Costa Rica, Mexico, and Chile by the survey firm of MORI International. The margin of error for the survey was 3.0 percent in Chile and Mexico, and 3.5 percent in Costa Rica at the 95 percent confidence level. All interviews were conducted face-to-face. In each country national probability samples were used, so the results accurately reflect the opinions of Costa Ricans, Mexicans, and Chileans.[5] Each respondent was asked the following question:

With which of the following sentences do you agree most?
1. Democracy is preferable to any other form of government.
2. For people like me, a democratic regime or a nondemocratic regime is the same thing.
3. Under some circumstances, an authoritarian government could be preferable to a democratic one.

While many survey questions can be ambiguous, this one is not. The respondent is forced to chose among clear alternatives.[6] In order to simplify the results and make the contrasts among the three countries as stark as possible, the responses were recoded so that the contrast is between those who said "Democracy is preferable to any other form of government" and those who chose one of the other two alternatives.[7] The results are shown in figure 1, and they conform very closely to the conventional wisdom regarding Costa Rican support for democracy as a way of governance. Nearly 85 percent of Costa Ricans prefer democracy to any other form of government, contrasted with only about half of Chileans and Mexicans. These results are not only statistically significant, but also obviously substantively significant, since strong contrasts such as these, consistent with impressionistic evidence, are not often found in survey data. Mexicans, of course, have had little direct experience with a fully democratic system, because the PRI (Institutional Revolutionary Party) exercised one-party hegemony for most of the twentieth century. Chileans had experienced democracy in the period prior to the Pinochet coup of 1973, but then lived under a stern and often brutal dictatorship for 17 years and today live under a system in which the military still retains ultimate control of key

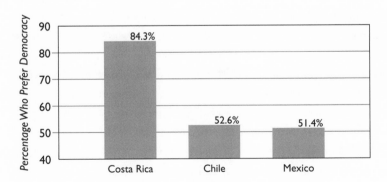

Sig. <.001; Valid N = Mexico, 1,158; Costa Rica, 954; Chile, 1,132

Fig. 1. *Preference for democracy*

political domains. Costa Ricans, in contrast, have enjoyed a competitive, democratic system for more than 50 years, and for most of this century they have lived under a democracy.[8]

If we are to trust these results as providing a good measure of the extent to which the citizens of Costa Rica, Chile, and Mexico support democracy over other forms of rule, it is vitally important to establish the reliability and validity of this survey question. In this chapter, I first do that, and then go on to attempt to test various theories about the reasons that Costa Ricans differ from the others interviewed in this project. I conclude with an overall test that compares each of the theories to the others.

RELIABILITY OF THE PREFERENCE FOR DEMOCRACY

Many social scientists are skeptical of survey questions because they doubt both their reliability and their validity. It is therefore important for me to establish both of these in this chapter. Fortunately, this is relatively easy to do. In order to determine the reliability of an item, it is often a good idea to repeat it in another survey to see if the results are similar. The preference-for-democracy item being analyzed in this chapter was included verbatim in the 1996 Latinobarómetro, a survey of more than 18,000 Latin Americans in 17 mainland countries of the region, excluding only Belize, Surinam, Guyana, and French Guiana.[9] Figure 2 shows the results of the 1998 Hewlett Foundation survey on citizen values for Tulane University alongside the 1996 Latinobarómetro. The consistency of responses strongly helps establish the reliability of the results. It needs to be kept in mind that these surveys were carried out by different organizations, and different sample frames were used for each. Moreover, two years passed between the Latinobarómetro survey and the Hewlett survey. So we were not expecting to be able to reproduce the exact same level in the two surveys. Yet in the case of Costa Rica, the results vary by only 0.2 percent, well within the level of confidence of the sample design. In the case of Mexico, the difference was greater—5.3 percent; in Chile the difference was only 4.1 percent, but that is only 1–2 percent greater than the expected variation based on the confidence interval of 3 percent. In all three countries, the preference for democracy in 1998 was lower than it was in 1996, perhaps an indication that factors are at work reducing confidence in democracy; but the drop in Costa Rica is entirely within the 3.5 percent confidence interval, so no substantive conclusion can properly be drawn. Overall, these results give us reason to have a great deal of confidence in the reliability of the survey and suggest that if the identical question were asked repeatedly of samples in these countries, very similar results would emerge.

A second finding from the data presented in figure 2 is that Costa Rica ranks at the

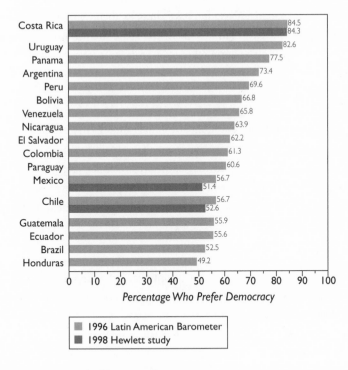

Country	Percentage Who Prefer Democracy
Costa Rica	84.5 / 84.3
Uruguay	82.6
Panama	77.5
Argentina	73.4
Peru	69.6
Bolivia	66.8
Venezuela	65.8
Nicaragua	63.9
El Salvador	62.2
Colombia	61.3
Paraguay	60.6
Mexico	56.7 / 51.4
Chile	56.7 / 52.6
Guatemala	55.9
Ecuador	55.6
Brazil	52.5
Honduras	49.2

■ 1996 Latin American Barometer
■ 1998 Hewlett study

Fig. 2. *Democracy is preferable to any other system*

very top of all countries in the survey, followed by Uruguay, the country that is often ranked closest to Costa Rica in its level of democracy. These findings suggest the validity of the survey question, linking popular preference to regime type. However, it is inappropriate to push this conclusion very far, because the very next country on the list is Panama, which had a long string of military dictatorships for most of this century and has developed a competitive democracy only since the U.S. invasion in 1989. Similarly, Peru ranks high on the list, yet President Alberto Fujimori, who was responsible for an executive coup that extinguished democracy in the early 1990s, has run the country with little attention to the democratic process. So we need to keep in mind that in this chapter we are not trying to predict the regime type, but only measure popular support for democracy—which may (or may not) translate into a democratic polity.

A third finding from the comparisons shown in figure 2 is that the three countries selected do exhibit variation on the preference-for-democracy item. As noted, Costa Rica emerges at the top of the list of 17, while Mexico ties for twelfth place with Chile based on the 1996 Latinobarómetro data. If the other countries in the region were to have retained their same preferences in 1998 as in 1996, then Chile and Mexico would fall near the bottom of the list, but it is likely that some shifting around would have occurred in the other countries during those two years, so it is very risky to draw that conclusion.

VALIDITY OF THE PREFERENCE FOR DEMOCRACY

Establishing the validity of a questionnaire item is always a more difficult task than establishing its reliability. A valid question is one that actually measures what we say it is measuring. In this case, we wish to know if the overwhelming preference for democracy in Costa Rica is a valid statement for a genuine belief in democracy. Fortunately, the survey gives us an ideal question for testing the validity of this item. The very first question in the survey asks:

In one word, could you tell me what democracy means to you?

The respondents were not read a list of options, but were asked to provide an answer of their own. The results for the three countries are displayed in figure 3. The contrast is stark: over two-thirds of Costa Ricans define democracy as "liberty," compared to less than one-third of Chileans and a little more than one-fifth of Mexicans. We can all debate what is the "correct" definition of democracy, but I think most scholars would agree that liberty is at the core. Responses such as "respect/legality," "voting/elections," "welfare/progress," and "type of government" are all definitions that fall wide of the mark, focusing on either process issues (e.g., elections) or on outcomes that may or may not be associated with democratic systems (e.g., economic welfare or

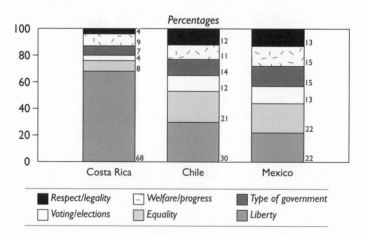

Fig. 3. Contrasting definitions of democracy

equality). Empirical research has consistently shown that democratic systems are no more likely to guarantee economic growth or equality (socially or economically) than other systems, however desirable those outcomes might be.[10] It is Costa Ricans alone among citizens of our three countries who have overwhelmingly captured and internalized the equating of democracy with liberty.

We can conclude from these exercises in reliability and validity that the questionnaire item selected as the basis for contrasting the three countries in this set of survey data is both reliable and valid. It is now appropriate to attempt to determine why it is that Costa Ricans favor democracy so much more strongly than do Chileans or Mexicans.

EXPLANATIONS FOR COSTA RICAN EXCEPTIONALISM

Tolerance

According to Robert Dahl, democratic political systems are ones in which the population is committed to belief in a system of both extensive and inclusive public contestation.[11] In such systems, the public accepts the right of widespread participation (i.e., universal suffrage) and also is willing to tolerate the rights of the opposition and minorities. Since the early part of the twentieth century, universal suffrage has become accepted throughout the world, but tolerance for the rights of the opposition and minorities has not. Intolerance is manifested on a daily basis in the civil wars that wrack the globe today. It is therefore reasonable to ask if the hallmark of Costa Rican democracy is a greater tolerance for the rights of others, when compared to the Mexican and Chilean systems.

The Hewlett survey includes a social tolerance measure that reads as follows:

I am going to read to you a list of people. Tell me whom you would prefer NOT to have as neighbors.
   a. Evangelicals
   b. Homosexuals
   c. Foreigners

In all three countries, foreigners are the most highly tolerated: 80 percent in Mexico, 88 percent in Costa Rica, and 89 percent in Chile. On this item there is so little expressed intolerance that it is not useful in distinguishing among the three countries. Tolerance of evangelicals as neighbors is also quite high: 77 percent in Mexico, 87 percent in Costa Rica, and 82 percent in Chile. Here again, tolerance is so widespread that we find that most respondents in the three countries express tolerance. Only with respect to homosexuals does the picture change. On this item, 67 percent of Mexicans, 57 percent

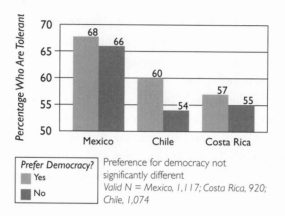

Fig. 4. Tolerance toward homosexuals

of Costa Ricans, and 57 percent of Chileans express a tolerant point of view. We can use this item to attempt to see if tolerance is the hallmark of Costa Rican democracy.

At first glance, it appears that on the three social tolerance measures generally, Costa Ricans do not stand out from Mexicans and Chileans. Costa Ricans were more tolerant of foreigners than were Mexicans but a bit less tolerant than Chileans; and they were tied with Chileans on tolerance of homosexuals. On only one of the three items, tolerance of evangelicals, were Costa Ricans higher than both of the other countries.[12] On the basis of those comparisons alone, Costa Rica does not stand out in its level of social tolerance.

In looking more closely at the data on social tolerance, the focus needs to be on the homosexual item, since that is the one in which the respondents most clearly distinguish themselves. If tolerance goes hand in hand with support for democracy, then it is reasonable to expect that the more tolerant respondents would prefer democracy more often than the less tolerant respondents. The comparisons displayed in figure 4 test this hypothesis for each of the three countries in our sample. The results show that while in each country those who prefer democracy are more likely to express tolerance toward homosexuals than those who do not prefer democracy, the differences are not statistically significant. In Mexico and Costa Rica the difference is only 2 percent, while in Chile it is 6 percent.[13]

The conclusion from this analysis is that social tolerance does not seem to be a critical factor in explaining Costa Rican exceptionalism. Fortunately, the survey contains another item that measures tolerance that will allow further testing of this hypothesis.

Respondents were asked:

Would you be in favor of or against one of your children (or siblings, if you do not have children) marrying a person of a religion different than yours?

The results of this question are presented in figure 5. Here there is additional evidence that tolerance does not explain Costa Ricans' preference for democracy. First, religious tolerance in Costa Rica is higher than in Mexico, but lower than in Chile. Thus, it is impossible to explain Costa Ricans' strong preference for democracy as a function of their level of religious tolerance. Second, within each country, those who favor democracy are no more tolerant than those who do not favor democracy.

The additional tolerance item clearly does not help us explain Costa Rican exceptionalism. We are forced to conclude, on the basis of the analysis of all four social tolerance items, that we must look elsewhere to explain the Costa Rican case.

Trust

Perhaps no other variable has garnered more attention in the recent literature on democracy than trust. Research on trust extends back over many years in the political psychology literature, but the big boost in attention came with the publication of Robert Putnam's 1993 book on democracy that focused on the importance of social capital, as well as Ronald Inglehart's 1997 studies of the World Values Surveys.[14] According to these studies, countries that build interpersonal trust among their popu-

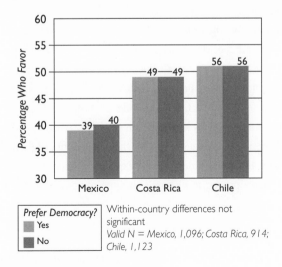

Fig. 5. Favor children marrying outside of religion

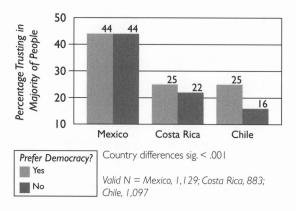

Fig. 6. *Interpersonal trust*

lation are more likely to be able to sustain democracy. It has also been argued that trust helps boost economic development, which in turn helps build democracy.[15] Trust is seen as an outgrowth of active participation in civil society, but since the Hewlett survey does not include data on such participation, we cannot determine the origins of trust within the sample. Nonetheless, since the causal arrows presumably go from civil society participation to trust, and from trust to democracy, we will have no difficulty in seeing if the more proximate variable, trust, is related to a preference for democracy.

Does high interpersonal trust explain Costa Rican exceptionalism? Figure 6 strongly suggests that it does not. Mexico, the country in the data set with the most limited democratic tradition, and the one in which the smallest percentage of respondents stated that they prefer democracy, had almost twice the trust level found in Costa Rica and more than twice the level found in Chile. Within both Costa Rica and Chile there is, however, some evidence that those who believe in democracy express higher levels of trust, with the stronger pattern found for Chile.

These results certainly cast strong doubt on the importance of interpersonal trust for democracy. When we combine them with the negative findings on tolerance, it is fair to conclude that the major candidates for explaining democracy in Costa Rica, tolerance and trust, have proven to be sorely disappointing. Are there other places to look?

Accountability

The classic work by Gabriel Almond and Sidney Verba *The Civic Culture* argued strongly that citizen efficacy is crucial to democracy.[16] Efficacy was defined in that study as citizens' feelings that they could have an impact on public affairs. Much has been done with efficacy over the years, but of late it has been less frequently used in the political psychology literature.[17] It has been pointed out that the difficulty with the efficacy questions is that they place the burden on the citizen rather than on the government. That is, citizens might *try* to make their voices heard, but if the government is "deaf," citizens can justifiably feel inefficacious in spite of their efforts.

The Hewlett survey overcomes this problem by avoiding the issue of the government's willingness to accept citizen input in decision-making, focusing instead on citizen behavior. The question was:

Would you personally be ready to do something to demand accountability from the politicians and bureaucracy: yes or no?[18]

The analysis compares those who responded to this item with "definitely yes" to those who were less certain about whether citizens should demand accountability. Figure 7 shows that here, at last, the data conform to our expectations. Costa Ricans are significantly more likely to believe in holding government officials accountable for their actions than are Mexicans or Chileans. Within Mexico and Chile, those who prefer democracy are more willing to hold their governments accountable. In Costa Rica, there is virtually no difference between those who prefer democracy and those who do not.

Accountability may turn out to be a very important feature of democratic systems.

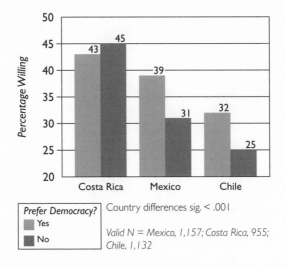

Fig. 7. Definitely willing to hold public officials accountable

When democracy was restored in countries such as Chile, Argentina, Uruguay, El Sal-vador, and Guatemala, there was a need to deal with the violations of human rights that had occurred during the military regimes. Yet in order to persuade the militaries to relinquish power, deals had to be cut granting widespread immunity from prosecu-tion. That is why former president Augusto Pinochet has totally escaped being held accountable within Chile for the actions of his government during his 17 years in pow-er; it is only international actors who have been seeking to have him stand trial for human rights violations. It may be that in Costa Rica the higher level of support for cit-izen responsibility to hold public officials accountable for their actions helps explain the resilience of democracy in that country.

Unfortunately, in the Hewlett data set there is only one item measuring accountabil-ity, which is a very slim reed on which to hang a theory. More questions are needed ask-ing about accountability at different levels of government (local, regional, and nation-al) and about accountability for different kinds of government actions (corruption, human rights violations, failed policies, etc.). Certainly, future studies of the attitudinal correlates of democracy should include a variety of measures of accountability.

Respect for the Rule of Law

Studies of democracy have focused mostly on citizen rights, but the responsibility side also ought to be examined. Citizens in a democratic system are expected to respect the rule of law, as well as other social norms. The Hewlett survey asked a series of ques-tions that attempted to measure this attitude. Respondents were asked:

I am going to read you a list of different things that people do. For each one of them, tell me if you believe that, in general, people who do these things are (1) very stupid; (2) somewhat stupid; (3) somewhat smart; or (4) very smart.
   a. Cutting in line
   b. Not saying anything if they get extra change
   c. Not paying fare in the subway or bus
   d. Going through a red light when there is no traffic
   e. Inventing a phoney excuse

This series includes items that measure attitudes toward actual violations of law (going through a red light and nonpayment for subway or bus service) but also items measuring adherence to social norms. Figure 8 shows the results.[19]

On four of the five items, Costa Ricans express significantly more respect for the law and for social norms than do Chileans or Mexicans. On only one item, going through a red light, are Chileans more law-abiding than Costa Ricans. It may well be, however, that Chilean police are especially vigilant when it comes to common traffic violations

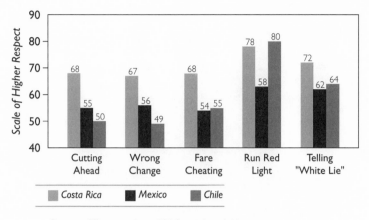

Fig. 8. Respect for rule of law

and that the results on this item do not reflect a general respect for the rule of law. Consider the results on fare cheating, where Chileans are far *less* likely to be honest than Costa Ricans. The other "crimes" are not punishable by law except for cheating on bus fares, and the punishment there must be very infrequent and minor. So, it would seem that Costa Ricans' respect for the rule of law extends to a generalized respect for the rights of others, even when punishment is not an issue.

Happiness

Do contented citizens have a preference for democracy? Certainly, the work of Inglehart based on the World Values Survey data has suggested this rather strongly. In the Hewlett survey, the following question was asked:

In general, would you say that you are very happy, somewhat happy, somewhat unhappy, or very unhappy?

Support for the Inglehart perspective emerges in this data set, as is shown in figure 9. Costa Ricans are far more likely to express a high level of happiness with life than the citizens of the other two countries. Within the countries, however, those who prefer democracy are no more or less likely to be happy.

What is unknown about the happiness variable, however, is whether it is the cause or the result of a preference for democracy. Perhaps citizens of democratic countries are happier than those under authoritarian-based regimes precisely because they live in a democracy. Since the survey data are a snapshot look at these attitudes, we cannot

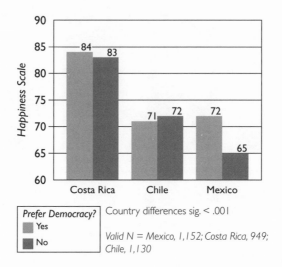

Fig. 9. *Personal happiness*

easily determine the direction of causality.[20] Satisfaction with the economy may, of course, be a factor explaining overall personal happiness. If this were the case, then the preference for democracy could actually be a function of the economic performance of the country. As will be shown below in the multivariate analysis, however, this is not the case.

MULTIVARIATE ANALYSIS

Only by turning to a multivariate analysis of the data can we determine which of the factors examined thus far have an impact on the dependent variable—preference for democracy—when we control for all others in the model. Perhaps more importantly, we can determine the importance of the variables identified here in explaining Costa Rican exceptionalism.

The approach in the regression analysis is to pool all three samples so that the impact of each of the predictors can be seen for the entire population. To do this, however, requires the creation of "dummy variables" to represent the country effect. Since there are three countries in the sample, two dummies were created, one for Mexico and one for Chile; Costa Rica is used as the base group against which the other two are compared.

Further additions needed for the regression analysis are demographic and socioeconomic factors. These have not been examined thus far in this chapter, in part because they carry little theoretical import, but also because—as will be seen shortly—they have little impact on the preference for democracy in these samples. Included in the regression analysis, therefore, are the variables of gender, age, education, and monthly family income.

In order to simplify the multivariate analysis, an index of support for the rule of law was created out of the five variables analyzed earlier. These form a reliable scale (with alpha coefficients of .78 in Costa Rica, .77 in Mexico, and .82 in Chile).[21] Similarly, an index of social tolerance was constructed for the three tolerance items analyzed above.[22] For this set of items, however, even though the inter-item correlations were positive for each country, the reliability of the scale was quite low. This suggests that a better scale of social tolerance needs to be utilized in future studies. Individual items could have been used in the multivariate analysis, but that would have unnecessarily complicated the model.

Finally, in order to facilitate comparison of the impact of each variable, they were all scored on a 0–100 basis, with the exception of education, age, and monthly family income. Those variables were left in their original form, since they relate directly to ranges in the survey instrument.

The multiple regression results are presented in table 1.[23] Model 1 incorporates each of the predictors examined in this study. The regression tells us, first of all, that although it is possible to explain variation in the preference for democracy among these samples with the variables examined here, the overwhelming explanatory factor is being a Costa Rican, versus being a Chilean or a Mexican. Being a Chilean *lowers* one's preference for democracy over authoritarian rule by 30 points on a 100-point scale, while being a Mexican lowers it by 31 points. All of the other variables in the study that make a significant difference in preference are greatly overshadowed by the impact of nationality. None of them has so much as a one-point impact on preference for democracy. More will be said about this finding in the concluding section of this chapter.

The second finding to emerge from model 1 is that demographic and socioeconomic factors have no impact on preference for democracy, except for income, which makes a slight negative contribution. It is of no import, therefore, whether the respondent is male or female, poorly or well educated, or young or old.

The third finding is surprising in the light of the analysis presented earlier. Once the impact of nationality is removed from the samples, then interpersonal trust, which had been discarded in the univariate analysis, becomes statistically significant. This is telling us that both Putnam and Dahl were on the right track when they pointed to

TABLE 1 *Predictors of a Preference for Democracy*

Predictors	Model 1		Model 2	
	B	t	B	t
(constant)	68.35	7.67	13.15	1.59
Interpersonal trust	.05*	2.21	.02	.79
Social tolerance	.04	1.33	.04	1.27
Accountability	.12***	4.35	.14***	4.95
Respect for the rule of law	.17***	4.99	.25***	7.19
Personal happiness	.07	1.89	.17***	4.76
Economic satisfaction	−.07	−1.94	−.01	−.28
Gender	.18	.10	−.94	−.50
Education	.08	.03	.08	.33
Age	−.64	−.52	−.40	−.32
Monthly family income	−2.60*	−2.02	2.64*	2.09
Chilean	−30.23***	−12.08	—	—
Mexican	−30.83***	−12.46	—	—
Adjusted R^2		.11		.04

Note: All variables coded on a 0–100 basis, except education, age, and monthly family income.

* Sig. < .05   ** Sig. < .01   *** Sig. < .001

these attitudinal variables as having an impact on democratic beliefs. By including the country dummy variables, we have removed from the analysis any impact of living under the political system of Costa Rica, Chile, or Mexico. Once this is done, we see that interpersonal trust does make a difference independent of the nature of the political system under which one lives. The difference, however, is very small.

A fourth finding, one consistent with the univariate analysis, is that respect for the rule of law and willingness to hold the government accountable for its actions do make a significant contribution to predicting a preference for democracy over authoritarian rule. Finally, even though personal happiness was found to help explain Costa Ricans' preference for democracy, in this multivariate analysis it does not. The control for economic satisfaction, similarly, turns out to have no significant impact. This may be because personal happiness is also included in the model, and the impact of economic satisfaction might erode the impact of personal happiness.

Model 2 analyzes the data without controlling for the impact of nationality. For that reason it clearly is an underestimated model, but it is useful for confirming some of the earlier findings. We see in model 2 that accountability, respect for the rule of law, and personal happiness each predict a preference for democracy. Interpersonal trust once again falls to insignificance. Finally, while demographic factors play no role, economic ones do, with higher income having a positive impact on preference for democracy.

This suggests that the old notion of working-class authoritarianism is not supported by these data. The variable that has the most important impact on preference for democracy (see the B's) is respect for the rule of law, followed by personal happiness and accountability.

IMPLICATIONS FOR THE EMPIRICAL THEORY OF DEMOCRACY

What are the implications of the findings of this chapter for democratic theory, and the field of political culture in particular? While studies of democratization abound, most of them fall into one of two nearly mutually exclusive categories. One set of studies focuses on institutions; the other set, including the chapters of this volume, concentrates on culture. The study of institutions has a long history in political science, but for many years it meant little more than comparing constitutions. Not much was learned about democracy by that effort. In the last 20 years, however, the "new institutionalism" has emerged as a powerful field in political science. As a result of the advances in that field, virtually all experts now agree that institutions do in fact matter. One question is, however, *when* do they matter? In other words, do certain institutional arrangements, such as parliamentarism versus presidentialism, matter in all cases, or only in advanced industrial democracies? More important still is the question of *how much* institutions matter. The dominant studies in the field have shown that certain electoral rules are responsible for the greater probability of particular electoral outcomes as opposed to others. When it comes to larger issues related to the stability of democracy, however, these studies have been less helpful.

It is in the area of the big questions that political culture research claims to make its contribution. According to political culture theory, the values of citizens determine, in very fundamental ways, the kind of political system they will have. Political culture does not have much to say about which candidate or party will win an election, unless a party or candidate presents a fundamental challenge to the system, as did Hitler's party in the 1930s. Under those circumstances, citizens predisposed to accept an authoritarian alternative to democracy might well support such candidates, voting to terminate the current system. On the other hand, if a majority of citizens support democracy, then such candidates cannot legally win office. Similarly, if coup plotters attempt to seize governmental power by unconstitutional means, citizens committed to democracy would be expected to protest, even at the risk of their personal safety, in order to resist such a blow to their vision of the good state. Indeed, this is precisely what happened in Costa Rica in 1948, when citizens took up arms as a result of the incumbent party's efforts to remain in power after a disputed election. While other factors played a role in the Costa Rican Civil War of 1948, the national lesson that was learned is that the electoral system is not to be tampered with.

The data presented in this chapter provide strong evidence that political culture matters when it comes to these big issues. It has been shown that Costa Rica, Latin America's most highly consolidated democracy, is one country in which political culture overwhelmingly favors democracy. To use the popular expression, in Costa Rica "democracy is the only game in town." Not so in Mexico and Chile, according to the data in our survey. In those two countries, it is an open question as to what kind of system citizens prefer. If political culture theory has any predictive power, it would predict that the stability of democracy in Mexico and Chile is far from assured.

What can we say about Costa Rican exceptionalism? We know that Costa Ricans have a much stronger preference for democracy than do the citizens of Mexico and Chile. We also know that variables such as respect for the rule of law and willingness to hold government accountable for its actions are factors that make Costa Ricans different from their counterparts elsewhere in Latin America.[24]

The larger message from the data analysis conducted here is that most of the variance that makes Costa Ricans much closer allies of democracy is not to be explained by the social-psychological attitudes analyzed here. Rather, the results strongly suggest that in Costa Rica there exists a deep-seated commitment to democracy that goes beyond issues of interpersonal trust and the like. All countries develop national myths; Costa Rica is a small and not especially prosperous country, but many scholars have noted that its citizens have developed a national myth that makes them proud of their country, and what they are most proud of is their democracy. One hears this on a daily basis in schoolrooms, one reads it in the press and hears it on television. Central to the Costa Rican myth is the country's identity as a democracy.[25] No other country in Latin America has had a stable democracy for so long, and no observer sees any serious threat to its continuation.

What lessons are there for other countries that wish to enhance the prospects of democratic stability? The Costa Rican case seems to be a persuasive illustration of the importance of developing a national myth (a political culture, if you will) about the centrality of democracy. Other countries develop national myths: in Chile, there is much celebration of the power of the armed forces, and in Mexico the myth has long centered on the Revolution. No doubt these myths, too, are important in defining national character, but their particular forms do little to encourage democracy.

Chapter 6

Transition to Democracy
A Mexican Perspective

Matthew T. Kenney

> *The most striking aspect of Mexican character, at first sight, is distrust.*
> *This attitude underlies all contact with men and things. It is present whether*
> *or not there is motivation for it.*
>
> Samuel Ramos, *Profile of Man and Culture in Mexico*

Mexico's transition to democracy, like so much in modern Mexican politics, has been characterized by uncertainty, contradictions, and doubts. The dominance of a single party and the political stability it has brought to Mexico for most of the twentieth century have made it an anomalous case not just within Latin America, but among Third World countries generally. While there is much enthusiasm inside and outside Mexico for its transition to democracy since 1994, this process has been a slow one and only now appears to be completed with the victory of Vicente Fox Quesada in the July 2000 presidential elections, not so much with the victory itself as with the context in which it occurred. However, as the Tabasco gubernatorial election in October 2000 demonstrated, Mexico still struggles—domestically and internationally—with the image of rigged elections.[1]

A useful theoretical model to help us understand the Mexican transition to democracy is one developed nearly 30 years ago by Dankwart Rustow. According to Rustow's dynamic model, there are four main sequential features in a country's transition to democracy. In the first, called the background condition, a country must achieve a sense of national unity. Mexico, one could reasonably claim, achieved this in the aftermath of its revolution in the last century. In the second feature, the preparatory phase, "the dynamic process of democratization itself is set off by a prolonged and inconclusive political struggle."[2] This phase, I would argue, began in the late 1960s and continued to at least 1994. Mexico today, I maintain, is in the decision phase, the third feature in Rustow's model, which is characterized by "a deliberate decision on the part of political leaders to accept the existence of diversity in unity and, to that end, to institutionalize some crucial aspects of democratic procedure."[3] Clearly, the crucial aspects that political leaders have focused on most have been in the area of electoral reform.[4] The fourth and final phase, called the habituation phase, lies, perhaps, in Mexico's future. In this phase, democracy becomes ingrained in a country's political culture and enjoys widespread popular and elite support as the most effective way to resolve societal conflict. In other words, we can view the habituation phase as one of consolidated democracy.

Costa Rica, where 80 percent of respondents in the 1998 survey preferred democracy over any other form of government, has reached this fourth phase, while Mexico and Chile, where only 50 percent of respondents preferred democracy, have not. On the question of interpersonal trust, however, ordinary Mexicans appear to be more trusting than not only Chileans, but even Costa Ricans as well.[5] Ordinary Mexicans, I argue, in terms of interpersonal trust and in terms of their view of individual responsibility, appear prepared to enter into the habituation phase of democracy. Offsetting this, though, are low levels of confidence in many governmental institutions. Mexicans' dissatisfaction with democracy in their country, and their lukewarm support for it over other forms of governance, can be attributed to the slowness with which political elites have pursued the democratic option.

In discussing Mexico's transition to democracy and the insights that the 1998 survey might give us, it is important to set this transition in a broader political and historical context. From my perspective, the Mexican transition to democracy began with the 1994 election of President Ernesto Zedillo. I base this view on what is perceived by most analysts to have been (at the time) the cleanest presidential election since the Mexican Revolution, and the democratic reforms subsequently pursued by the Zedillo administration.[6]

Until the 1980s, popular elections in Mexico, especially those for federal offices and governorships, represented something very different than a democratic struggle for power. With the overwhelming dominance of the Institutional Revolutionary Party (PRI) in local, state, and national elections, to be chosen as a PRI candidate was a virtual guarantee of securing office.[7] Instead of providing voters with the opportunity to make meaningful choices regarding their future representatives, elections before the 1980s mainly served other, more symbolic purposes related to the preservation and mythology of Mexico's revolutionary past as a democratic, popular state dedicated to the rights of peasants, workers, and other Mexicans.

In the 10 to 15 years prior to 1994, elections in Mexico became increasingly competitive (though still marred by fraud), especially in 1988, when Carlos Salinas de Gortari was elected president with just over 50 percent of the popular vote amid charges of widespread electoral fraud. In fact, many claimed that opposition candidate Cuauhtémoc Cárdenas had won the election but was denied victory because of electoral fraud engineered by the PRI.[8] However, in the midterm congressional elections, which also took place in the summer of 1988, opposition parties—notably the conservative National Action Party, or PAN, and the coalition of parties that supported Cárdenas, a former PRI governor in the state of Michoacán—made unprecedented gains in the Chamber of Deputies. As a result, for the first time in the PRI's history, the president and his party had to work with opposition politicians to amend the constitution. This was an important step in making the legislature a more representative and deliberative body, not simply a rubber stamp for the president.

Despite the pivotal political events of 1988, I do not locate the beginning of Mexico's transition to democracy in this year, because of the widespread allegations and perceptions of electoral fraud at the time. Additionally, the centralization of power during the Salinas presidency from 1988 to 1994 and his use of extralegal measures to assert his control were antithetical to a genuine transition to democracy.[9] Moreover, the 1991 midterm elections were once again marred by numerous allegations of fraud as the PRI recouped its losses from 1988.[10] Salinas, who accelerated the neoliberal economic restructuring and partial dismantling of the Mexican state begun by his predecessor, Miguel de la Madrid, pursued a policy of political liberalization rather than democratization. Both his economic and political initiatives were largely engineered from the executive level of government, an approach entirely consistent with the tradition of strong Mexican presidentialism.[11] Two examples of his manipulation of Mexican politics were the National Solidarity Program (a federal assistance program targeting the poor that was the centerpiece of Salinas's social policy initiative) and his replacement of certain PRI state governors with opposition candidates, in all cases from the PAN as opposed to the left-of-center Democratic Revolutionary Party, or PRD (most of whose members were former PRI supporters).[12]

The steady erosion of social services since the 1980s—resulting from financial crises and neoliberal economic policies that impose harsh austerity measures on the Mexican population—has, as one scholar has written, had the unintended consequence of creating new political space and opportunities for groups that normally would have been co-opted or simply ignored by the state. According to Judith Teichman, "The political impact of market liberalizing reforms before 1988—an impact that was unanticipated by the reforms' practitioners—triggered the unraveling of the traditional mechanisms of corporatist and clientelist control."[13] This unraveling, I would add, has also introduced considerable instability into the Mexican political system at the elite level, principally as a result of the weakening of the PRI and its ongoing loss of legitimacy.[14] Undemocratic as many state actions and practices were in Mexican politics during most of the twentieth century, they were instrumental in maintaining a remarkably stable political system since the end of the Mexican Revolution, especially during periods of sustained economic growth. The decision by Mexican political leaders to link Mexico's future to global markets represented an about-face from the statist and protectionist economic policies of the past and also, importantly, a distancing of the current generation of technocratic rulers from Mexico's revolutionary and populist political traditions.[15] This process, begun in earnest by de la Madrid, reached its zenith under Salinas, as he aggressively and successfully fought for the inclusion of Mexico in the North American Free Trade Agreement and the reform of the constitution to allow for the sale of communal farms, or *ejidos*.

Elections, as some of my earlier remarks imply, are the hallmark of democracy. According to Samuel Huntington, "The central procedure of democracy is the selection of leaders through competitive elections by the people they govern."[16] Clearly, qualifications need to be made. For elections to be democratic, they must be free, fair, and open, and nearly all adult citizens must be allowed to vote. Moreover, they must occur on a regular basis. Elections have certainly occurred on a regular basis in Mexico in the past seven decades, and today nearly all adult citizens in Mexico have the right to vote. It is only in recent years, and especially since 1994, that elections have become cleaner and more competitive to the point that they can be called democratic. As Jesús Rodríguez Zepeda notes, "Without forgetting the need to resolve the remaining problems of equality in electoral competition, we can say that the foundation for considering the Mexican political system a polyarchy has been laid."[17]

There is a tendency among some analysts, I find, to downplay the importance of voting and elections and to place greater emphasis on citizen participation, democratic attitudes, and associational life.[18] While these are no doubt important, especially in the consolidation of democracy, I do not view them, in theoretical terms, as necessary to a country's transition to democracy, and certainly not as sufficient in themselves to bring about the transition from nondemocratic to democratic forms of governance. Still, a public that is supportive of democracy and prepared to alter its behavior to achieve greater democracy is likely to gain the attention of political leaders who are themselves in a better position to change the system. Additionally, to quote from Ronald Ingle-hart, "Although it does not seem to be the immediate cause of the *transition* to democracy, political culture does seem to be a central factor in the survival of democracy. In the long run, democracy is not attained simply by making institutional changes or through clever elite-level maneuvering. Its survival also depends on what ordinary people think and feel."[19] Or, as John Stuart Mill noted over a century ago, "political checks will no more act of themselves, than a bridle will direct a horse without a rider. If the checking functionaries are as corrupt or as negligent as those whom they ought to check, and if the public, the mainspring of the whole checking machinery, are too ignorant, too passive, or too careless and inattentive, to do their part, little benefit will be derived from the best administrative apparatus."[20]

At present, I believe that Mexicans are more apt to accept a minimalist definition of democracy that emphasizes the importance of clean and fair elections. When they were asked in 1998 to identify the principal task of a democracy, the most frequently selected response was the task of electing rulers. Significantly more Mexicans (33 percent) identified this response than was the case in the Costa Rican or Chilean samples (24 and 18 percent, respectively). Given the history of electoral fraud in Mexico, this should not surprise us. Also, it perhaps reflects disillusionment among Mexicans about government's ability to redistribute wealth or protect minorities. This could represent an important shift—and perhaps a realistic and necessary one—away from the revolutionary and populist rhetoric of the PRI, which has historically portrayed the state as not only the guarantor but also the provider of social justice for all Mexicans. If so, this shift would also explain the declining fortunes of the PRD, especially at the national level, with its promotion of a more interventionist state.

A question from the 1998 survey that can be used to support the claim that Mexicans may expect less from the state than in the past asked respondents to indicate with which of the following two statements they most agreed: (1) the government should look after the well-being of individuals, or (2) each individual should look after his or her own well-being. Only 30 percent of Mexicans answered that the government should look after the well-being of individuals, compared to 41 percent of Costa Ricans and 57 percent of Chileans. We can interpret the Mexican responses as perhaps indicating disillusionment with government and its ability to respond to a broad range of

TABLE 1 *Levels of Confidence in Government, 1998* (percent)

	Low	Medium	High
Chile	24.4	38.0	37.7
Costa Rica	34.8	34.9	30.2
Mexico	46.9	40.5	12.6

Source: 1998 Hewlett survey. (N = 3,397)

individual and societal needs. If correct, such an interpretation would be all the more significant when set against the historically strong role of the Mexican state in the economy and other aspects of social life.

In fact, when we look at responses to five questions relating to confidence in government and governmental institutions (i.e., the police, schools, courts, and congress), we find that Mexican respondents score lower than Chileans and Costa Ricans on these variables. Table 1 presents the results from a scale made up of scores from these variables, which I use to measure overall confidence in government. Each of the five variables was recoded "1" for responses indicating some or much confidence, and "0" for little confidence, no confidence, or "don't know." I then classified respondents on this six-point scale using the following break points: 0–1 for low, 2–3 for medium, and 4–5 for high levels of confidence.

The most striking figure in table 1 is the relatively small percentage (12.6) of Mexicans who fall into the high-confidence category. Also surprising, and encouraging for Chilean democracy, is the relatively high legitimacy of governmental institutions indicated by the Chilean data. It seems reasonable to expect that until Mexicans' confidence in government rises, the likelihood that democracy will become habituated in their country remains uncertain. It is also worth noting that in the 1998 survey, just over 22 percent of Mexicans identified the government as the main obstacle to democracy, a figure twice that of the Costa Rican sample and nearly four times as high as the Chilean sample.

Seventy-five percent of respondents in both Mexico and Costa Rica in the summer of 1998 expressed the opinion that many or nearly all people in government are corrupt, and respondents from both countries were more than twice as likely as Chileans to identify corruption as the greatest threat to democracy in their countries. A key difference between the Mexican and Costa Rican respondents is that the latter generally view elections as clean (as do Chileans) and overwhelmingly consider democracy preferable to other forms of government—just the opposite of what we find among Mexican respondents, where only 33 percent answered that elections are clean. This is very important, because it leaves open the possibility for Costa Ricans to elect politicians who are perceived to be less corrupt. To reiterate the importance of free and fair elections to modern democracies, their absence—or the presence of elections marked by fraud and other abuses—is a sure sign that the political system under consideration is not a democracy.

Turning to 1997, we see that federal and state elections in Mexico in that year were important for two main reasons.[21] First, as in the 1988 presidential election, Cárdenas was again the focal point as he scored a clear, and this time undisputed, victory in Mexico City's first mayoral race, on June 6, 1997. Mexico City dominates the country's political, economic, and cultural landscape, and the significance of an opposition candidate's becoming its first elected mayor (this position had previously been filled by presidential appointment) can hardly be overstated. Second, on the same day the PRI, for the first time in its history, failed to win an absolute majority in the Chamber of Deputies. As a result, the lower house has been able to function as an effective and meaningful legislative body and counterweight to executive power, thereby continuing a process that began with opposition gains in the 1988 midterm elections (only to be reversed in 1991). In short, Mexicans used their votes to send a clear message to the PRI that its stranglehold on the electoral process was incompatible with Mexican democracy. Three years later, in the 2000 presidential election, this message was delivered in a more definitive fashion.

I believe that we are witnessing a time lag between improved electoral politics in Mexico and perceptions by its citizens that elections have become cleaner. This caution is understandable and even wise, given the long history of electoral fraud in Mexico. The 1998 survey showed that 61 percent of Mexicans still considered elections to be fraudulent, a figure more than twice that for Costa Rican respondents and nearly three times that for Chileans. Still, the Mexican figure of 61 percent is a significant decrease from the 79 percent of respondents who answered that elections were generally fraudulent when interviewed in a national survey in 1995.[22] Given the widespread view that the 2000 national elections in Mexico were both free and fair (relatively speaking), I predict that polls in the near future will show that significantly fewer Mexicans perceive elections to be fraudulent.

This ongoing transformation in the national balance of power toward a genuine system of checks and balances, as spelled out in the constitution, is further evidence of Mexico's transition to democracy. Further narrowing the gap between its formal and informal constitutions represents an important challenge to Mexico's ability to become a habituated democracy. If opposition candidates can now enter and compete in the political arena with a real chance of winning office, as demonstrated by Fox's recent victory, certainly this bodes well for democracy and will give greater voice to citizen-voters who were previously denied input into governmental policies unless they operated within PRI or government-controlled channels and institutions established by PRI politicians. As John Bailey and Arturo Valenzuela noted in the aftermath of the July 6, 1997, elections, "[c]itizens have experienced a new empowerment. They can punish incumbents without fear, casting votes to reflect their interests as members of an increasingly complex and diverse society."[23]

Although, as has been argued, Mexico has completed the transition to democracy, democratic consolidation remains an uncertainty. Some of the most obvious threats to this consolidation (or, in Rustow's terminology, habituation) are the continuing unrest in the southern state of Chiapas, corruption, extreme poverty, the escalation of drug trafficking and the social ills it engenders, and the expanding role of the military in domestic political affairs. There also appear to be serious flaws in Mexico's political system that hamper its effective functioning as a democracy. For example, representatives in the Chamber of Deputies serve only three years and have little time or opportunity to gain expertise and influence in specialized legislative areas. Compounding this problem is the constitutional ban on reelection of officeholders at the federal, state, and local levels of government.[24] Once elected, politicians frequently have little incentive to respond to their constituents' concerns and preferences, thus undermining a key purpose of democracy, which is for politicians to represent the interests of as wide a spectrum of society as possible and to be held accountable for their actions while in office. Once again, 45 percent of Mexicans interviewed in 1998 reported that they felt poorly represented by their deputies, compared to only 20 percent of Costa Ricans and 34 percent of Chileans.

Zedillo's increased reliance on the military to resolve domestic matters was one of the most troubling and puzzling features of his administration. Among democratic theorists, a substantial and continuing reliance on the military by civilian leaders to solve domestic problems is a threat to the long-term stability of democracy, a thesis with which Zedillo was certainly familiar.[25] By continuing to turn to the military even as scandals, arrests, and allegations of corruption involving the armed forces mounted, Zedillo exhibited a stubborn determination to pursue this option. Mexicans and non-Mexicans are justified in asking why such an apparent advocate of democracy as Zedillo favored a higher political profile for the military.

This concern notwithstanding, the central figure in Mexico's transition to democracy was, I argue, Ernesto Zedillo. Given the history of authoritarian presidentialism in Mexico and its central position in postrevolutionary politics, it is perhaps both ironic and fitting that a Mexican president should play such a pivotal role. While sharing much in common with his technocratic predecessor on the issue of economic reform, Zedillo differed greatly from Salinas in the political reform he sought. Salinas, as has been argued, preferred to place economic reform before political reform in the belief that without the former, the latter might lead to unacceptable chaos and disorder.[26] Whether this is true or not, political reform under Salinas was largely reactive and certainly top-down. In contrast to Salinas, Zedillo, in a 1995 speech to the American Society of Newspaper Editors, told his audience, "I came to office believing that we could never have a permanently sound economy if we had a hollow, token democracy—or an unjust judicial system."[27]

Zedillo, in his 1995 Development Plan, made frequent reference to the need to reform the office of the presidency in Mexico by balancing executive power against other branches of government. He noted that Mexican presidentialism and the excessive centralization of power had been fostered, in part, by an insufficiently mature political culture and the absence of adequate counterweights to executive powers and privileges, all of which contributed to authoritarian and nondemocratic tendencies in the Mexican political system.[28]

Zedillo's decision not to use and abuse powers and privileges at his disposal stemming from his combined position as president and as a member of the PRI was an important sign of his desire to introduce a new dynamic between the presidency and the PRI. His intent, I believe, was not to weaken the party, but rather to expose it to the challenges and uncertainties that come with operating in a democratic arena characterized by, for example, cleaner elections, a more competitive party system, and a system of checks and balances among the three branches of government. His reasoning seemed to be that in meeting these challenges, the PRI would become both stronger and more democratic.

One of the most significant and symbolic acts that Zedillo refused to perform was the naming of a successor at the end of his term. With the *dedazo,* or pointing of the finger, Mexican presidents since the 1920s had named the next presidential candidate for their party, who, until the assassination of Luis Donaldo Colosio in 1994, was invariably elected. Over the objections of many within his own party, Zedillo viewed the selection of the presidential candidate as a decision of the party and not the president.

Overall, I believe that many of the criticisms leveled against Zedillo stemmed in part from a perceived weakness based on his refusal to exercise the considerable powers that previous presidents had used.[29] Aware of this perception, Zedillo appeared unfazed by it. In a 1996 interview he said that "[b]ecause nobody can accuse me of being a thief or corrupt or abusive, they say I am weak. That's fine. I answer my critics with deeds and tough decisions I have had to make without ever considering my index of popularity."[30] One can interpret his political reform as representing a challenge to the Mexican people to take more responsibility for their nascent democracy. The theme of responsibility was a recurring one in Zedillo's political speeches and can be traced, arguably, to his humble upbringing in a lower-middle-income family in Mexicali. Even in his Yale doctoral dissertation, Zedillo "contended that Mexico's staggering debt was a result of government irresponsibility, rather than of the inflexibility of foreign banks, as many preferred to believe."[31]

Zedillo, in a manner reminiscent of Mexican intellectuals such as Samuel Ramos and Octavio Paz, has emphasized that for Mexican democracy to succeed, Mexicans must undergo a more personal evolution: "What we need is not confidence in the government. We need confidence in ourselves, confidence in the abilities, in the will, in the integrity, in the resolve of all Mexicans."[32] As was alluded to earlier, most Mexicans— nearly 68 percent in our survey (a figure comparable to that in the 1990 and 1996 World Values Survey results from Mexico)—have little or no confidence in the government.[33] By contrast, the 1998 figures for Chile and Costa Rica were 48 and 56 percent, respectively. However, I do see an important change, and one that bodes well for the future of democracy in Mexico—provided that political elites are able to stay the democratic course—in the growing trust that Mexicans now seem to express in others.

Interpersonal trust, as theorists and researchers have long argued, is essential to the long-term stability of democracy. Robert Dahl, who prefers the term *polyarchy* over *democracy*, notes that "[i]n the first place, polyarchy requires two-way or mutual communication, and two-way communication is impeded among people who do not trust one another."[34] In their study of political attitudes and democracy in the late 1950s, Gabriel Almond and Sidney Verba concluded that "[t]he role of social trust and cooperativeness as a component of the civic culture cannot be overemphasized. It is, in a sense, a generalized resource that keeps a democratic polity operating."[35] And more recently, Ronald Inglehart, who has examined the relationships between values and political regimes for the last three decades, finds a strong correlation between interpersonal trust and stable democracy.[36]

The 1998 study showed that 44 percent of Mexicans surveyed said that other people could be trusted, compared to only 22 percent of Costa Ricans and 20 percent of Chileans. We can compare this figure of 44 percent in 1998 to past national surveys. In 1990, 34 percent of Mexicans said that other people could be trusted, while in 1981 only 18 percent expressed this opinion. This means that levels of interpersonal trust in Mexico have more than doubled since 1980. It must be pointed out, however, that the wording for the interpersonal trust question in the World Values Survey differs from that used in the 1998 Hewlett survey. In the former, respondents were asked whether people could be trusted or whether one can't be too careful when it comes to trusting others. In fact, 1996 World Values Survey results for Mexico show a decline in levels of interpersonal trust, to 28 percent of valid responses (i.e., excluding "don't know" and missing scores). In the Hewlett survey, by contrast, interviewees were given the choice of responding yes or no (or not at all) when asked if other people could be trusted. While this difference may well explain some of the jump in the Hewlett results for Mexico, we do find consistency on interpersonal trust results for Chile between the 1998 Hewlett Survey and 1996 World Values Survey data, where 21 percent of valid responses in both data sets indicated trust in other people. In the 1990 World Values Survey in Chile, approximately 23 percent of respondents expressed trust in other people.[37]

Today, I would argue, while trust is hardly the most striking aspect of the Mexican character, its apparent increase during Mexico's transition to democracy is not mere coincidence. Rising levels of interpersonal trust can be seen as a by-product of the democratic institutions that are slowly taking shape in Mexico. This, however, is only a partial explanation.[38] A more powerful one may be, as data on individual responsibility seem to suggest, that Mexicans are coming to realize that they can no longer expect the state to solve the country's problems and that they must instead turn to one another. This involves a distancing from the revolutionary and populist rhetoric that has characterized Mexican politics over the last seven decades. The Almond and Verba study showed that most Mexicans expressed high levels of dissatisfaction with governmental programs in the late 1950s. Since the 1980s, this process has been accelerated as a result of continuing corruption in government and, perhaps, of the neoliberal economic policies pursued by Mexico's technocratic leaders, which have resulted in the reduction of social services.

Almond and Verba also noted that Mexicans were generally supportive of many democratic values and principles, although they failed to act on these beliefs in their daily lives. Accordingly, these authors characterized Mexican political culture as largely aspirational.[39] By 1991, there was considerable evidence to show that Mexicans had at last begun to act on these beliefs, as political participation rates rose sharply above levels seen a decade earlier—leading some to argue that a convergence of values was taking place among Mexicans, Americans, and Canadians.[40] Together with rising levels of interpersonal trust, attitudes toward individual responsibility, and the impact of democratic reforms under the Zedillo administration, then, ordinary Mexicans now appear well positioned for the next stage of democratization in Mexico—habituation.

Chapter 7

Legacies of Authoritarianism
Political Attitudes in Chile and Mexico

Joseph L. Klesner

Any study of contemporary Latin American political culture must address the authoritarian heritage of many of the nations of this hemisphere. Costa Rica's record of democracy is exceptional among its neighbors; all major Latin American countries have experienced military or civilian authoritarian rule within the memory of many or most of their citizens. Chile and Mexico are among the latest Latin American nations to have made the transition to electoral democracy and hence provide valuable cases through which we can explore the legacy of authoritarian rule for the attitudinal foundations of democracy. Their experiences of authoritarianism, however, were sufficiently different that we might gain not only general insights into that legacy, but also specific insights into the impact of particular dimensions of authoritarian rule.

This study of the bases of democracy does not see support for democratic institutions as being purely instrumental. I will argue that certain underlying political orientations tend to be more conducive to democratic stability.[1] Some of those political orientations are more prominently represented in Mexican and Chilean political culture; others seem to be in deficit in our two cases. Hence, this chapter will conclude by expressing worries about the attitudinal foundations of democracy in Mexico and Chile.

That said, I share most of the concerns expressed by Alan Knight in his contribution to this volume about the relatively ephemeral character of many of the attitudes that respondents express when queried by pollsters and about the absence of a single, national political culture in a country as geographically and socially complex as Mexico. I follow Gabriel Almond and Sidney Verba's understanding of political culture:

"The term political culture . . . refers to the specifically political orientations—attitudes toward the political system and its various parts, and attitudes toward the role of the self in the system."[2] An individual may have either relatively fixed, long-held views about politics and the political, or relatively fleeting attitudes. Because the term *political culture* often connotes orientations toward politics that are more or less static, I prefer to avoid using the term. The phrase *political attitudes* does not connote such fixity of political values; hence I will use it, because I believe many of the political orientations I will explore in this chapter are, as Knight suggests, views held at this moment—maybe during this period in Chilean or Mexican history, but not necessarily enduring.

In *The Civic Culture,* Almond and Verba also state, "The political culture of a nation is the particular distribution of patterns of orientation toward political objects among the members of the nation."[3] They go on to argue that their view of political culture hence does not assume that a nation has a homogeneous set of political orientations, but rather that within a nation there will be a mix of attitudes. Of course, there may be many ways to try to divide up a national society into different political subcultures. Knight suggests we should appreciate regional and local differences in political attitudes in a society such as Mexico's. While not denying the merit of his view (indeed, I have sought to explore regional differences in views held by Mexicans about neoliberalism and economic integration in another article),[4] my approach in this chapter will be to examine the extent to which those whom we might expect to have been supporters of the authoritarian regimes hold political values, particularly about democracy, that are significantly different from those held by opponents of the authoritarian regime.

CHILE AND MEXICO: THE CASE FOR COMPARISON

Juan Linz defined authoritarianism as a political system with limited, not responsible, political pluralism; without an elaborate and guiding ideology (but with distinctive mentalities); without intensive or extensive political mobilization (except at some points in its development); and in which a leader (or occasionally a small group) exercises power within limits that are formally ill-defined but actually quite predictable.[5] By this definition, Chile's military regime clearly fits the authoritarian appellation.[6] Mexico, too, has been called authoritarian by many observers.[7] Yet both have had democratic institutions in place for most of this century.

That said, the twentieth-century records of Chile and Mexico with respect to democratic institutions could hardly be more different. With a brief exception from 1925 to 1932, Chile enjoyed the functioning of stable democratic institutions from the 1870s until 1973, when the socialist government of Salvador Allende was overthrown by the military coup led by General Augusto Pinochet. Pinochet ruled in a harsh personalist military dictatorship until 1988, when his quest to continue his rule for eight more years failed in a national plebiscite. The Chilean transition back to democracy came rapidly by comparative standards, so that in the 1990s electoral democracy was back in full bloom in that nation of 15 million in the Southern Cone.

In contrast, twentieth-century Mexico did not know competitive elections until the 1990s. Although both pre- and postrevolutionary Mexico had the formal trappings of democracy—an elected president, a congress with powers to legislate for the nation, regular elections—alternation in power has been unknown. From the formation of the Institutional Revolutionary Party (Partido Revolucionario Institucional, or PRI) in 1929 until Vicente Fox's surprise victory in July 2000, no other party had taken the presidency nor the majority of the Senate, and only in 1997 did the PRI yield its majority in the Chamber of Deputies, the lower house of the federal congress. Yet from 1988 onward, the PRI's rule was subjected to serious challenge from opposition parties on both the left and the right. In the past five years, the autonomy of the federal electoral authorities has been established, and the press has become willing to criticize the PRI and the government in a way previously unknown in this century.

Thus, Chile and Mexico each have a track record of about a decade of competitive politics following a significant period of authoritarian rule—seventeen years in Chile's case, most of the last century in Mexico's. Fully 34.6 percent of Mexicans and 20.2 percent of Chileans in the samples surveyed by MORI International for this study have come to the age of majority since 1988, the year in which the authoritarian regime in Chile was transcended and the year in which the ruling party in Mexico was first truly challenged. Only 49.8 percent of the Chilean sample had had the experience of democratic citizenship prior to Pinochet's coup. Each case thus offers a sample of citizens who have either come to adulthood after being brought up and socialized under authoritarian rule or who lived much of their young adult lives in an authoritarian setting. How each nation has adopted democratic attitudes after that experience could be a compelling study. That is, how have the authoritarian "mentalities," to use Linz's term, shaped democratic values in these two nations? Unfortunately, given that the survey conducted for this study only provides a snapshot of the Chilean and Mexican electorates in 1998, I cannot undertake such a rigorous, longitudinal analysis of the emergence of democratic values here. However, I can offer some comparative observations about the extent of acceptance of democratic values in Chile and Mexico, about the continued presence of attitudes unsupportive of fully democratic rule, and about how the different experiences with authoritarianism in these two nations have had separate consequences for the emerging political cultures of Mexico and Chile. Moreover, I can provide some evidence about the different views held about democracy by those who are likely to have supported authoritarian rule and those who likely opposed it.

The different specific characteristics of the authoritarian regimes that governed these two nations, to which I just alluded, are key to explaining the different attitudes prominent among these peoples. Both the years just preceding Pinochet's coup in 1973 and the era of the military regime itself were extremely divisive for Chileans, so much so that one major study of Pinochet's Chile and the society emerging from it is titled *A Nation of Enemies*.[8] Many from Chile's middle and upper classes consider Allende's administration to have engaged in unconstitutional seizures of their property and misguided efforts to change the country's development path. Chile had reached a state of latent civil war when the military intervened in September 1973.[9] However, the military regime, far from healing those divisions, made them only deeper by killing or disappearing well over 2,500 Chileans in its violent effort to root out radicalism.[10] When given the opportunity to vote Pinochet out of office and the military out of power in 1988, 43 percent chose to support eight more years of the general's rule.

Many Chileans have wished to deny the violent character of Pinochet's government, but stories of the use of torture and of the disappearances of the children of acquaintances make that denial impossible. Chileans have thus known that some significant share of their countrymen supported the dictatorship while another significant part of the population experienced exile, imprisonment, torture, or even death under the military. Also, the harshness of the military's treatment of its enemies, both those who were politically active under the Allende administration and those who objected to military rule in the 1970s and 1980s, discouraged many Chileans from participation in politics.[11] Chile entered the 1990s democratic but divided, with profound depoliticization (or, as Louis Goodman describes it in his chapter, political alienation) among a large part of the population, especially those benefiting from the robust economic growth engendered by Chile's new export-oriented development strategy.

For decades, Mexicans either actively supported or tacitly accepted PRI domination, especially during the years of the Mexican miracle after the Second World War, when the economy grew at a rapid rate. The government's repression of the 1968 student movement introduced widespread disaffection with the regime, but even then the PRI's organizational advantages and the willingness of the two subsequent administrations to engage in populist spending strategies kept the PRI in firm control of electoral politics, bolstered by the significant though not decisive use of electoral fraud.[12] Economic crisis in the 1980s, however, led to an upsurge in support for opposition parties, which the PRI countered by more blatant reliance on electoral fraud and campaigns lavishly financed by what many suspected were government funds.[13] In 1988, the ruling PRI suffered the defection of some of its leaders over the neoliberal development path the previous administration had chosen to follow, and only the blatant use of fraud and intimidation took the presidential election for the PRI. One of the bases of the PRI's success was the extensive clientelist network that spread throughout the society. Almost everyone knew people benefiting personally from government expenditures, and one's individual advancement depended much on personal connections with others in this clientelist system. One consequence of clientelism was widespread corruption, as many thousands of Mexicans, from petty functionaries and police officers to the country's highest officials, sought to use the public sphere and the state for private gain.[14]

Thus, while some similarities make a compelling case for comparing Chile and Mexico, especially the roughly similar timetable of political transition in each over the past decade and their respective governments' embrace of neoliberal economic development strategies (Mexico now has a decade and a half of experience with neoliberalism, while Chile's approaches a quarter century), the specific experience of authoritarian rule differed in important characteristics in the two nations. Chile suffered under a harsh military dictatorship that proved divisive to the society. Mexican authoritarianism was much milder and more reliant on the recruitment of many, many civilians into government roles, civilians who essentially bought into the Mexican political regime. Further, Chile has an earlier heritage of democracy, while Mexicans have only just begun to enjoy democratic institutions. One additional difference with important political implications results from the experience of the neoliberal economic strategies pursued in each country. Mexico has within the past five years suffered an economic setback associated with the December 1994 devaluation of the peso. Although this might not necessarily be a direct result of the neoliberal model, it may be perceived as such by the Mexican people. In contrast, Chile's recent experience with neoliberalism has been mostly positive, with steady and rapid rates of growth.[15] The likelihood that Mexicans will view the economic depression of the mid-1990s as being a legacy of authoritarian rule is thus real: it is another example of the failure of the authoritarian presidency.

POLITICAL ATTITUDES IN CHILE AND MEXICO: GLOBAL SIMILARITIES AND DIFFERENCES

Authoritarianism does seem to have had consequences for the political attitudes of Chileans and Mexicans. As other contributors to this volume have noted, particularly

TABLE 1 *Assessments about Extent of Democracy* (percent)

How much democracy would you say this country has?	Mexico (N = 1,200)	Chile (N = 1,194)	Costa Rica (N = 1,002)
Much	11	11	40
Some	36	32	26
Little	30	37	24
None	20	16	7
Don't know/no answer	2	4	3

Source: Hewlett Foundation/MORI Internacional, 1998.

Mitchell Seligson, the contrast between Costa Rica on the one hand and Chile and Mexico on the other is a marked one, especially in regard to responses to a set of broad questions about democracy posed in the Hewlett survey conducted for this book. Perhaps the most important of these contrasts is the residual preference for authoritarianism in Chile and Mexico noted by Seligson (fig. 2). More than a quarter of Mexican and Chilean respondents in the Hewlett survey expressed indifference between democratic and nondemocratic regimes, and nearly 20 percent of each nation's respondents said that in some circumstances, an authoritarian regime can be preferable to democracy.[16] As Seligson also points out (fig. 3), Mexicans and Chileans were less likely to equate democracy with liberty than were Costa Ricans, being more inclined to link democracy with particular substantive outcomes (equality or economic progress, for instance).

Chileans and Mexicans do not perceive their countries as being very democratic. In each case, only 11 percent of the sample surveyed replied that there was much democracy in the country, and less than half said that much or some democracy existed in their country (see table 1). In contrast, two-thirds of Costa Ricans believe they live in a country with much or some democracy. Hence, a majority of Mexicans and Chileans seem not to believe that their nation has made a transition to truly democratic rule. Similar percentages of Mexicans and Chileans felt that their local governments were not especially democratic. Interestingly, while the definition individual Mexicans gave for democracy (in terms of process or of substance) was unrelated to their tendency to rate the current regime as democratic, Chileans who defined democracy in process terms were more inclined to say the regime was much or somewhat democratic, and those who defined democracy in terms of substance were more likely to view the current regime as being relatively undemocratic. This suggests that Chileans remain divided about the very definition of democracy and about the purposes of government, a division that contributed mightily to the breakdown of democracy in 1973.

Perhaps more interesting from a comparative perspective than these similarities in the authoritarian heritages of Chile and Mexico are some key differences in the attitudes held by people in those nations. Again, I grant Knight's point that responses to survey questions can tap either passing political attitudes or deeply ingrained aspects of political culture. Nevertheless, these two societies differ in their political perceptions in three ways that might be related to their experiences with authoritarian rule. Perhaps these experiences will lead to the consolidation of a set of values about politics that we can label a political culture. At this point, the survey responses we have indicate some profoundly different values that may be temporary in nature but that may also be political cultures in formation, political cultures shaped by their history of authoritarian rule.

First, Chileans and Mexicans differ about the purposes and priorities of government (see table 2). These responses may be the most fleeting of the values on which these nations differ and may be reflective of contemporary problems in each society. For instance, Mexicans are more inclined to say that fighting crime is the main task of democracy than are Chileans; indeed, nearly one-third of Mexicans offer this response. Why fighting crime is a particular responsibility of *democracy* rather than of any government, the respondents don't seem to have stopped to ask themselves. However, Mexico has recently experienced significant growth in crime, so perhaps this response is understandable and temporary. Of the responses available on the question "If you had to choose, which of the following would you say is the *main* task of democracy?" that truly pertain to *democratic* regimes, Mexicans are more inclined to see democracy in electoral terms—electing governors—than Chileans, who are more concerned about the protection of minorities and the distribution of wealth. Mexicans' focus on elections probably reflects the recent history of electoral fraud and the longer history of one-party domination—now subsiding—in that country, while Chileans' lesser interest in electoral aspects of democracy may have to do with the sense that electoral politics is not so tenuous there.

Table 2 also suggests that Chileans have acquired from their experience with a dictatorship that focused on promoting economic growth a similar obsession with economic prosperity. Mexicans, struggling to promote a more democratic regime while remembering a recent economic downturn, are more likely to want to have it both ways—a government that improves both the economy and democracy. Again, these seem to be passing political preferences, not deeply held values of the nation.

Perhaps less ephemeral are values that relate to interpersonal trust, engagement in the political process, and confidence in government. A second key difference between

TABLE 2 *Priorities of Government* (percent)

If you had to choose, which of the following would you say is the main task of democracy?	*Mexico* *(N = 1,194)*	*Chile* *(N = 1,200)*
To combat crime	31	26
To elect governors	33	18
To distribute wealth	17	28
To protect minorities	16	25
None	1	1
Don't know/no answer	2	2

Which is more important to you: to have a government that improves democracy or that improves the economy?		
Improves democracy	20	18
Improves the economy	51	68
Both	26	13
None	2	0
Don't know/No answer	1	1

Source: Hewlett Foundation/MORI Internacional, *Visión Latinoamericana de la democracía.*

TABLE 3 *Politicization and Trust* (percent)

How important would you say politics are?	*Mexico* *(N = 1,194)*	*Chile* *(N = 1,200)*
Much	36	19
Some	38	41
Little	16	22
None	7	14
Don't know/no answer	2	3

Generally speaking, would you say that people are trustworthy or not trustworthy?		
Yes, trustworthy	44	20
No, not trustworthy	54	76
Don't know/no answer	3	4

Source: Hewlett Foundation/MORI Internacional, 1998.

Chile and Mexico seems to be the willingness of people to participate politically and to trust their fellow citizens (see table 3). Interpersonal trust was identified by Gabriel Almond and Sidney Verba as a value significant for developing the civic cooperation that forms the basis of democratic practice.[17] Mexicans scored low on interpersonal trust in Almond and Verba's 1959 survey and in those of several researchers who followed them.[18] As Matthew Kenney suggests in his contribution to this volume, Mexicans appear to be more trusting of each other today than in the past. This can only be a positive development in Mexican political culture, even if one is willing to argue that political cooperation can be generated in the absence of high levels of interpersonal trust.[19] Here the contrast between apparently distrustful Chileans and more trustful Mexicans is striking.

Almond and Verba linked high levels of interpersonal distrust to political alienation.[20] Table 3 also shows that perceptions of the importance of politics are much lower in Chile than in Mexico. The perception of the importance of politics serves as one indicator of political alienation in Chile, of the disinclination to participation. Likewise, as Goodman notes in his chapter, many Chileans are more inclined to indicate no sympathy with a political party and to say that they don't vote. In addition, those with low levels of trust are more likely to be among the depoliticized in both countries, but the relationship is especially strong in Chile. Chileans, hence, have entered democracy with low levels of interpersonal trust and a considerable part of the population uninvolved in politics. While the Hewlett survey cannot demonstrate that Chileans are depoliticized and exhibit distrust because of their experience with authoritarian rule, the contrast between the politicization of the years before 1973 and the alienation from politics of many Chileans today is striking. However, there seems to be little or no relationship between age and interest in politics in either Chile or Mexico, except that Chileans under the age of 30 (that is, those who came of political age under Pinochet— those now age 30 would have been five years old when the dictator assumed power) are much more likely to say that they do not usually vote than are their older countrymen.[21]

Mexicans' principal attitudinal legacy from authoritarian rule seems to be very low levels of confidence in national political institutions. Rather than being alienated from one another, as are Chileans, Mexicans are alienated from their political system. Table 4 reports levels of confidence held by both societies in several national institutions. While Mexicans and Chileans are both confident in schools and both distrustful of political parties, most remarkable in table 4 are the low levels of confidence Mexicans have in their government, their national legislature, their police, and even their press. Nearly two-thirds of Mexicans report little or no confidence in the major national institutions of their political system. Chileans are less confident in these institutions than would be ideal, but they lag quite far behind Mexicans in their lack of confidence. This is a third key difference in the values the two nations seem to have inherited from authoritarian rule.

TABLE 4 *Confidence in National Institutions* (percent)

How much confidence do you have in:	Mexico (N = 1,200)	Chile (N = 1,194)
The police		
Much or some	33	61
Little or none	65	38
Schools		
Much or some	64	89
Little or none	35	10
The government		
Much or some	30	51
Little or none	68	48
The press		
Much or some	29	57
Little or none	66	41
Congress		
Much or some	28	43
Little or none	61	51
Political parties		
Much or some	30	27
Little or none	63	70
The army		
Much or some	45	53
Little or none	49	44

Source: Hewlett Foundation/MORI Internacional, 1998.

TABLE 5 *Perceptions of Corruption* (percent)

In your opinion, how many government officials are corrupt and accept bribes?	Mexico (N = 1,200)	Chile (N = 1,194)
Few or none	21	36
Many or most	76	58

In your opinion, what has been the major obstacle to democracy in this country?		
Corruption	42	20
The government	22	6
Political parties	11	16
Poverty	8	20
People's passivity	6	7
Lack of education	7	13
Other	1	11
Don't know/no answer	3	7

Would you say that elections are regularly clean or fraudulent?		
Clean	33	68
Fraudulent	61	23
Don't know/no answer	6	9

Source: Hewlett Foundation/MORI Internacional, 1998.

Mexicans similarly exhibit a strong opinion that corruption is rampant and that it forms the major obstacle to democracy in their nation (table 5). Three-quarters of Mexicans believe that many or most government officials accept bribes and are otherwise corrupt. Importantly, electoral fraud is perceived by Mexicans to be widespread, apparently reflecting their nation's recent electoral history, in which the PRI has often been accused of stealing elections. Fewer Chileans see government officials as being corrupt or elections as being fraudulent. Interestingly, however, those Chileans who do see government officials as corrupt or elections as fraudulent tend to have low confidence in all major social institutions, including the church and the family. In short, a significant portion of Chileans seem to be simply alienated from and cynical about all social and political institutions. In contrast, Mexicans more carefully delineate which institutions should be distrusted because of corruption—the government in general, the police, the army, and political parties. The Mexican congress, for instance, a largely impotent body in the past, is not held accountable for corruption and electoral fraud.

PARTISANSHIP, PARTICIPATION, AND
AUTHORITARIAN LEGACIES

How can we explain the different attitudes that Chileans and Mexicans seem to have brought with them into their new democracies? As I suggested at the outset, neither Chileans nor Mexicans are of one mind about fundamental political values pertaining to democracy and its practice. We might immediately hypothesize that those Chileans who supported the Pinochet regime or those Mexicans who followed the PRI would hold values fundamentally different from those of their fellow nationals.

The Hewlett survey does not directly ask respondents whether they *were* supporters of the authoritarian regime, but it does ask which party a respondent would vote for if an election were to be held tomorrow. Only the top three parties in each congress are clearly identified in the data set, but those serve adequately to identify pro-authoritarian-regime and anti-authoritarian-regime respondents. In Mexico, the PRI clearly has been identified with the old regime, while the two major parties of opposition, the center-right National Action Party (Partido Acción Nacional, or PAN) and the center-left Democratic Revolutionary Party (Partido de la Revolución Democrática, or PRD), have run on antiregime platforms as much as anything. In Chile, the Christian Democratic Party (Partido Demócrata Cristiano, or PDC) is definitely identified with opposition to the Pinochet dictatorship; having the largest congressional delegation and having elected the two presidents since 1989, it is, more than any other, the party of the government. The two other Chilean parties with whom the Hewlett data set provided respondents a clear opportunity to identify are both in some way associated with the dictatorship and the right. Renovación Nacional (National Renewal, or RN) "represent[s] modern values associated with democracy, a professional military and respect for human rights," while the Independent Democratic Union (Unión Democrática Independiente, or UDI) "stress[es] total faith in the market model, a complete defence of the Pinochet era, combined with a certain degree of populism and less than total conviction in the virtues of democracy."[22] Many would thus see RN as the conservative party, leaving authoritarian rule with a goal of integrating into the new democracy, and would see the UDI as the unrepentant right—those not convinced of democracy's virtues.

Chileans willing to indicate that they would vote for the right tend to be more mistrustful of others than the national average and than Christian Democrats (see table 6). The polarization of society associated with Allende's socialist experiment and Pinochet's purges seems to have led those most supportive of those purges to remain uncertain about the reliability of their fellow nationals. More compelling is the differ-

TABLE 6 *Partisanship, Politicization, and Trust in Chile* (percent)

How important would you say politics are?	PDC	RN	UDI	None	National
Very	23	18	12	13	20
Some	49	54	40	34	42
Little	20	16	22	29	23
None	9	12	26	24	15
$N =$	288 (25%)	87 (8%)	104 (9%)	341 (29%)	1,160
Generally speaking, would you say that people are trustworthy or not trustworthy?					
Yes, trustworthy	22	15	17	16	20
No, not trustworthy	78	85	83	85	80
$N =$	289 (25%)	89 (8%)	102 (9%)	339 (30%)	1,147

Source: Hewlett Foundation/MORI Internacional, 1998.

PDC = Christian Democratic Party

RN = National Renewal

UDI = Independent Democratic Union

Other parties and don't know/no answer responses excluded.

ence within the right between the more conciliatory RN and the more unreconstructed UDI on perceptions of the importance of politics. RN supporters are more like PDC voters than not, and both see politics as more important than the national average. However, UDI voters are like the nonvoters in that they are more likely to see politics as having little or no importance. Thus, an important segment of the right in Chile has adopted the attitude that politics is unimportant, or should be unimportant—a value that General Pinochet sought to drill into his subjects. These findings hint that despite the effective functioning of democratic institutions in Chile for nearly a decade, the society remains divided.

In Mexico, even supporters of the ruling party (the PRI) are more likely to express little or no confidence in national political institutions than to say they have some or much confidence in them (see table 7). But opposition supporters are even less trustful of national political institutions than PRI supporters. In particular, the opposition supporters have little or no confidence in the government and the congress—far less confidence than PRI supporters, even though the lower house of congress was in the hands of the opposition when the Hewlett poll was taken in July 1998. Likewise, opposition supporters are more likely to indicate that they find corruption rampant in Mexico (see table 8). But while the perception among PRI supporters that the governmental appa-

TABLE 7 *Partisanship and Confidence in National Institutions in Mexico*
(percent)

How much confidence do you have in:	PRI	PRD	PAN	National
The police				
Much or some	40	34	31	36
Little or none	60	66	69	64
N =	386 (33%)	203 (17%)	288 (24%)	1,181
The government				
Much or some	40	25	28	33
Little or none	60	75	72	67
N =	393 (33%)	202 (17%)	287 (24%)	1,180
Congress				
Much or some	40	31	26	33
Little or none	60	69	74	67
N =	352 (33%)	190 (18%)	258 (24%)	1,064
Political parties				
Much or some	38	36	30	35
Little or none	62	64	70	65
N =	370 (33%)	199 (18%)	277 (25%)	1,123

Source: Hewlett Foundation/MORI Internacional, 1998.
PRI = Institutional Revolutionary Party
PRD = Democratic Revolutionary Party
PAN = National Action Party
Other parties, none, and don't know/no answer responses excluded.

ratus is full of bribe-takers is not significantly different from that held by the supporters of the two main opposition parties, there is a great difference between likely PRI voters, on the one hand, and likely voters for the PRD or the PAN on the issue of electoral fraud. Likely PRI voters are much more inclined to see electoral politics as clean and fair than are supporters of the opposition. This pattern of responses suggests that while all Mexicans have questions about national political institutions and the national political process, for those not identifying with the political regime and its electoral organ, the PRI, national politics is even less legitimate. Consolidating democracy in this context may require significant efforts to restore public confidence in the government, in the political parties, and in the electoral process.

While the relationships I have just displayed do not definitely identify supporters of the previous authoritarian regimes as the main holders of attitudes inimical to democ-

TABLE 8 *Partisanship and Perceptions of Corruption in Mexico* (percent)

In your opinion, how many government officials are corrupt and accept bribes?	PRI	PRD	PAN	National
Few or none	23	19	21	20
Many or most	77	81	79	80
N =	387 (33%)	203 (17%)	285 (24%)	1,174

Would you say that elections are regularly clean or fraudulent?				
Clean	47	30	34	39
Fraudulent	53	70	67	61
N =	377 (34%)	192 (17%)	280 (25%)	1,125

Source: Hewlett Foundation/MORI Internacional, 1998.
Other parties, none, and don't know/no answer responses excluded.

TABLE 9 *Voting Intention and Regime Preference* (percent)

	Regime Preference			
Voting intention	Democracy	Indifferent	Authoritarianism	Vote Share
Mexico				
PRI	52	29	19	33
PRD	46	32	22	17
PAN	56	24	20	24
N =	596 (51%)	317 (27%)	246 (21%)	1,158
Chile				
PDC	62	20	17	24
RN	43	14	43	8
UDI	25	48	27	9
N =	595 (53%)	329 (29%)	208 (18%)	1,132

Source: Hewlett Foundation/MORI Internacional, 1998.
Other parties, none, and don't know/no answer responses excluded.

racy today, they do suggest that a substantial subset of Chileans and Mexicans have not embraced the attitudes that would be most supportive of democracy. Interestingly, though, in Mexico voting intention has no relationship to one's regime preferences; PRI supporters are as likely to say that democracy is the best form of government as are PRD or PAN supporters (see table 9). This may reflect different understandings of what democratic practice entails—the PRI, after all, has long argued that the regime it headed was democratic. In contrast, in Chile, the right is clearly more ambivalent about democracy than are the Christian Democrats. RN supporters are as likely to choose authoritarianism as democracy, and almost a majority of UDI supporters are indifferent between democracy and authoritarianism. A majority in both parties of the right do not choose democracy as the preferable regime. Of course, supporters of the UDI and the RN make up less than 20 percent of this sample, so their numbers are limited; nevertheless, a hard core of nondemocrats remains among the Chilean public.

CONSEQUENCES OF ATTITUDES INHERITED IN CHILE AND MEXICO

What do these attitudes mean for the overall legitimacy of contemporary democracy in Chile and Mexico? It should not be surprising that the attitudes I have been exploring here tend to be related: the depoliticized tend to be distrustful of their fellow citizens, the distrustful tend to have low confidence in national institutions, and so forth. Of special interest is the extent to which these attitudes about trust, interest in politics, perceptions of corruption, and confidence in national institutions are related to the degree of satisfaction with the current democratic regime and to the preference for alternatives to democracy.

Table 10 shows a remarkable correlation between trust in the reliability of others and satisfaction with the functioning of democracy. This relationship does not indicate the direction of causality; that is, does being trustful lead one to assess the functioning of democracy in a positive way, or does a positive assessment of democracy's functioning lead one to be trustful? That cannot be shown merely with statistical tools. Howev-

TABLE 10 *Interpersonal Trust and Satisfaction with Democracy* (percent)

Are people trustworthy or not?	Very Satisfied	Somewhat Satisfied	Neither	Somewhat Dissatisfied	Very Dissatisfied	Total
Mexico						
Trustworthy	67	53	49	40	35	45
Not trustworthy	33	47	51	60	65	55
N =	81 (7%)	275 (24%)	152 (13%)	314 (27%)	328 (29%)	1,151
Chile						
Trustworthy	41	32	16	15	10	21
Not trustworthy	59	68	84	85	90	79
N =	50 (4%)	383 (34%)	77 (7%)	368 (33%)	259 (23%)	1,136

Header over data columns: Are you satisfied or dissatisfied with the way democracy is working?

Source: Hewlett Foundation/MORI Internacional, 1998.

TABLE 11 *Perceptions of Corruption and Satisfaction with Democracy* (percent)

How many people in the government are corrupt?	Are you satisfied or dissatisfied with the way democracy is working?					
	Very Satisfied	Somewhat Satisfied	Neither	Somewhat Dissatisfied	Very Dissatisfied	Total
Mexico						
Almost no one	5	2	4	2	0	2
Few	61	25	27	14	8	20
Many	16	46	35	37	29	35
Almost everyone	18	27	34	47	62	43
N =	79 (7%)	282 (24%)	151 (13%)	314 (27%)	330 (29%)	1,156
Chile						
Almost no one	20	8	6	11	8	9
Few	43	39	17	31	11	28
Many	15	36	44	41	34	37
Almost everyone	23	17	32	18	47	26
N =	46 (4%)	373 (34%)	61 (5%)	367 (33%)	263 (24%)	1,110
Are elections regularly clean or fraudulent? (Mexico only)						
Clean	52	49	40	30	21	35
Fraudulent	48	51	60	70	79	65
N =	79 (7%)	268 (24%)	146 (13%)	301 (27%)	315 (28%)	1,108

Source: Hewlett Foundation/MORI Internacional, 1998.

er, in whichever way the arrows of causality point—and most likely the relationship is bidirectional—the high levels of distrust in these two societies does not bode well for the deep legitimacy of the regimes in Chile and Mexico. In both countries, those who view people as being unreliable are very likely to be dissatisfied with the current state of democratic practice. The scale of this problem for democracy is great. Nearly half of Chileans, for example, fall into the boxes in table 10 in which they are both somewhat dissatisfied with democracy and find others unreliable (28 percent) or very dissatisfied with democracy and distrustful (21 percent). While the elites currently occupying positions of authority in the Chilean government and/or the political parties may not have such high levels of distrust for one another, thus allowing democracy to function well at the level of political institutions and politicians, these levels of dissatisfaction and distrust at the mass level could be problematic for the interaction of elites and masses or the interaction of mass groups should political crisis reemerge in the Chilean political system. The levels of dissatisfaction and distrust are moderately lower in the Mexican case, but still high enough to portend high levels of political conflict should a crisis arise.

Equally troubling is the apparent link between perceptions that the occupants of government positions are corrupt and the level of satisfaction with democracy (see table 11). In both countries, a majority of the sample responded that many or almost all of those occupying government positions are corrupt; in fact, three-quarters of Mexicans held this view. The same respondents who see corruption rampant in the government are likely to be somewhat or very dissatisfied with the functioning of democracy in their nation. Again, while mere cross-tabulations of responses to these two questions cannot establish a causal link between corruption and the delegitimation of these two regimes, a strong hypothesis might be that the perceptions of corruption tend to lead people to be unhappy with the regime in place—in these cases, democratic regimes. And again, the numbers of respondents who both perceive corruption to be rampant and are dissatisfied with the regime are relatively large shares of the sample. For example, almost half of Mexicans see many or almost all of those in the government as corrupt and also are somewhat or very dissatisfied with the functioning of Mexican democracy.

In Mexico, the link between perceptions of the integrity of the electoral process and satisfaction with democracy seems especially strong. The bottom rows of table 11 would seem to demonstrate a clear linear relationship between those two variables: those who perceive elections to be fraudulent are more likely to be dissatisfied with democracy's practice. Again, the numbers of those who perceive electoral fraud and who are dissatisfied (somewhat or very) are high, in this case over half (51 percent) of respondents.

Going beyond the general legitimacy of the regime to examine some key aspects of democratic practice, we find some additional worrisome relationships. For example, the significant percentage of depoliticized Chileans tends to include large numbers of both nonvoters (see table 6) and non–party identifiers (see table 12). Although an excessively politicized population can produce severe political conflict, as Chileans learned in the early 1970s, a very depoliticized population with large numbers of nonvoters and many floating voters does not contribute to strong political institutions. Chile already suffers from a fragmented party system; only 24 percent of the Hewlett sample said they would vote for the nation's largest political party (the PDC) were elections to be held tomorrow, and the other parties have much smaller followings (see table 9). In this situation, with 41 percent of the population admitting to having no partisan identity, electoral volatility is a distinct possibility should a crisis arise. Chile has

TABLE 12 *Politicization and Strength of Partisan Identity* (percent)

How important are politics?	Strong Partisan Identifier	Weak Partisan Identifier	No Partisan Identity	Total
		Strength of Partisan Identity		
Mexico				
Much	42	36	30	38
Somewhat	37	39	40	38
Little	16	17	20	17
None	6	8	10	8
$N =$	408	578	159	1,145
	(36%)	(51%)	(14%)	
Chile				
Much	26	23	13	20
Somewhat	47	46	36	42
Little	16	24	38	23
None	11	7	24	15
$N =$	318	358	461	1,138
	(28%)	(32%)	(41%)	

Source: Hewlett Foundation/MORI Internacional, 1998.

had the good fortune of experiencing political and economic stability since its transition to democracy in 1989. The PDC politicians at the center of the new regime and their socialist allies in the Concertación have powerful incentives to avoid a crisis, given the distribution of nonvoters and independents that this survey has identified.

In Mexico, an issue central to the consolidation of democracy will be institutional arrangements at the national level, particularly the relationship of the presidency to the legislature (specifically, how a president of one party will work with a congress in which his party does not have a majority) and the merits of alternation in the presidency (which has not occurred thus far). Although I have noted that Mexicans display higher levels of interpersonal trust than Chileans, a majority of Mexicans nevertheless respond that they don't find others reliable. Those who distrust others are far more likely to be uncomfortable with the new institutional arrangements that would have to take hold were Mexico to consolidate its democracy than are their more trusting countrymen. As table 13 indicates, both Mexicans and Chileans who do not trust others are more likely to assess alternation in power as being bad or very bad, while those who are more trusting are more likely to find alternation in the presidency a good thing. In the Mexican case (but not for Chile), those who find others to be reliable are more likely to consider divided government to be good, while those who are distrustful show greater doubts about the merits of divided government. While mass views about the reliability

TABLE 13 *Interpersonal Trust and Institutional Preferences* (percent)

	Do you think it is good or bad that the president of the republic is sometimes from one party and sometimes from another?					
Are people trustworthy or not?	Very Good	Somewhat Good	Neither	Somewhat Bad	Very Bad	Total
Mexico						
Trustworthy	53	51	39	34	34	45
Not trustworthy	47	49	62	66	66	55
N =	276 (25%)	360 (32%)	184 (16%)	187 (17%)	119 (11%)	1,127
Chile						
Trustworthy	34	24	24	19	10	21
Not trustworthy	66	76	76	81	90	79
N =	95 (9%)	312 (28%)	210 (19%)	264 (24%)	219 (20%)	1,100

	Do you think it is good or bad that the president of the republic belongs to one party and the majority of the congress to another?					
	Very Good	Somewhat Good	Neither	Somewhat Bad	Very Bad	Total
Mexico						
Trustworthy	48	52	40	34	35	44
Not trustworthy	52	49	60	66	65	56
N =	232 (21%)	403 (37%)	148 (14%)	221 (20%)	99 (9%)	1,103
Chile						
Trustworthy	27	22	23	19	19	21
Not trustworthy	73	78	77	81	81	79
N =	48 (4%)	308 (28%)	161 (15%)	384 (35%)	210 (19%)	1,110

Source: Hewlett Foundation/MORI Internacional, 1998.

of others are not likely to influence the evolution of the national institutions in question, in the Mexican case, where these national institutions are in a moment of evolution, the fact that many citizens seem uncomfortable with this change is another reflection of mass uncertainties about the country's political future, especially on the part of those Mexicans who are cynical about public life and generally uncomfortable with public interaction.

PROSPECTS FOR THE FUTURE

The transition to and consolidation of democracy is a process that has both elite and mass dimensions. In the absence of elite willingness, mass preferences for democracy cannot be easily practiced, as an earlier study of Mexico by John Booth and Mitchell Seligson demonstrated.[23] Conversely, many studies of the democratization of Latin American nations have focused on the efforts of elites to arrive at negotiated settlements of their differences.[24] Mass attitudes play a role in the latter process only by providing support to different sides in those negotiations. Thus, democratic consolidation is not solely a matter of mass attitudes—the political culture of a country, as it were—and they may not even be the most important factors in shaping democratic practice in subsequent years.

However, high levels of interpersonal distrust, lack of confidence in major national institutions, perceptions that the government and important political processes are pervaded by corruption, and low levels of interest in politics cannot be healthy for emerging democracies. In these situations, democratic legitimacy has to be built *despite* the widespread presence of such values. As democratization continues in Mexico, for instance, national leaders will have to find ways to convince Mexicans that the government can be trusted, that political parties have worth, that important agencies of the government are not just out to enrich themselves (such as the police or the army). Otherwise, the inclination of citizens to take part in the formal political processes—for example, through elections—and to approach the government for redress of some wrong or to address some need will be minimized. Democratic substance can hardly be accomplished without violence unless democratic process is followed. The inclination to seek to use political processes other than the formal rules of Mexican democracy remains widespread and even popularly supported in Mexico. The Zapatista uprising in Chiapas is merely the best known of many guerrilla movements and social movements.

Elites have made the Chilean transition to democracy one of the smoothest yet observed in Latin America. Important segments of the Chilean public remain unconvinced that democracy has been achieved, however. Goodman has indicated that the challenge to Chilean elites is precisely "the management of fear, division, and alienation." Chileans are now more inclined to nonparticipation than are Mexicans, to simply not accord politics (narrowly or broadly understood) much importance. As I have argued above, this inclination could change if Chile were to face a political or economic crisis. To avoid that circumstance, Chilean political leaders need to figure out how to heal the divisions within the country, how to give Chileans a sense that they can trust others, and how to draw uninvolved citizens into the political process at some level.

As Mexicans and Chileans entered the 1990s and a new political era, in neither case was the political culture a tabula rasa. Years of authoritarian practices produced a variety of attitudes not always functional for democracy. Some segments of the population of each country remain antidemocratic in profound ways that reflect the characteristics of the authoritarian regimes from which they emerged. Of course, all democracies incorporate such people (witness the United States' experience with the Ku Klux Klan and other hate groups), but they can produce strains in democratic practice and test the tolerance of those who are profoundly democratic in their values. This is a challenge that both Chile and Mexico will face in the years to come.

Chapter 8

Color and Democracy in Latin America

Miguel Basáñez and Pablo Parás

Color differences in the United States are very clear. Their impact on society, politics, and business is evident every day. This is not the case in Latin America. In the United States, there are antidiscrimination laws, protection for minority workers, and a variety of ways of expressing the intensity of the social division by color. Political and advertising campaigns are designed with a very clear perception of color differences. Perhaps the most conspicuous example in advertising is the "United Colors of Benetton" campaign.

Why is the effect of color not studied in Latin America? Why not even in countries such as Mexico, in which barely 15 percent of the population is white? Because such an effect doesn't exist? Finding out people's propensity for democracy or authoritarianism by color may help us to understand some features of Latin American political development. The exploration may shed some light on whether democratization is a process led by the elites or by the masses. These are points that we will address in this chapter.

The results of the last congressional election in the United States suggested that three "R's" (race, religion, rural-urban) were the strongest factors in determining voter preferences—much stronger than sex, age, marital status, education, geography, income, family economic situation, political party preference, political orientation (liberal-conservative), or prior voting record.[1] Differences are sometimes greater than 40 percentage points, as can be seen in table 1.

More than twice as many African Americans as whites (89 percent versus 43 percent) preferred Democrats, and more than five times as many whites as African Americans (57 versus 11 percent) preferred Republicans. Party preferences by religion and

TABLE 1 *U.S. Congressional Election Vote, 1998* (percent)

	Total	Race (Color)			Religion			Rural-urban		
		White	Hispanic	African-American	Protestant	Catholic	Jewish	Metro	Cities	Rural
Democrat	49	43	63	89	42	53	79	82	52	38
Republican	51	57	37	11	58	47	21	18	48	62

Source: New York Times, November 9, 1998, p. 20.

rural-urban show similarly large contrasts. Do these strong differences of opinion exist in Latin America? Differences by rural-urban have been explained in modernization theory as part of the urbanization process. Religious and cultural differences have been approached from a variety of viewpoints[2] and are beginning to be explored empirically.[3] However, color as a factor influencing opinion seems to be almost unexplored in the region. In a bibliographical search of titles published about Latin America, we found mainly tangential references. In contrast, the literature on the United States is direct and abundant.[4]

Color differences are presumed to be nonexistent in countries such as Mexico, at least in the dominant institutional culture. This is not without explanation. Mestizo pride and feelings of equality have undoubtedly been a positive outcome of the Mexican Revolution of 1910 and have contributed to broadened opportunities and therefore to upward social mobility. But have the differences and their consequences been erased? Has there been an equalization of opportunity among people of color and whites in professional positions, politics, business, and social class? Distinguished scholars such as Daniel Cosío Villegas in Mexico felt that even the exploration of the subject was useless.[5]

To try to answer our central questions, we used the poll conducted with the support of the Hewlett Foundation in July 1998 among 3,396 adults in Mexico, Costa Rica, and Chile. In all of the poll's questions, the differences of opinion between whites and *morenos* (people of color) are notable. The differences do not exceed 40 percent, as they do in the United States, but they are statistically significant. Table 2 highlights some items. What especially stands out are the opinions on preference for democracy versus authoritarianism, the importance given to politics, and whether elections are clean. In general terms, the strongest differences appeared in political opinions, confidence, civility, and knowledge.

An initial review of the data in table 2 shows that the preference for democracy is

TABLE 2   *Contrast of Opinions by Color in Mexico, Costa Rica, and Chile* (*percent*)

	White (N = 1,270)	Moreno[a] (N = 2,126)	Difference
Prefers democracy to authoritarianism	68	53	14.9
Politics is very important	43	31	11.9
Always participated in family decisions	26	15	10.9
Self-placed on the right	25	16	9.3
Democracy is liberty	37	29	8.4
Equality is the most important political right	20	29	−9.3
Elections are fraudulent	28	44	−15.6
Would never participate in a boycott	83	75	8.1
No confidence in the army	37	24	12.7
Much/some confidence in the courts	45	33	12.3
Much confidence in small enterprise	31	19	12.3
Much/some confidence in the press	56	44	11.9
Much confidence in the schools	50	41	8.6
Much/some confidence in congress	42	33	8.6
Very foolish to run a red light at night	56	43	12.6
Very foolish not to pay subway/bus fares	39	27	11.6
Very foolish to cut in line	39	28	10.6
Very foolish to keep extra change	36	26	10.2
Identifies the executive branch by name	40	28	11.9
Identifies the judicial branch by name	43	32	11.5
Identifies the legislative branch by name	42	33	8.8
Personal economic situation somewhat good	39	29	9.8
Gets news from the press	24	15	8.6

a. Under the term *moreno* (brown) are grouped light colored, dark colored, indigenous, and black.

greater among whites (68 percent) than among *morenos* (53 percent). Does this mean that elites (predominantly made up of whites in Mexico and Chile) drive the process of democratization more than a social demand by the majority of the population, made up of *morenos?* Does an elite-led process mean an unstable path to democracy? As we proceed with the analysis, a more complex picture will emerge.

A study conducted by María Teresa Ruiz of sixth graders in Costa Rica and Panama found high levels of discrimination and even racism among high-income whites, as well as low levels of self-esteem among blacks interviewed.[6] Does this point to feelings of social distance? In their examination of Mexican authoritarianism, John Booth and Mitchell Seligson found that the average industrial worker has democratic values.[7] On the other hand, Silvia del Cid found when comparing whites, indigenous people, and ladinos in Guatemala that "ethnicity may jeopardize democracy and democratic stability."[8] In summary, there is not a consistent picture when looking at color in the region.

POLITICAL CULTURE

The analysis of differences in values and attitudes falls under the field of political culture. The study of political culture has been a subject of attention and debate since the late 1960s, particularly after the publication in 1963 of *The Civic Culture* by Gabriel Almond and Sidney Verba.

Criticisms of the study of political culture range from charges that it is "elitist" (only certain societies hold true democratic values and attitudes) to accusations of "cultural determinism" (culture causes structural changes; authoritarian heritage is responsible for undemocratic attitudes and beliefs, or for undemocratic and unstable institutions) and "reductionism." Scholars such as Samuel Huntington call culture a "residual category," a soft, nonquantifiable and nongeneralizable explanation "when hard ones do not work," since cultural explanations are vague. For an update on criticisms and problems with respect to this topic, see Alan Knight's chapter in this book.

Proponents of the idea of political culture claim, on the other side, its usefulness in understanding cultural factors rooted in previous historical experiences, events, and socialization processes. For them, cultural values are quite stable, though they are subject to change. Culture is not seen as destiny. Political culture influences other structural factors but does not determine them.

Almond and Verba's *The Civic Culture* continues to be the classic reference for subsequent comparative works on values and attitudes in societies with different levels of economic development. For Almond and Verba, political culture is not a theory but a set of variables that may be used to construct theories. The explanatory power of political culture variables is seen as an empirical question, open to hypotheses and tests. In spite of criticisms and reevaluations of their original work, and after a period of disenchantment with the potential of cultural factors as a causal explanation of different levels of democracy, political culture studies have seen a renewal in academic interest in the last 10 years.

For Ronald Inglehart, cultural variables are often thought of as ethereal simply because we usually have only vague, impressionistic measures of them. When measured quantitatively, basic orientations are quite stable.[9] Robert Putnam's work has been seen as an important contribution on the causal linkages between economic and cultural factors. In an analysis of Italy using regional data from the past century to the 1980s, he found that high levels of social capital in some regions were linked to the economic development achieved in those regions. Thus, cultural factors (civic involvement levels in the past) had effects on the working of institutions in the present.[10] Inglehart and Putnam treat political culture as both an independent and a dependent variable, causing structure and behavior and being caused by them.

Frederick Turner suggests that political culture in the 1990s must be interpreted in a broader context than it was in *The Civic Culture*, avoiding characterizations that use a model drawn from countries such as the United States or the United Kingdom. As he points out, whether Latin America has one political culture or whether the elements of political culture differ among those nations is a fundamental issue to be addressed by the empirical analysis of values and orientations to politics in the region. He acknowledges that an interesting development in many countries is the proliferation of survey research around the world, which facilitates the testing of hypotheses and theories with respect to culture and politics.[11]

Mitchell Seligson points out that, in spite of limitations in the availability of survey data and archives for survey research in Latin America, and the strong resistance to doing political culture research by Latin American scholars—due to their humanistic tradition, as opposed to the positivist, empirical approach of North American social science—there is an increased interest in political culture research in the region. This is partly due, he argues, to the inability of economic theories of democratization to predict regime change in the area, coupled with the transition to democratic regimes throughout Latin America.[12]

Peter Smith suggests that the "uniqueness" of the Latin American region must be reformulated as a proposed subject for empirical investigation, rather than being considered an automatic premise. He argues that Latin American social science has a cyclical tendency to embrace and discard theoretical schemes. In the 1960s, the basic views of modernization theories (economic development leads to pro-democratic attitudes) were weakened by reality. Economic development exacerbated the concentration of wealth, and the political outcome was an authoritarian turn in several of the most developed countries of the region (Brazil in 1964, Argentina in 1966, and Chile in 1973).[13]

Dependency studies then came to the forefront with alternative explanations for underdevelopment. In the 1980s, reality also challenged expectations: while suffering economic depression, countries with authoritarian regimes embarked on processes of liberalization and democratization. Thus, dependency theory was weakened, and the role of the elite was seen as a key factor in the transition. As liberalization began to change the political landscape in the 1980s, new methodologies and regular research on public opinion began to appear. Since then, public opinion polling has been closely related to the process of democratization.

PROBLEMS AND LIMITATIONS

Using color as a category of analysis has problems as well as operational and conceptual limitations. A first problem is, What are we really measuring—differences in color, or differences in class? That is, the category *color* hides the complexity of levels of education, income, and occupation, among other factors associated with the concept of *class*. Conceptually, there are also problems. What does it mean to be in the white majority (as in the United States) or to be in the white minority (as in some countries in Latin America or in South Africa)? Ask the same question for people of color. What does it mean to be of color in Mexican society as compared to that of Chile or Costa Rica? Is it possible to attempt to compare? Is it relevant to delineate the differences?

The poll upon which this study is based is operationally limited because color was determined by interviewer observation and also because no national representation of indigenous population was sought. Interviewers were given instructions to classify the respondents' color. Making such a classification is easier the stronger the color contrast is. However, it is less easy when grading light shades of *morenos*. Under the term *moreno* we group those who were classified as light colored (these can also be identified as mestizo or ladino), dark colored, indigenous, or black. Taking only two categories as the basis of our analysis—whites and *morenos*—helps with the reliability and validity of the contrast. There is a need to experiment with ways to help get a better classification of color.

The impact of differences in opinion based on color should vary between countries simply because of differences in internal social composition in the region. Whites in Mexico, as shown in table 3, constitute a clear minority (16 percent); in Chile they make up a plurality (38 percent); and in Costa Rica they are in the majority (61 percent). Additionally, levels of education, income, and occupation within each country vary by color. Table 3 separates the profiles of *morenos* (mestizo or light colored) and *mulatos* (dark colored) interviewed in the poll, although in the rest of this chapter, light and dark *morenos* are treated aggregately.

The first question about whether there are differences of opinion based on color has an affirmative answer in Table 2. Table 3 shows that there are also educational and income differences by color. The differences are largest in Mexico, followed by Chile and then Costa Rica. In Mexico, 22 percent of whites received only primary education, as opposed to 53 percent of *mulatos*. Conversely, higher education was achieved by 41 percent of whites but only 11 percent of *mulatos*. A similar profile emerges with respect to income. In Costa Rica, the figures for primary education only show practically no difference (50 percent and 54 percent), and higher education does not show such a

TABLE 3 *Education and Income by Color* (percent)

	Mexico			Costa Rica			Chile		
	White N = 200 (16%)	Moreno N = 590 (49%)	Mulato N = 378 (31%)	White N = 613 (61%)	Moreno N = 272 (27%)	Mulato N = 87 (9%)	White N = 457 (38%)	Moreno N = 544 (46%)	Mulato N = 178 (15%)
Education									
Primary (1 to 6 years)	22	36	53	50	54	54	35	38	50
Secondary (7 to 12 years)	32	38	30	26	22	23	38	38	40
Higher (13+ years)	41	24	11	18	10	7	26	24	9
Income									
Low	25	39	53	31	40	38	29	36	55
Middle	16	25	21	29	28	31	23	25	21
High	60	37	26	40	32	31	47	38	24

strong contrast. However, in Mexico the percentage of people with higher education is much larger than in the other two countries.

What needs to be done now is to find out (1) whether the differences are attributable to color or to class; and (2) whether they have a positive or negative effect on democracy. To clarify these questions and to measure the impact of belonging to one or the other of these groups, we look at the answers to question 4 in the survey, about preference for democracy or authoritarianism. Each respondent was asked: "With which of the following phrases do you agree most? 1. Democracy is preferable to any other form of government; 2. I am indifferent to a democratic or a nondemocratic regime; 3. In some circumstances, an authoritarian regime can be preferable to a democratic one."

To simplify the results and to highlight the contrasts, we gave +1.0 to those who prefer democracy (answer 1) and –1.0 to those who are indifferent or who accept authoritarianism (answers 2 and 3). The 4.5 percent who do not know are eliminated. The seven-interval scale in figure 1 thus assigns a positive value of +1.0 to the most democratic end of the scale and a negative value of –1.0 to the most authoritarian end of the scale.

The mean answers to this question by country, level of education, income, and color appear in table 4. It can be seen that Costa Ricans fall in the category *democratic*

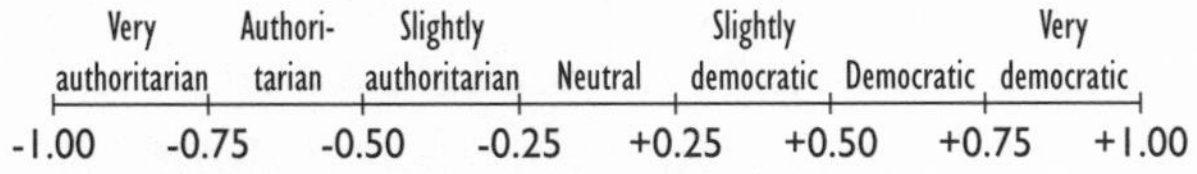

Fig. 1. Authoritarian-democracy orientation scale

TABLE 4 *Authoritarian-Democracy Orientation by Education, Income, and Color* (means)

	Mexico	Costa Rica	Chile
Total	0.03	0.69	0.05
Education			
Basic	–0.08	0.67	–0.04
Secondary	0.05	0.70	0.08
Higher	0.23	0.72	0.26
Income			
Low	–0.11	0.70	0.09
Middle low	0.00	0.68	–0.03
Middle high	0.14	0.70	0.06
High	0.34	0.79	0.05
Color			
White	0.32	0.68	0.13
Moreno	–0.03	0.70	0.00

Note: –1.0 = authoritarian, 0 = neutral, +1.0 = democratic

(+0.69), while Mexicans and Chileans are *neutral* (+0.03 and +0.05). It is evident that the higher the level of education, the more positive the feelings toward democracy in each of the three countries. Income and color show more complex relations.

The least educated Mexicans and Chileans are neutral, leaning slightly toward authoritarianism (–0.08 and –0.04), whereas the least educated Costa Ricans are clearly democrats (0.67) at almost the same level as the more highly educated *ticos* (0.72). It is notable that differences due to education are small in Costa Rica (within 5 points) and large in Mexico and Chile (within 31 and 30 points, respectively). Income shows a pattern similar to that of education. Costa Rica shows a 9-point difference; Mexico, a 45-point difference. Chile follows a strange pattern closer to the Costa Rican one.

In contrast, the picture is complex when viewed by color. *Morenos* in Mexico and Chile show a neutral profile (–0.03 and 0.00), while in Costa Rica whites and *morenos* are equally democratic (+0.68 and +0.70). White Mexicans are slightly democratic (0.32), while white Chileans are neutral but more democratic than *morenos* (0.13).

In summary, greater education and income show a clear tendency toward support for democracy in all three countries. The higher the individual's education and income, the more likely the person is to hold democratic opinions. Color is of no significance in Costa Rica for a democratic attitude, but it is very important in Mexico (35 points difference) and in Chile (13 points difference).

On the basis of the data above, it is not possible to know whether the differences of opinion are a product of color or are the effect of social class. To clear up this uncertainty, we must control for country and class. To control for class, we selected *level of education*, closely linked with income: 75 percent of high-income people are in the higher education brackets, and 64 percent of lower-income people fall into the low education bracket.

Table 5 breaks down the table 4 values for color controlling by education in each country.[14] It confirms that color has an important effect on democratic preference in Chile and Mexico, but not in Costa Rica. Less educated Mexicans score −0.13 for *morenos* and +0.35 for whites (48 points of distance in the scale), while in table 4 the figure for basic education is −0.08. A similar pattern is seen among the highly educated Mexicans (*morenos* score +0.21 and whites +0.30); but the distance in the scale is reduced to only nine points, and *morenos* shift to the democratic side of the scale. Hence, in Mexico, for the same level of education *morenos* lean toward authoritarianism and whites toward democracy. However, among white Mexicans, education has a slightly negative effect on the preference for democracy.

Less educated Chileans behave as Mexicans do. *Morenos* scored −0.12 and whites +0.09, which means that both are neutral, but *morenos* lean toward authoritarian and whites toward democratic. The distance between them is 21 points on the scale. The trend is the same as in Mexico, but to a lesser degree, as the distance is smaller (48 versus 21 points). Nevertheless, among the highly educated Chileans, it is *morenos* who are more democratic than whites. *Morenos* score +0.37 and whites score +0.15, a distance of 22 points on the scale. Thus, in Mexico the color effect is stable, but in Chile the effect is mixed.

In summary, it is not possible to establish a color effect in Costa Rica, as differences

TABLE 5 *Authoritarian-Democracy Orientation by Color, Controlled for Education* (means)

Education	Mexico	Costa Rica	Chile
White			
Basic	.35	.67	.09
Higher	.30	.72	.15
Total	.32	.68	.13
Moreno			
Basic	−.13	.68	−.12
Higher	.21	.69	.37
Total	.03	.70	.00

Note: −1.0 = authoritarian, 0 = neutral, +1.0 = democratic

are minor and fall within the survey's margin of error. In Mexico and Chile, it is indeed possible to establish such an effect. Among Mexicans, being *moreno* produces an inclination toward authoritarianism as compared to whites, independent of education level. In Chile, that is true only for the less educated. On the other hand, education has little effect on whites in Mexico and Chile, but it has a very significant impact on *morenos* in both countries.

FACTORS IN DEMOCRACY

To find democratic orientations, this chapter has so far focused on the responses to question 4. We now turn to the 26 questions in the survey that have been boiled down by factor analysis to six factors that explain 50 percent of variance (see details in the appendix to this chapter). The resulting index is a more refined tool with which we can look more closely at the ingredients of democratic preferences. It examines the respondents' level of confidence, legality, participation (conventional and nonconventional), socialization, and tolerance. The general assumption is that the higher the respondent's score on each factor, the more inclined the individual is toward democracy. However, Mexicans show a clear lack of confidence in institutions, which is explained more by the performance of the institutions than by the attitudes of the respondents. Nevertheless, because the main focus of the analysis is finding the relative distance by color for each factor, their absolute values are less important.

Table 6 displays the means by country and color for each of the six factors, together with the means for democratic versus authoritarian orientation. Mexico has the largest orientation variation between whites and *morenos* (35 points). However, Mexicans show relatively smaller differences in the democratic factors (41 points total). Chile, in turn, shows the largest differences in the democratic factors (85 points total) and only 13 points' distance in orientation. Costa Rica is the lowest of the three countries in both measures.

Besides showing differences by color, the use of factors helps to describe shades of democracy in each country. Chileans and Costa Ricans have much more confidence in their institutions than do Mexicans. Costa Rica is the most legalistic of the three. In Mexico there is a greater tendency to participate in politics in both conventional and nonconventional ways; in Costa Rica there is more of an inclination to participate in conventional activities; and in Chile the inclination to participate at all is markedly less. Costa Rica is the most socialized country, followed by Mexico and Chile. Lastly, we can observe that the Chilean and Costa Rican societies are more tolerant than Mexican society.

TABLE 6 *Color Differences in Authoritarian-Democracy Orientation and Factors by Country* *(means)*

Color	Orientation	Confidence	Legality	Conventional participation	Noncon-ventional participation	Socialization	Tolerance	Factors Av. Difference
Mexico								
White	0.32	−0.34	0.03	0.12	0.06	0.12	−0.17	
Moreno	−0.03	−0.32	−0.18	0.03	0.10	0.12	−0.13	
Difference	0.35	−0.02	0.22	0.10	−0.04	0.00	−0.03	41/6 = 6.8
Costa Rica								
White	0.68	0.16	0.30	0.08	-0.08	0.40	0.02	
Moreno	0.70	0.04	0.31	0.05	−0.02	0.32	0.11	
Difference	−0.02	0.12	−0.01	0.03	−0.06	0.07	−0.09	38/6 = 6.3
Chile								
White	0.13	0.39	−0.01	−0.16	-0.12	−0.36	0.03	
Moreno	0.00	0.13	−0.17	−0.06	−0.01	−0.47	0.13	
Difference	0.13	0.26	0.17	−0.10	−0.11	0.11	−0.10	85/6 = 14.2

The largest difference is in the confidence factor, where Chilean *morenos* show a mean 26 points lower than that of whites. Next is the legality factor, where Mexican *morenos* show a mean 22 points lower than for whites. Third is legality again, among Chileans, where *morenos* have a mean 17 points lower than for whites. In summary, differences in orientation toward democracy do exist among the three countries.

TOWARD EXPLANATION

The last phase of our work on color and democracy in Latin America is the regression shown in table 7. We want to clarify which of the factors examined have an effect on the authoritarian-democratic orientation (dependent variable question Q4) when controlling for all other variables. Q4 is input in the regression analysis in its original format with five categories (white, light colored, dark colored, indigenous, and black) in order to make use of all its power. In model 1, we regressed four sociodemographic variables (color, education, income, and city size). In model 2, we added the six factors included in table 6. Finally, in model 3 we added the country variable for Mexico and Chile.

The regression shows, first of all, that the strongest explanatory factors for *not* being a democrat are being Mexican or being Chilean. Second, all factors of democracy are statistically significant, except socialization; and four out of the six (excluding socialization and nonconventional participation) contribute positively to choosing democracy

TABLE 7 *Authoritarian-Democracy Orientation: Regression Analysis*

Standardized Beta Coefficient	Model 1	Model 2	Model 3
(Constant)	3.355	3.385	4.115
Education	0.054**	0.036*	0.050**
Income	0.059**	0.055*	0.027
City size	−0.131***	0.119***	−0.020
Color	−0.117***	−0.091***	−0.039*
F1—Confidence		0.097***	0.085***
F2—Legality		0.114***	0.087***
F3—Conventional participation		0.109***	0.095***
F4—Unconventional participation		0.062***	−0.055***
F5—Socialization		0.008	−0.029
F6—Tolerance		0.061***	0.055***
Mexico			−0.224***
Chile			−0.234***
Dependent variable: 4			
Adjusted R^2	0.035	0.074	0.102

* sig < .05 / ** sig < .01 / *** sig < .001

over authoritarianism. However, no definite conclusions can be drawn without sepa-rating this analysis for the three countries. Third, color has a negative impact on demo-cratic attitudes, which shows consistency and significance in the three models and is stronger than the impact of education and income. The darker the person's color, the less democratic their view. Fourth, city size also has a negative impact, but it loses sig-nificance in model 3. Fifth, education has a positive impact, though weaker than the impact of color, in explaining favorable attitudes toward democracy. Sixth, income behaves very similarly to education, but it loses significance in model 3.

CONCLUSIONS

At the beginning of this chapter we posed several questions: Why aren't color differ-ences in Latin America studied? Because they don't exist? If they did exist, what impact would they have on democracy? If there were a difference in propensity toward democ-racy between whites and *morenos,* what impact would it have on the democratization process—is that process led by the elite or by the masses?

The explorations in this chapter seem to indicate that there are differences based on color, but their impact varies among the three countries studied. The differences are clear in Mexico and Chile, but not in Costa Rica. Nevertheless, it should be noted that these differences are much less intense than in countries such as the United States.

The slight contrasts may be one of the reasons that the topic has not been explored in the region. Additionally, it could be an effect of the *mestizaje* produced by the Spanish conquest and Catholic evangelizing. In countries such as Mexico, the existence of powerful symbols such as Benito Juárez, the *moreno* president, reinforces the feelings of equal opportunity that he symbolizes.

It is not yet possible to come to a general conclusion about the effect that color exercises on orientation toward democracy. In the case of Mexico, whites show a slightly greater propensity toward democracy than do *morenos,* independent of their level of education. This seems to be a controversial finding and may point to inequality of opportunities for *morenos.* However, in Chile the effect is mixed, and in Costa Rica no effect can be established. In view of the above, only in the case of Mexico, where the *moreno* population is a clear majority (85 percent), can it be said that the process of democratization has greater support from the white minority than from the *moreno* majority.

The democratization process in Latin America may take longer than many would like, but it may rest on a more solid foundation. Institutions, not only culture, seem to be the key.

APPENDIX: METHODOLOGY

Question for the Authoritarian-Democracy Orientation Scale (Q4)

With which of the following phrases do you agree most? 1. Democracy is preferable to any other form of government; 2. I am indifferent to a democratic or a nondemocratic regime; 3. In some circumstances, an authoritarian regime can be preferable to a democratic one.

Questions in the Factor Analysis

Factor 1—Confidence: *Q36* How much confidence do you have in . . . (2. police; 4. government; 5. press; 6. tribunals; 7. unions; 8. congress; 9. television; 10. political parties)? A lot = 5; Somewhat = 4; Little = 2; nothing = 1

Factor 2—Legality: *Q30* I'm going to read to you a list of different things that people do. For each one of them, tell me if you believe that people in general think that those who do them are (1) very stupid, (2) somewhat stupid, (3) somewhat smart, or (4) very smart (a. cutting in line; b. not saying anything if they get extra change; c. not paying the subway or bus fare; d. going through a light when there is no traffic; e. make up false excuses). Very stupid = 5; somewhat stupid = 4; somewhat smart = 2; very smart = 1

Factor 3—Conventional participation: *Q21* Would you personally be ready to do something to demand accountability from government officials: yes or no? Definitely yes = 5; Maybe yes = 4; It depends = 3; Maybe not = 2; Definitely not = 1 / *Q22* I'm going to read you some forms of participation in politics (a. sign a protest letter; b. attend a demonstration; c. participate in a forbidden strike). Have done any = 5; Would do any = 3; Never = 1

Factor 4—Nonconventional participation: *Q22* I'm going to read you some forms of participation in politics (c. participate in a forbidden strike; d. take over a building or factory; e. participate in a boycott). Have done any = 5; Would do any = 3; Never = 1

Factor 5—Socialization: *Q12* From what you remember, with what frequency did your parents allow the children to participate in family decisions? Always = 5; Almost always/often = 4; Only sometimes/little = 2; Never/almost never = 1 / *Q16* From what you remember, with what frequency did your teachers at school allow students to participate in decisions concerning the class? Always = 5; Almost always/often = 4; Only sometimes/little = 2; Never/almost never = 1 / *Q20* In general, how often do employees participate with management in decisions concerning their jobs? Always = 5; Almost always/often = 4; Only sometimes/little = 2; Never/ almost never = 1

Factor 6—Tolerance: *Q8* Would you be in favor of or opposed to one of your children (or siblings, in case you don't have children) marrying a person of a different religion than yours? Very much in favor = 5; Somewhat in favor = 4; Neither = 3; Somewhat oppose = 2; Very much oppose = 1 / *Q10* I'm going to read to you a list of people. Tell me whom you would prefer NOT to have as a neighbor: evangelicals, homosexuals, foreigners. Mentioned = 1; Not mentioned = 5

Factor Analysis Method

Extraction by principal axis factoring / Replacement of missing values with the mean / Direct oblim rotation / We started by categorizing as more democratic those respondents who answered that they are more in favor of, or are more in agreement with, or prefer, or recall, or express: (1) confidence in institutions; (2) legality to effectiveness; (3) participation in collective actions; (4) participating in decisions at home, school, and work; (5) tolerance to intolerance; (6) liberty to order; (7) journalistic investigation to remaining silent; (8) democracy to prosperity; (9) alternation of power to continuity; (10) distribution over centralization of power between the executive and congress; and (11) accountability. The higher the score, the higher the inclination toward democracy.

From the many questions originally included, 26 contributed positively to the six factors that we present. The score for each respondent to each factor is saved as a new variable to find the means that are the basis of the analysis.

Final Statistics

Variable	Communality	*	Factor	Eigenvalue	Pct. of Var.	Cum. Pct.
IPT12	.54777	*	1	3.40478	13.1	13.1
IPT16	.52115	*	2	2.79914	10.8	23.9
IPT20	.42179	*	3	2.57406	9.9	33.8
IPT21	.45467	*	4	1.55611	6.0	39.7
IPT22_A	.60136	*	5	1.46098	5.6	45.4
IPT22_B	.63798	*	6	1.09713	4.2	49.6

	Factor 1 Confidence	Factor 2 Legality	Factor 3 Conv. Participation	Factor 4 Non conv. Participation	Factor 5 Socialization	Factor 6 Tolerance
IPT12	−.00866	.00772	.03867	−.00576	.73599	.06654
IPT16	.05197	.05300	−.02997	.02712	.71612	.03428
IPT20	.00691	.01489	.08974	−.02621	.63864	−.07015
IPT21	−.04529	.04704	.65464	−.04448	.12265	.06954
IPT22_A	−.04106	.00516	.73772	.23065	−.01242	−.04551
IPT22_B	.02939	−.04798	.75215	.25954	−.01209	−.03968
IPT22_C	.00572	−.02467	.49863	.60992	.01818	.02005
IPT22_D	−.03995	−.03285	.16373	.82889	.00851	−.01314
IPT22_E	−.02914	−.04832	.09554	.82371	−.02346	−.02744
IPT36_10	.57160	−.02956	.03580	.05111	.08174	−.06010
IPT36_2	.56339	.01921	−.17014	.02531	−.06636	.04891
IPT36_4	.71764	.01916	−.07077	.04164	.02156	.02130
IPT36_5	.66160	.06707	−.01987	−.04028	−.03842	.05360
IPT36_6	.67764	.06576	.03664	−.05191	.11437	−.04264
IPT36_7	.59445	.00277	.06715	.01306	.04601	−.02454
IPT36_8	.71557	−.00132	.03612	−.07247	.01008	−.00441
IPT36_9	.61369	−.02754	−.01606	−.05373	−.09511	.02951
IPT8	.07783	−.06473	.06920	.01264	.10901	.39185
IPT10_1	−.04308	.10817	−.06517	−.05853	−.00819	.71466
IPT10_2	−.02403	−.02422	−.06306	.05290	−.01276	.51350
IPT10_3	−.01932	.02471	.06017	−.06557	−.09016	.71002
IPT30_A	−.00659	.74478	−.07234	.05472	.07629	.06861
IPT30_B	.02804	.76143	−.04612	.04219	.12793	−.02620
IPT30_C	.02823	.79905	−.07769	.01227	.05250	−.00141
IPT30_D	.04627	.57942	.12506	−.11693	−.16345	−.01495
IPT30_E	.00222	.71919	.07738	−.10032	−.00744	−.0182

Part IV

Does Democracy Cross Boundaries?

Latin America versus North America

Chapter 9

Mexico and the United States
Two Distinct Political Cultures?

Frederick C. Turner and Carlos A. Elordi

Political scientists have long assumed that the political cultures of Mexico and the United States differ fundamentally, reflecting the different historical experiences of the two countries. This has provided an easy explanation as to why the institutions of politics have remained so distinct north and south of the Rio Bravo/Rio Grande during the twentieth century, with patterns of politics far more authoritarian in Mexico than in the United States. Challenging this perspective, however, are at least two types of information. First, if we look at what citizens of Mexico and the United States say that they want in their political systems, their responses are often very similar. Second, at the end of the twentieth century, the Mexican political system is opening up, at least somewhat, challenging the dominance that the Partido Revolucionario Institucional (PRI) has maintained for seven decades. If an authoritarian political culture once undergirded an autocratic political system in Mexico, then of what use is the concept when we see this system beginning to change?

In the context of these issues, how are we to understand, to measure, and to evaluate the concept of political culture in the two nations? Can political culture change over time, and, if so, how and why does it do so? These questions deserve careful analysis, but in order to provide meaningful answers one must first consider the concept of political culture and the nature of political values in the two countries in some detail. Since a large literature on political culture already exists, and since scholars have approached political culture in a variety of ways, it should be possible to draw out insights from a number of past findings in order to compare the situations of Mexico and the United States more effectively.

One way to approach these questions concretely is to compare values, attitudes, and political behavior in Mexico and the United States. This can be done through careful comparisons of survey data, so long as the data are collected through the same questions, asked of comparable samples of respondents in the same periods of time. The three waves of the World Values Survey, ranging from 1981 to 1995–97, provide such data for Mexico and the United States. These data turn out to furnish some insights, as well as some surprises, concerning the political cultures of the two nations. Before turning to the data themselves, however, one must confront the wider debate over the meaning of political culture and the relevance of this concept in Mexico and the United States.

ASSUMPTIONS ABOUT POLITICAL CULTURE

During the final decades of the twentieth century, most social scientists have assumed that attitudes and values differ significantly among people in various countries, and that patterns of these attitudes and values come to constitute distinctive "political cultures" in each nation. In their classic study *The Civic Culture*, Gabriel Almond and Sidney Verba selected the United States and Mexico as two of the five nations whose cultures and whose patterns of politics they contrasted. For them, the civic culture involved a balance between political participation, acceptance of the rule of law, and a high level of interpersonal trust.[1] They concluded that "[t]he civic culture appears to be particularly appropriate for a democratic political system,"[2] and they found the attitudes and values of citizens in the United States to approximate those of the civic culture far more than did those of Mexicans. After this study, other social scientists have confronted the same issues that concerned Almond and Verba.

Before considering some of their interpretations, however, it may be useful to question how much we can learn from the survey findings involved. For example, the meaning of "political culture" as measured by questions in public opinion surveys may not be as clear as it at first seems to be. Some Mexican social scientists claim that, despite increasing verbal support for democracy and for democratic norms in opinion polls, Mexicans remain deeply authoritarian in their underlying perceptions and personal relationships.

One such scholar is Lourdes Arizpe, a distinguished Mexican anthropologist. Arizpe contends that, whatever public opinion surveys say, most Mexicans learn authoritarian patterns within their families, unquestioningly accepting the authority of their fathers, and later in life transferring this acceptance of authority to the president of Mexico, the symbolic father of the Mexican family.[3] This helps to explain the exceptional power of the president within the Mexican political system, which for the last seven decades of the twentieth century effectively included even the right to name his successor. Distinguished writers on U.S. politics such as Huntington in the past have agreed that Mexicans are brought up to obey authority whereas U.S. citizens are brought up to fear it,[4] so that, as Domínguez and McCann write, the president of Mexico enjoys a "godlike public role."[5]

In evaluating the perspective of Arizpe, a contrast appears between disciplinary approaches and between ways of knowing as well as between alternative interpretations of Mexican culture. Anthropologists typically work through participant observation, living among those that they study over long periods of time and therefore coming to understand intimately the motivations and behavior of small numbers of people. Survey researchers, on the other hand, look to national, regional, or local polls of opinion, being careful to interview representative samples of particular communities, tending to accept the answers that respondents give to survey questions for which the response categories have been structured in advance.

Paradoxically, the perspectives on Mexican culture of anthropologists and survey researchers may both contain elements of truth. Many Mexicans may be more accepting of authority—both within their families and vis-à-vis the President of the Republic—than they are willing to admit to interviewers in opinion polls. During the long decades of PRI rule, the official rhetoric of the PRI favored norms of democracy, and it also upheld the anti-authority images of the Mexican revolutionaries of 1910 that school textbooks and Mexican popular culture have inculcated for so long. In the face of this nominal support for democracy in both popular culture and PRI rhetoric, the responses of Mexican citizens to pollsters almost have to favor democratic norms, even though these responses may still mask the acceptance of more authoritarian perceptions and patterns below the surface. This is not to say that we must reject the findings of Mexican opinion polls or that we can learn nothing by comparing them with similar polls in the United States. It is to say, however, that we must be modest in our claims for what such questions really tell us, aware that they reflect only some dimensions of Mexican political reality.

As perceived and measured in different ways, therefore, Mexican political culture contains some dimensions that are more authoritarian, and others that are more democratic. This raises the centrally important issue of change in political cultures. The whole concept of political culture has frequently been criticized as static and determin-

istic, but in fact it is neither. Indeed, one of the most intellectually fascinating and politically significant aspects of political cultures is their tendency to modify the norms that
they embodied at some point in the past.

Cultures, including political cultures, can and do change over time. Just as Smith
demonstrates that "most opinion change can be plausibly explained,"[6] so too can most
shifts in political cultures. As Eckstein points out in the cases of the political cultures of
France and Tory Britain, changes in some dimensions of culture may in fact be necessary in order to keep in place key elements of the political culture and the institutional
structure of a political community.[7] Political cultures are not immutable, therefore,
and the fact that a culture favors limited political participation at one point in time
does not mean that the culture of the nation in question will do so to the same degree
several decades later. Referring to the institution of more democratic norms, Przeworski notes that "there is little, if anything, that should lead us to believe that cultural
obstacles to democracy are immovable."[8] We should look, therefore, for evidence of
gradual changes in the various dimensions of citizens' values and attitudes that are generally assumed to shape their political culture.

Since dimensions of the political culture of a nation may thus change over time, a
central question in studying political culture must be how much the culture of given
nations has changed, and over what period of time. De Tocqueville, for example, specifically contrasted Mexico and the United States. As noted by Inkeles, de Tocqueville
wrote that "[t]he manners [character] of the Americans of the United States are the *real*
cause which renders it the only one of the American nations that is able to support a
democratic government."[9] Yet de Tocqueville's perceptions were those of the 1830s,
and certainly a century and a half later the political cultures of the two nations may
have come more into line. Almond and Verba, on the basis of survey data collected in
1959 and 1960, saw major differences in the political cultures of Mexico and the United
States, but they also wrote that "the aspirational aspect of the Mexican political culture
suggests a potentiality for a civic culture, for the orientation to participation is present."[10] Over the decades since the 1950s, such shifts may have occurred, so that it
becomes especially important to consider survey findings over this period of time.
Only by investigating more recent data, and thinking carefully about their implications, can we see whether the political cultures of Mexico and the United States are
coming at least somewhat more together.

Some evidence suggests that this is true. McCann points out that, while two-thirds
of Mexicans said that they had little or no interest in politics in the late 1980s and early
1990s, this was also true for nearly half the respondents in national polls in the United

States.[11] Basáñez notes that children in the United States are taught to question and criticize far more than are children in the family structures and the schools of Mexico, yet he also points to increasing social participation and increasing respect for fellow citizens in Mexico. This can be seen, for example, in the orderly lines that Mexicans have come to form while they wait for buses, or buy tortillas, or enter movie theaters, as well as from the systematic registration of more than 11,000 soccer teams among the two million residents of the economically impoverished community of Nezahualcóyotl near Mexico City.[12] Far from the sphere of survey research, these observations evidence how Mexican norms are changing and how norms in the United States and Mexico are becoming more similar.

Such indications appear in survey data also. In contrast to the distinctions that Almond and Verba drew between the United States and Mexico, studies in the 1980s and 1990s have pointed to similarities in attitudes in the two countries. Booth and Seligson demonstrate that, like U.S. citizens, urban Mexicans show strong support for democratic liberties. For the residents of Guadalajara and six northern industrial centers in Mexico, they find that social class importantly helps to predict support for widespread political participation, while the educational levels of Mexican respondents in public opinion surveys most influence their support for the right to dissent.[13] As Booth and Seligson sum up their findings from data gathered in 1978 and 1979, "our data have uncovered a largely democratic political culture within an essentially authoritarian regime."[14]

This finding not only suggests that Mexican political culture may be much more like that in the United States than scholars had earlier assumed. It also calls into question the widespread assumption of a causal link between political culture and the structures of government, since one interpretation of Booth and Seligson's finding is that the democratic orientations of Mexican political culture simply failed to impact the authoritarian institutions of the Mexican political system. On the other hand, however, another interpretation may point to an incipient effect for Mexican political culture in the 1970s and 1980s. When Mexicans in these decades said that democracy was the best system of government and evidenced support for a democratic political culture, the norms of that culture may over time have been a fundamental reason for the significant openings toward democracy in Mexico during the 1990s.

Data from that decade point to further similarities between Mexico and the United States in the relationship between public opinion and economic reform. On the basis of surveys conducted in Mexico between 1992 and 1995, Kaufman and Zuckermann conclude that patterns of support for reform policies in the United States and Mexico are strikingly similar. In Mexico, as has previously been found in the United States, judgments concerning the economy, support for the president, and support for the party in power have major effects on whether or not people support policies of reform.[15]

Such comparisons raise the long-term issue of whether or not Mexico will move toward adopting a more truly democratic political system, and, if so, what the role of political culture may be in this process. Inglehart, who writes that "political culture may be a crucial link between economic development and democracy," finds two essential reasons for the rise of democracy in so many countries over recent decades. To run a technologically advanced economy, in Inglehart's view, a modern nation-state requires a well-educated labor force in which people exercise considerable personal autonomy, and such technological modernization in turn creates shifts in culture, as citizens can rely on greater economic security and so come to make new types of demands on their political leaders.[16] Before the collapse of the authoritarian system of the Soviet Union, Inglehart emphasized that this process was going on there, and, without pushing the analogy too far, one might note that Russia and Mexico have often been compared in the twentieth century, as countries that had massive revolutions early in the century and highly autocratic political systems for the remainder of it. Of course, as Knight and others remind us, observers who have predicted the demise of PRI dominance in Mexican politics have been disappointed over and over again, as this dominance has remained stubbornly resistant to change.[17] But at least this situation should make us look carefully at the Mexican case, asking whether in fact the political culture of the Mexican people is becoming at least somewhat more like that of their neighbors to the north.

THE VALUE OF TRUST

As we turn empirically to compare issues of political culture in Mexico and the United States, it is useful to differentiate attitudes from values. While Almond and Verba noted that political culture involves "value standards and criteria," they emphasized that the term refers specifically to "attitudes toward the political system and its various parts, and attitudes toward the role of the self in the system."[18] In contrast, specialists in survey research now differentiate attitudes and values more sharply, finding that values are far harder to change. For instance, Lipset, Worcester, and Turner describe attitudes as "currents below the surface of opinion, held for longer periods and with more conviction," while they define values as "the deepest, most powerful tides underlying opinions and attitudes, learned early in life from parents and nearly invulnerable to change."[19] As Alduncin wrote in his classic study of values in Mexico, "it is only through the values of a culture that the short-term, medium-term, and long-term goals of a society are established."[20] From this contrast, we may expect elements of the political culture of a nation that relate to attitudes to modify as the attitudes of citizens shift over time, but those dimensions of political culture that relate to values to alter much more gradually. Of course, it should be noted that values, and the culture that expresses those values, are not independent of their social context, and that under periods of rapid social, political, or economic change, such as those experienced by Mexico in the late 1980s and early 1990s, the measures that we have of values are likely to be affected. Inglehart provides a good example of this situation in his study of value change and its interaction with changing economic conditions, including those reflected by rising price levels or the increase in unemployment.[21] Furthermore, because comparable data for Mexico and the United States are limited, our analysis will suffer from the shortcoming of having only a few points in time for analysis, therefore making it difficult to disentangle period effects from long-term trends in value change.

With these considerations in mind, it is useful to turn to the concept of interpersonal trust and attempts to measure it through survey research. In trying to gauge this concept, we seek measures of an underlying value that relates centrally to whether citizens feel that they are bound to a larger, more impersonal community, such as those that characterize modern national states. Without this feeling of trust, it would be harder for people to accept the rules by which these larger communities abide. This is especially important in democratic societies. As Lasswell wrote, to build a "democratic character" among citizens, it may be "essential to have *deep confidence in the benevolent potentialities of man,*" to have an "affirmative trust" that leads citizens to accept and to act in terms of the norms of democratic institutions.[22] Furthermore, as Inkeles notes, empirical evidence from a number of countries "is highly suggestive of a strong positive association between economic development and a psychological disposition to trust other people."[23] What is the evidence for Mexico and the United States? With its far higher level of per capita income, is the United States a country where citizens trust one another far more than they do in Mexico?

The data in table 1 offer a puzzling answer to these questions, an answer that may be better understood once we contemplate the changing context in both countries and some methodological problems, such as conducting the survey in different languages and using a single indicator to measure an underlying value. The data come from three waves of the World Values Survey, where the same survey questions were asked in Mexico, the United States, and a number of other countries in 1981, 1990, and 1995–97. For

TABLE 1 *Respondents Who Agreed That Most People Can Be Trusted* (percent)

	1981	1990	1995–97
United States	41	51	36
Mexico	17	33	28

Source: 1981, 1990, and 1995–97 World Values Surveys. The question read, "Generally speaking, would you say that most people can be trusted or that you can't be too careful in dealing with people?" Sample size for Mexico is 1,837 in 1981, 1,531 in 1990 and 1,511 in 1996–97. Sample size for the United States is 2,325 in 1981, 1,839 in 1990, and 1,839 in 1995.

both Mexico and the United States, the table shows that the percentage of respondents agreeing that "most people can be trusted" went up in the decade of the 1980s and then went down somewhat during the mid-1990s. Most importantly, the level of interpersonal trust is significantly higher, and remains significantly higher, in the United States than in Mexico.

If values are by definition comparatively stable, and if we use this question as a rough measure of interpersonal trust, then how can we explain these apparent changes in interpersonal trust between 1981 and 1997? There are at least three answers to this question, and these relate to measures of values, to language, and to the contexts of the surveys in question.[24] Investigation of the World Values Survey data for Mexico and the United States reveals virtually no generational differences in regard to interpersonal trust; since this interpretation can be rejected, the other interpretations of the data in table 1 take on somewhat greater significance.

In the first place, the question on interpersonal trust used in the World Values Survey is not a perfect measure of the "value" of interpersonal trust. It is, however, the best measure that is available for these two countries over this period of time. When respondents answered this question on trust, some dimensions of their answer related to this underlying value, but other considerations undoubtedly influenced their answers as well. In the social sciences in general, and through survey research in particular, it is not possible to measure values as clearly as we would like to do. In prospect, we can try to formulate even better survey questions. In retrospect, we must use the questions that are available to us.

Second, language and question order also enter into the interpretation of these data, as they so often do in cross-cultural research. The English word *trust* connotes an affective orientation, but when we translate this word into Spanish as *confianza*, this comes closer to the English word *confidence,* which implies an orientation to performance. In Spanish, *confianza* is the best approximation to the English word *trust*, but the fact that there is really no Spanish word for "trust" in fact illustrates an underlying contrast between the cultural contexts of an English-speaking country like the United States and a Spanish-speaking country like Mexico. When seen in the data of the World Values Survey, the Spanish-language question that mentions *confianza* is more likely to capture changes in the political environment than is the English-language question that speaks of "trust." Furthermore, from a methodological perspective, another part of the fluctuation evident in table 1 may be explained because the question did not appear in the same order in the questionnaires conducted in the three waves of the World Values Survey. Because it is the only (and therefore the best) indicator that we have at hand for measuring this dimension of trust, we have to deal with the shortcomings of this question and accept the fact that there will be a large portion of error in our measure.

Third, we can therefore expect issues of the political context in which this question was asked to affect the respondents' answers, particularly in the case of Mexico. Here, the change is understandable if we accept the proposition that the general context in which a survey is conducted naturally affects people's perceptions of others and of their political system, therefore also influencing their responses. During the late 1980s and early 1990s, competitive politics made impressive strides in Mexico, with the 1988 elections serving as an aperture for cleaner and more open elections. The liberalization of the political scenario was also accompanied by strong economic performance, especially during Carlos Salinas de Gortari's tenure in office (1988–94). This changing context should help to explain the apparently rising levels of interpersonal trust in the period that goes from 1981, when our first survey was conducted, through 1990, when the second wave of the World Values Survey was carried out. The ensuing years were rocky ones, with the peso crisis in December 1994 and the Mexican recession a year later. Politically, too, the environment was decomposed because of the assassination of Donaldo Colosio, the PRI candidate, in 1994, and later on because of the self-imposed exile of former president Salinas and the prosecution of members of his family for acts of corruption. Together, both the political and the economic stress that Mexicans underwent during these years help to explain why levels of interpersonal trust apparently declined when we look at our final measure, which is taken from a survey conducted in 1996 and 1997.

In the case of the United States, the explanation of such fluctuations seems to be less straightforward, and the matter is still an issue for debate. Certainly, here too the survey question is an imperfect measure of the underlying value of political trust. Also, while the initially increasing levels of interpersonal trust coincided with the optimism that reigned during the Reagan era, the sharp decline from 1990 to 1995 is harder to explain. Speculations abound for the apparent decline in trust, and they frequently relate to the changing role of the media and its impact on the public during these years. Since people acquire most of their information from the media, the critical and sensationalistic nature of most media coverage in these years may explain a more cynical view among the public in general, which shows up in the data as an apparently lower level of interpersonal trust. This hypothesis remains to be adequately tested, however, providing an important matter to be explored.

However we in fact measure it, the level of interpersonal trust in a society has long been seen as a key element of a participant political culture. But what is the causal relationship between trust and democracy? That is, does a high level of interpersonal trust provide an impulse for a nation to acquire democratic structures of government, or do those structures in turn work to create higher levels of trust over time? The careful work of Muller and Seligson shows the latter to be the case.[25] Since trust grows in a political community in which democratic institutions have ameliorated conflicts of interest over many years, and since those structures have long been in place in the United States but not in Mexico, it is natural for the political culture of the United States to reflect far higher levels of interpersonal trust. In this sense, it is the democratic institutions of the United States that have inculcated a high level of interpersonal trust among U.S. citizens, and, as the institutions of the Mexican polity come to allow more effective participation, it is to be expected that the level of interpersonal trust in Mexico will increase thereafter.

SUPPORT FOR GRADUAL REFORM

While interpersonal trust thus appears to result from long experience of a polity with democratic institutions, some attitudes of the population are also important in encouraging the initial realization of such institutions. An attitude that appears to be especially important in this regard is the degree of support for gradual reform in a society. When citizens are asked whether they advocate radical reform, gradual reform, or the defense of the status quo, political scientists since the 1960s have interpreted the proportion of the population that supports the option for gradual reform to be a fundamental measure of a democratic political culture. When citizens uphold norms of gradual change, as opposed to violent change or the mere defense of the status quo, they are in effect backing the sort of change associated with democracy.

The data in table 2 reveal strong similarities between the United States and Mexico

TABLE 2 *Support for Radical Reform, Gradual Reform, and the Status Quo*
(percent)

	Mexico			United States		
Position Supported	1981	1990	1996–97	1981	1990	1995
Radical reform	11	14	11	5	6	4
Gradual reform	68	61	52	66	70	69
Defend the status quo	10	11	26	20	16	18
Don't know	12	14	11	10	8	9

Source: 1981, 1990, and 1995–97 World Values Surveys. The question read, "On this card are three basic kinds of attitudes concerning the society we live in. Please choose the *one* which best describes your own opinion. CODE ONLY ONE." The card read, "(1) The entire way our society is organized must be radically changed by revolutionary action. (2) Our society must be gradually improved by reforms. (3) Our present society must be valiantly defended against all subversive forces. (4) Don't know." Sample size for Mexico is 1,837 in 1981, 1,531 in 1990 and 1,511 in 1996–97. Sample size for the United States is 2,325 in 1981, 1,839 in 1990, and 1,839 in 1995.

in this regard. In 1981, almost exactly the same proportion of Mexicans and U.S. citizens—two-thirds of the respondents in both countries—said that they backed gradual reform, as compared to only between 5 and 11 percent favoring radical reform and between 10 and 20 percent defending the status quo. Even as support for the gradual reform option fell in Mexico by 1995, between half and three-quarters of the populations of both countries still opted for gradual reform. These data thus point more to similarities than to differences in the political cultures of Mexico and the United States.

Nevertheless, the data in table 2 also indicate intriguing differences between the United States and Mexico in regard to the options for reform. While the proportion of Mexican respondents backing the gradual reform alternative decreased steadily between 1981 and 1995, the percentage in the United States increased somewhat. The change in Mexico during these years, as the data in table 2 document, was not a rise in support for radical reform. Instead, it was an increase in the defense of the status quo. Probably, the high percentage of Mexicans saying in 1995 that they wanted to defend the status quo (26 percent) was in part an artifact of their economic situation in the year of the survey. With the dramatic downturn in the Mexican economy at the end of 1994, Mexicans became concerned to maintain what income they had at a time when real per capita income was dropping significantly. This created more conservative reactions in the short run, significantly affecting the proportion of Mexicans who supported gradual reform.

What does this say about Mexican political culture and about opportunities for greater democracy in Mexico? On the one hand, support for gradual reform has been found to be an element of civic culture that significantly impacts democratization.[26] In nations where a substantial part of the population supports gradual reform, this fact encourages the growth of democratic institutions. Yet how can one reconcile this perspective with the Mexican experience? Between 1981 and 1995, support for gradual reform declined in Mexico, yet the elections of 1997 demonstrated a substantial opening toward a more democratic system.[27] Mexicans clearly support this opening of their political system, yet this is not what we would predict on the basis of the decline in support for gradual reform. What is going on here?

There are several possible answers to this question. On the one hand, in the early 1980s Inglehart found that Mexico was one of the lowest countries among the two dozen that he studied in its level of support for the status quo, while more generally support for the status quo was highest in countries with higher levels of per capita income.[28] Therefore, as Mexican income rose over time, it is natural to assume that the proportion of Mexicans supporting the status quo would rise as well. On the other hand, another interpretation would suggest that, after the wrenching economic downturn of 1994–95, Mexican respondents in 1996 and 1997 were concerned to defend at least what remained of their personal and family income. For some of those interviewed in the World Values Survey, this may have made their responses to the social change question temporarily more conservative, thereby affecting the key measure of support for gradual reform. This pattern of responses did not alter their support for democratization, even though it did significantly affect their responses to the question about attitudes toward reform and social change. This emphasizes, once again, that we need to look carefully at the specific situation of respondents during the period in which survey questions are asked.

Still another answer to the apparent paradox may be that elite attitudes are even more important than the general attitudes of the population in regard to encouraging the rise of democratic structures of government. Muller and Seligson anticipate this nicely, arguing that elites may be the most important initiators of more democratic structures.[29] If so, the general attitudes in the population as a whole may correlate with increased democratization not because they directly impact democratization, but because the general population holds the same attitudes toward gradual reform as do the elites. Naturally, elites may convince the general population to follow their lead, to share their perceptions of the need for change, and/or the need for continuity. As Knight writes with the case of Mexico in mind, "A crisis is really only a crisis if enough people so perceive; it becomes a crisis *manqué* (a turning point when history fails to turn) if incumbent elites can reassure their alarmed subjects and preserve the status quo."[30]

Under these assumptions, it is the acceptance of gradual reform among the elites that really matters for the initiation of more democratic structures. Bollen defines democracy as "the minimization of elite power and the maximization of nonelite power" over the national governing system,[31] and this definition may be particularly useful in the case of Mexico. It emphasizes how difficult it is for elites to champion the advent of democracy, in effect greatly reducing their own power. Also, we unfortunately have much less information on elite attitudes than we do on the attitudes of the general population, so that it is not possible at this point to test the assumption of a correlation between democratization and elite support for gradual reform. But the assumption is logical, and it also squares with the fact that Mexican elites felt the economic hardships in the 1980s and 1990s far less than did most Mexicans. The wealth of the elites spared them from the ravages of declining incomes that other Mexicans felt acutely, so that, without an overwhelming need to defend their own privileges, and feeling pressure for change from other segments of the population, some members of the elites came to support at least a partial opening of the political system.

Thus, even though it would be very useful to have more systematic information on the values and attitudes of Mexican elites, the comparison of attitudes toward gradual reform in Mexico and the United States may be broadly revealing. Table 2 demonstrates majoritarian support in both countries for the option of gradual reform. The increasing difference between the two countries by 1995 in regard to this measure may relate especially to conservatism based on economic growth in Mexico in the 1980s and early 1990s, as well as on the economic downturn of 1994–95. The Mexican responses also caution us to look more closely at this particular measure of political culture, since the economic conditions of a nation both before and at the time when the "gradual reform" question is asked may have a strong effect upon how respondents answer. Also, these patterns of attitudes alert us to the importance of elites in the processes of social change and democratization. Ideally, in the future we will have more survey data on the values and attitudes of elites, allowing comparisons to be made between the political cultures of the elites and those of the rank-and-file populations of various countries.

We also lack information on regional differences in Mexico. In 1980 Craig and Cornelius rightly stressed the importance of gathering and analyzing such information,[32] but so far little has been done to bring together comparable data on political culture in the distinctive regions of Mexico. Support for the three major parties varied substantially by region in the 1990s, so that it would be especially interesting to compare this support by region with data on dimensions of political culture. Unfortunately, the coding of the 1996–97 Mexican data from the World Values Survey has so far made this impossible with these data,[33] although they could be recoded to make them consistent. Moreover, further information may be gleaned from the hundreds of Mexican surveys collected since 1988 at the Roper Center, and future surveys can be designed to have enough coverage in the major regions of the country to make valid comparisons possible. When this is done, new appreciations of Mexican political culture should emerge, perhaps indicating a national context where regional variations in political culture are substantially sharper than they are in the United States.

GROUP DIFFERENCES IN REGARD TO POLITICAL CULTURE

While we do not have comparative data on the attitudes and values of matching samples of the elites of Mexico and the United States for the issues of trust, support for reform, and political culture more generally, we can compare the perspectives of different occupational groups from each country. Such comparisons appear in tables 3 and 4. Here, the data from the 1990 and 1995–97 waves of the World Values Survey are combined, so that more respondents can be included in each occupational group. In this way, the tables can more accurately reflect perspectives of people in the two groups.[34]

One important point that appears in these tables is that, at least in regard to interpersonal trust and backing for gradual reform, the political cultures of the United States and Mexico are quite well generalized. Vast differences do not appear in regard to these measures among most occupational groups in the two countries. Nevertheless, some interesting and suggestive contrasts do emerge.

TABLE 3 *Respondents Who Agreed That Most People Can Be Trusted, by Occupational Group* (percent)

	Mexico	United States
Professionals	28	58
Managers	28	53
Foremen	33	43
Skilled workers	26	32
Unskilled workers	32	29
Agricultural workers	36	25

Source: 1981, 1990 and 1995–97 World Values Surveys. The question read, "Generally speaking, would you say that most people can be trusted or that you can't be too careful in dealing with people?" The managers in this table are those who work in firms employing more than 10 persons. Sample size for Mexico is 1,531 in 1990 and 1,511 in 1996–97. Sample size for the United States is 1,839 in 1990 and 1,839 in 1995.

TABLE 4 *Support for Different Kinds of Reform by Occupational Group* (percent)

	Mexico			United States		
	Support Radical Change	*Support Gradual Reforms*	*Defend Our Present Society*	*Support Radical Reform*	*Support Gradual Reforms*	*Defend Our Present Society*
Professionals	13	68	14	3	78	13
Managers	4	62	28	2	76	14
Foremen	11	52	17	4	74	17
Skilled workers	14	58	18	7	65	20
Unskilled workers	15	52	16	8	60	19
Agricultural workers	8	44	22	5	70	20

Source: 1990 and 1995–97 World Values Surveys. The question read, "On this card are three basic kinds of attitudes concerning the society we live in. Please choose the *one* which best describes your own opinion. CODE ONLY ONE." The card read, "(1) The entire way our society is organized must be radically changed by revolutionary action. (2) Our society must be gradually improved by reforms. (3) Our present society must be valiantly defended against all subversive forces. (4) Don't know." The managers in this table are those who work in firms employing more than 10 persons. Sample size for Mexico is 1,531 in 1990 and 1,511 in 1996–97. Sample size for the United States is 1,839 in 1990 and 1,839 in 1995.

One of these relates to interpersonal trust in the United States. Here, more than half of the people with higher incomes and higher levels of education, such as professionals and managers, agree that most people can be trusted. On the other hand, unskilled workers and agricultural workers in the United States reveal levels of interpersonal trust even lower than those of their counterparts in Mexico. Interpersonal trust varies by occupation in the United States, but not in Mexico.

This makes sense, because higher levels of interpersonal trust arise from long experience with democratic institutions. Professionals and managers in the United States operate in working contexts in which they understand the give-and-take of democratic norms and structures, but many unskilled workers and agricultural workers do not. Their jobs are not so different in Mexico and the United States, and neither are their feelings of trust. Between two-thirds and three-quarters of the unskilled and agricultural workers in the two countries still live and work in contexts where they do not develop generalized attitudes of interpersonal trust. A fundamental reason, therefore, that the United States appears in aggregate national statistics to be a country of high interpersonal trust is that the occupational structure of the country has become one in which relatively few unskilled and agricultural workers remain.

Tables 3 and 4 also show agricultural workers in Mexico to be quite a traditional group. They show somewhat more trust than do members of the other occupational groups, perhaps because of traditional religious norms or because of an ability to rely on their families and friends. Also, Mexican *peones* show a greater tendency to defend the status quo than do wealthier groups, such as foremen or professionals. While their incomes are low, the *peones* live at or near the margin, so that for them the prospect of change may seem threatening or dangerous.

In both countries, the professionals are an intriguing group as well. Composed of lawyers, teachers, accountants, and other professionals, they are the group closest to a sampling of the elite that the World Values Survey can provide. In both Mexico and the United States, they are also the group most likely to support gradual reform. This at least implies that segments of the elites in both countries similarly support the option of gradual reform. Since backing for gradual reform is a dimension of a political culture that favors the institutionalization of democratic structures, this lends support to the thesis that important segments of the elites in both countries favor democratic institutions. Since the "Mexican elite" has so often been characterized as self-interested and resistant to change, these findings make it all the more worthwhile to study Mexican elites in greater detail, differentiating more clearly among them and among their perspectives.

POLITICAL PARTICIPATION

The "participant" political culture, the one that Almond and Verba found to be most compatible with democracy, was that in which citizens not only understood what government could do for them, but also saw how they could affect government decisions, and in which they took active measures to do so. Both Mexico and the United States contain, of course, citizens with widely different political orientations, including those who relate to more authoritarian or more democratic political cultures. U.S. supporters of German National Socialism rallied inside Madison Square Garden before the United States entered World War II, just as the Gold Shirts in Mexico also supported European fascism. Dedicated democrats have led both countries, back to the times of Abraham Lincoln and Don Benito Juárez. The question is not whether democrats and autocrats exist in both countries, but rather what are the proportions of each group, and how do citizens in each country perceive their own opportunities to affect political decisions and processes.

In these terms, Mexico and the United States reveal both similarities and differences. As table 5 indicates, some measures of participation reflect the differences in political culture that were evident in the Almond and Verba data from the end of the 1950s. If we measure political participation by the percentage of citizens in each country who have signed a petition or joined a boycott, then the level of active political participation appears to be far greater in the United States. Nevertheless, between 1981

TABLE 5 *Political Actions Taken* (percent)

	Mexico			United States		
	1981	1990	1996–97	1981	1990	1995
Signed a petition	8	31	28	61	70	70
Joined a boycott	1	6	9	14	17	18
Attended a lawful demonstration	8	20	10	12	15	15
Joined an unofficial strike	2	7	6	3	4	4
Occupied a building or a factory	1	5	4	2	2	2

Source: 1981, 1990, and 1995–97 World Values Surveys. The question read, "Now I'd like you to look at this card. I'm going to read out some different forms of political action that people can take, and I'd like you to tell me, for each one, whether you have actually done any of these things, whether you might do it or would never, under any circumstances, do it." The response categories were "(1) Signing a petition. (2) Joining in boycotts. (3) Attending lawful demonstrations. (4) Joining unofficial strikes. (5) Occupying buildings or factories." Sample size for Mexico is 1,837 in 1981, 1,531 in 1990, and 1,511 in 1996–97. Sample size for the United States is 2,325 in 1981, 1,839 in 1990 and 1,839 in 1995.

and 1995, the level of participation as measured by these two actions rose significantly in Mexico. For both countries, the level of political participation rose for these two measures in the decade and a half after 1981.

As also appears in table 5, Mexicans during this period became much more likely to join an unofficial strike or to occupy buildings and factories. While the proportions of Mexicans and U.S. citizens who took these actions were quite comparable in 1981, by the 1990s Mexicans did so much more commonly. These actions placed those who took them outside the law, and Mexicans proved far more willing to stand outside the law in order to make political statements than were their counterparts north of the Rio Bravo.

The countries thus differ in intriguing ways. In both, citizens have come to feel that their actions matter, and to take actions designed to affect government decisions. The nature of these actions and the degree of their legality differ substantially in the two nations, however. Mexicans are more willing to take illegal actions in order to protest government policies, while U.S. citizens tend to confine their protests to those that are within the law. Since the Mexican political system in the 1980s and 1990s remained far more authoritarian than that of the United States, one can argue that Mexicans had to be more willing to step outside the boundaries of the law in order to engineer political change. Peaceful actions, such as signing petitions and joining boycotts, increased in Mexico, but so did illegal strikes and the occupation of buildings and factories. These actions differentiate the political cultures of the two countries in fundamental ways, and they also point to the very different nature of the political systems involved.

An underlying cause for these differences in political participation may come from the lasting symbolic impact of the Mexican Revolution of 1910—the fact that Mexicans for generations have been brought up to feel that it was right and necessary for the heroes of 1910 to take up arms against the dictatorship of Porfirio Díaz. This orientation is reinforced when cultural leaders in Mexico such as Carlos Fuentes declare that the opening of the Mexican political system in the 1990s would not have occurred without the public revulsion against the killing of some 500 protesting Mexican students in the Plaza of the Three Cultures in 1968. In contrast, despite the high levels of street crime in many parts of the United States, education in this country has stressed that protests must remain within the law, that "the rule of law" must be sacrosanct. The resignation of Richard Nixon and the impeachment of Bill Clinton emphasize that even presidents of the republic cannot stand outside the law. Thus, while both Mexico and the United States provide contexts in which citizens advocate participation and do in fact participate vis-à-vis government, the forms of that participation differ, and the contrasting forms of participation say a good deal about the cultural norms inculcated in the two nations.

SUPPORT FOR AUTHORITARIANISM

Mexicans are also more likely to support authoritarianism than are U.S. citizens. Arizpe and others who question survey research findings may be correct in believing that Mexicans hold authoritarian values even more than they are willing to admit to pollsters, but such values certainly show up in public opinion polls as well. For

TABLE 6 *Respondents Who Felt That Democracy Is Better than Any Other Form of Government* (percent)

	Mexico	United States
Strongly agree	19	47
Agree	47	40
Disagree	17	7
Strongly disagree	2	1
Don't know	15	5

Source: 1995–97 World Values Survey. The question read, "I'm going to read off some things that people sometimes say about a democratic political system. Could you please tell me if you agree strongly, agree, disagree, or disagree strongly, after I read each one of them?" The statement reflected in this table was, "Democracy may have problems, but it's better than any other form of government." Sample size for Mexico is 1,511. Sample size for the United States is 1,839.

TABLE 7 *Support for Having a Strong Leader Who Does Not Bother with Parliament and Elections* (percent)

Feelings about Having Such a Leader	Mexico	United States
Very good	10	3
Fairly good	28	20
Fairly bad	33	25
Very bad	13	47
Don't know	15	5

Source: 1995–97 World Values Survey. The question read, "I'm going to describe various types of political systems and ask what you think about each as a way of governing this country. For each one, would you say it is a very good, fairly good, fairly bad, or very bad way of governing this country?" The statement reflected in this table was, "Having a strong leader who does not have to bother with parliament and elections." Sample size for Mexico is 1,511. Sample size for the United States is 1,839.

TABLE 8 *Support for Having the Army Rule* (percent)

Feelings about Having the Army Rule	Mexico	United States
Very good	5	1
Fairly good	17	5
Fairly bad	37	16
Very bad	27	74
Don't know	14	3

Source: 1995–97 World Values Survey. The question read, "I'm going to describe various types of political systems and ask what you think about each as a way of governing this country. For each one, would you say it is a very good, fairly good, fairly bad, or very bad way of governing this country?" The statement reflected in this table was, "Having the army rule." Sample size for Mexico is 1,511. Sample size for the United States is 1,839.

TABLE 9 *Support for Experts' Making Decsions Rather Than the Government* (percent)

Feelings about Having Experts Make Decisions	Mexico	United States
Very good	13	7
Fairly good	40	26
Fairly bad	26	27
Very bad	7	33
Don't know	14	6

Source: 1995–97 World Values Survey. The question read, "I'm going to describe various types of political systems and ask what you think about each as a way of governing this country. For each one, would you say it is a very good, fairly good, fairly bad, or very bad way of governing this country?" The statement reflected in this table was, "Having experts, not government, make decisions according to what they think is best for the country." Sample size for Mexico is 1,511. Sample size for the United States is 1,839.

instance, the data from the World Values Survey for 1995 indicate that Mexicans are more likely than U.S. citizens to agree that in democracies, the economic system runs badly, there is too much indecision and squabbling, and there is not enough maintenance of order. Mexicans are less likely to say that it is very good for a country to have a democratic system of government. As table 6 points up, Mexicans also remain strikingly less likely than people in the United States to say that democracy is better than any other form of government. Whereas half the people in the United States agree strongly with this statement, the proportion is only two out of ten in Mexico, and another two Mexicans in ten are willing to say that they do not think democracy is the best form of government.

Other support for authoritarianism appears in tables 7, 8, and 9. As table 7 shows, 10 percent of Mexicans say that it is very good to have a *caudillo,* a strong leader who does not bother with parliament and elections, while only 13 percent say that this is very bad. In contrast, nearly half of the people in the United States categorically reject such a leader, and three-quarters of them reject such authoritarian leadership in some degree. Even more strikingly, table 8 indicates that one Mexican in five supports rule by the Mexican army. In the United States, three-quarters of the people find the prospect of army rule to be very bad, as compared to only about one-quarter of the Mexican people. Here indeed are some of the most striking contrasts in the political cultures of the two countries.

Why should such authoritarian values persist in Mexico at the end of the twentieth century? Perhaps because values change very slowly, because Mexicans greatly admired strong government in the nineteenth century, and because the devastating Revolution of 1910 convinced a generation of Mexicans and their descendants that strong government was necessary to prevent chaos and civil war. Indeed, many scholars have interpreted the seven decades of PRI rule and the acceptance of the authoritarian ethos accompanying it to be the inheritance of Mexican history and the revolution. Historians such as Meyer have long interpreted the dictatorship of Porfirio Díaz as the precursor of the PRI system,[35] as both the Porfiriato and the PRI institutionalized only limited pluralism. Stevenson and Seligson indicate that the violence of the Revolution of 1910 had a deep effect on Mexican political culture and that this effect has carried over to those born long after the revolution who nevertheless had lost family members in it.[36]

The data in table 9 lead to the same conclusions, as they show that in 1996–97, Mexicans were much more likely than were people in the United States to favor a situation in which experts—rather than the government—make decisions according to what they think is best for the country. Again with resonance in Mexican history, these "experts" resemble the *científicos* of the Porfiriato and the technocrats of the PRI era, perhaps even calling to mind presidents such as Carlos Salinas de Gortari (educated at Harvard) and Ernesto Zedillo (educated at Yale). More than half the Mexicans in the survey supported decisions' being made by the experts, and 13 percent of them qualified it as very good. Whereas fully one-third of the U.S. respondents rejected such a situation as very bad, only 7 percent of the respondents in Mexico did so.

These data point not only to fundamental differences between Mexicans and U.S. citizens in regard to whether "experts" should make fundamental decisions in society. Because the question specifically says that experts as opposed to "government" should make the decisions, agreement with the question also serves as an indirect measure of support for authoritarianism as well. When first looking at the table 9 data, one might suppose that they reflect partisan differences in Mexico—that is, that those opposed to the PRI would reject decisions made "by government," because government and the PRI have been synonymous for seven decades. But, in fact, this is not the case. Analysis of the table 9 data shows that there is not much difference in terms of party loyalty between those who agree or disagree with experts' making the decisions. Instead, positive responses to the question on experts versus government reflect the views of Mexicans who feel that technocrats can run a system that remains above politics, one in which a "government" is not really necessary to manage conflict. In contrast to the one-third of Mexican respondents who reject this conclusion, nearly two-thirds of those in the United States do so, reflecting the common assumption in the latter country that in fact government and politics are the natural and necessary means of conflict resolution.

Before turning to other issues, it may be helpful to look at tables 6, 7, 8, and 9 with "parochials" in mind. Almond and Verba cite the parochial as someone who "tends to be unaware, or only dimly aware, of the political system in all its aspects."[37] Such citizens fail to understand much of either what government can do to or for them or what they can do to or for government. In tables 6 through 9, some 14 or 15 percent of the Mexican respondents fall into the "don't know" category, as contrasted with only 3 to 6 percent of the U.S. respondents. That is, a fairly sizeable proportion of the Mexican population simply appears to be unable to respond meaningfully to these questions on what sort of government is preferable, especially as compared to the United States, where far fewer respondents choose the "don't know" option. While considerable controversy among pollsters has surrounded the issue of the "undecided" voters in Mexican electoral polls who say that they "don't know" for whom they will vote,[38] it seems clear in the context of the questions cited above that many Mexicans simply felt that they could not give meaningful answers to these somewhat abstract and complicated questions. Here again is evidence that the proportion of "parochials" remains far higher in Mexico than in the United States.

PERCEPTIONS OF THE POLITICAL SYSTEM

Various perceptions of the political system also relate to political culture. Unlike interpersonal trust, these do not result from citizens' experience of democratic structures over long periods of time. Unlike support for gradual reform or specific acts of political participation, they do not form part of the aggregate of attitudes and actions that make up dimensions of political culture per se. Nevertheless, they do give us more perspective on how citizens see their political system, including its political culture.

One such measure is the level of satisfaction with how democracy is functioning in Mexico and the United States. As table 10 suggests, the differences between the two countries are not as great as one might expect. The question here really asks for citizens' evaluations of politics and politicians at the present time, rather than relating to their underlying feelings about democracy per se. In this context, citizens in the United States are more satisfied than those in Mexico, but four out of ten Mexicans in 1998 still expressed at least some satisfaction with the way that democracy was "working" in their country. This may relate to the tentative opening of the Mexican political system in the 1990s, to the fact that many Mexicans came to see in the 1997 elections more effective competition among political parties and candidates than had existed during

TABLE 10 *Satisfaction with How Democracy Is Working, 1998*
(percent)

Levels of Reported Satisfaction	Mexico[a]	United States[b]
Satisfied	41	52
Neither satisfied nor dissatisfied		
(volunteered by the respondent)	9	—
Dissatisfied	48	44

a. From the national survey of 3,396 respondents conducted in Mexico in 1998 by Roderic Ai Camp for the Hewlett Foundation. The question read, "In general, would you say you are satisfied or dissatisfied with the way democracy is working in this country? (INSIST): Very much or somewhat?" This table combines those who are "very much" or "somewhat" satisfied with democracy in Mexico into the "satisfied" category and those who are "very much" or "somewhat" dissatisfied with democracy in Mexico into the "dissatisfied" category.

b. From a national telephone survey of 852 respondents conducted December 19–20, 1998, by the Gallup Organization. The question read, "Are you satisfied or dissatisfied with the way democracy is working in this country?" These data are taken from the Public Opinion Location Library (POLL) of the Roper Center for Public Opinion Research.

the seven decades of PRI dominance. It may also reflect the higher levels of political participation that Mexicans had come to exercise and the satisfaction that many citizens took in that participation. Whatever the cause, satisfaction with the functioning of democracy is another measure in which citizens take quite similar stands north and south of the Rio Bravo.

A different result appears when citizens are asked whether they are willing to fight to defend their countries. This issue serves as an overall measure of loyalty to the nation-state, reflecting how citizens evaluate their nation as well as how much they are willing to sacrifice personally for it. As table 11 indicates, different trends were evident for this measure in Mexico and the United States between 1981 and 1995–97. With the Vietnam War an increasingly distant memory, about seven in ten U.S. respondents in this period said that they were willing to fight for their country, and the proportion remained steady over this decade and a half. In contrast, the proportion of Mexicans

TABLE 11 *Respondents Willing to Fight for Their Country*
(percent)

	1981	1990	1995–97
United States	66	70	77
Mexico	79	59	59

Source: 1981, 1990, and 1995–97 World Values Surveys. The question read, "Of course, we all hope that there will not be another war, but if it were to come to that, would you be willing to fight for your country?" Sample size for Mexico is 1,837 in 1981, 1,531 in 1990, and 1,511 in 1996–97. Sample size for the United States is 2,325 in 1981, 1,839 in 1990, and 1,839 in 1995.

TABLE 12 *Respondents Who Show Confidence in Four
Political Institutions (percent)*

	1981	1990	1995–97
United States	30	15	12
Mexico	16	17	15

Source: 1981, 1990, and 1995–97 World Values Surveys.The question read,
"Please look at this card and tell me, for each item listed, how much confidence you have in them. Is it a great deal, quite a lot, not very much or none at
all?" The four institutions are the legal system, the police, the legislature and
the civil service. Sample size for Mexico is 1,837 in 1981, 1,531 in 1990, and 1,511
in 1996–97. Sample size for the United States is 2,325 in 1981, 1,839 in 1990,
and 1,839 in 1995.

ready to do so fell dramatically from 1981 to 1990, leveling off at the lower plane during
the 1990s.

Another important dimension of citizens' perceptions of their nation and its political system is the level of confidence that they manifest in its political institutions. In
recent decades, the debate over ever-lower levels of institutional confidence has created
a large literature on the "crisis of confidence" in many nations.[39] The percentage of
Mexicans expressing confidence in basic institutions has often been lower than that in
other countries of Latin America. For example, in 1996–97 the percentage of Mexicans
expressing some confidence or much confidence in the police and in the judiciary was
lower than that for Argentines, Brazilians, Chileans, Paraguayans, and Uruguayans.[40]
Popular perceptions have a good deal to do with the effectiveness of the institutions
within each country; in Latin America, for example, evaluations of the Church are consistently high and those of the police are low.

When confidence in political institutions is compared for the United States and
Mexico, the United States turns out to be the more striking case. Table 12 summarizes
evaluations of four political institutions: the legal system, the police, the legislature,
and the civil service. All three waves of the World Values Survey contained questions
on confidence in these four institutions, and a factor analysis of them demonstrates
that they relate closely together in the perceptions of respondents. As table 12 suggests,
the aggregate level of confidence in these institutions remained low but constant in
Mexico between 1981 and 1996–97. In contrast, the level of confidence in the United
States dropped sharply.

This decline in confidence does not threaten institutional structures or stability in
the United States, and, as Inglehart has recently written, "the erosion of state authority
has been accompanied by a rising potential for citizen intervention in politics."[41] That

is, with higher levels of education and a more widespread sense of personal security, citizens increasingly distrust traditional institutions, while they increasingly take actions on their own, such as signing petitions and participating in boycotts. At this point, levels of institutional confidence are similarly low in the United States and Mexico, and in both nations the proportion of citizens signing petitions and boycotting products is increasing. Fundamental perceptions of institutional effectiveness have deteriorated far more in the United States than many observers of politics once assumed to be possible, but this has brought perceptions in Mexico and the United States more into line.

CONCLUSIONS

In broad outline, what can one conclude after comparing the data on the political cultures of Mexico and the United States? One clear conclusion must be that these nations maintain two distinct political cultures. The level of interpersonal trust stands higher in the United States than in Mexico, and this appears to result from the long experience of democratic structures of government in the United States and their effective absence south of the Rio Bravo. In terms of standard measures of political participation, such as signing a petition or joining a boycott, people in the United States remain substantially more likely to take these actions, even though the proportion of Mexicans doing so has increased materially since the early 1980s. Finally, the level of support for a *caudillo*, for authoritarianism, and even for rule by the army remains much greater in Mexico than in the United States. On several measures, those admiring *caudillaje* or army rule number about one Mexican in five, but this proportion points to substantially higher support for authoritarianism in Mexico than in the United States.

While the political cultures of Mexico and the United States thus stand distinct in terms of traditional measures of political culture, they also resemble one another in a number of ways, some of which we would not at first expect. Between half and three-quarters of the population of both nations supports gradual reform as opposed to either radical reform or defense of the status quo, and this orientation is fundamental to the initiation and maintenance of democratic institutions. If larger segments of Mexican elites in time come to back gradual reform as the primary option for policy and institutional change, this would support a continued opening of the Mexican political system. The failure of the system to move to more effective liberalization by the mid-1990s may help to explain another difference in the participant dimension of political culture in the two countries: whereas in 1981 Mexicans were less likely than people in the United States to have joined an illegal strike or to have occupied a building or a factory, by the 1990s Mexicans had become far more likely to have taken one or the other of these actions.

Perceptions of the political systems of the two countries also indicate a number of similarities between them. The level of satisfaction with the functioning of democracy was only somewhat higher in 1998 in the United States than in Mexico, even though U.S. respondents several years earlier had become considerably more likely to say that they would be willing to fight for their country. While confidence in basic political institutions in Mexico remained at a low level between 1981 and 1996–97, confidence in the same institutions in the United States fell dramatically during the same period, so that by the 1990s it stood even below the level in Mexico.

The issue of causation is intriguing here. For most of the twentieth century, some North Americans have felt that Mexico would—and some have said should—become politically more like the United States. The proximity of the U.S. colossus, the pervasiveness of its media inside Mexico, the number of U.S. tourists in Mexico, and the numbers of Mexican workers and students in the United States—all these would seem likely to nudge Mexican perceptions and attitudes toward those of the United States. This appears to be true for some dimensions of political culture in Mexico, but it is decidedly not true in terms of institutional confidence, where levels in the United States have fallen below those in Mexico. This suggests that, in fact, fundamental attitudes in both countries may be reacting to similar types of causation, rather than one nation's simply adopting more of the attitudes of the other. This interpretation is less ethnocentric, and therefore a good deal more satisfying, than the older assumption that Mexico would in time follow the path of the United States.

Clearly, the contrasting conclusions outlined above lead to a series of new questions. Elements of political culture do change over time, although attitudes shift more rapidly than do underlying values. Measures of citizen participation in Mexican political culture, such as the acts of signing a petition or joining a boycott, increased strongly in the 1980s and the 1990s, even though the levels of this participation in Mexico remained well below those in the United States. Both intellectually and politically, such trends warrant careful scrutiny in the future, and they may lead to new interpretations of the possible convergence of values in the two nations. As Inglehart, Nevitte, and Basáñez conclude, Mexico and the United States may be evolving toward accepting more similar democratic institutions, not only because citizens in these countries want those institutions, but also because the institutions themselves "are the most effective way of coordinating technologically advanced societies."[42]

Finally, while it is commonplace for scholars to bemoan the lack of agreement on exactly what constitutes a participant political culture,[43] in a sense the absence of agreement remains an asset rather than a liability. It encourages researchers to search for a variety of measures of political culture, and in the process of doing so they are likely to reveal different dimensions of the phenomenon. International comparisons of political culture in two or more countries have become vastly easier with the rise of coordinated, multination survey projects, such as those of the World Values Survey, the Latin American Barometer, and the International Survey Project. As elite and regional data are gathered and compared over time to survey data for general populations, new dimensions of political culture studies will become possible. In time, their significance may well match that of what we have learned so far in comparing the political cultures of representative samples of the general populations of various nations, including Mexico and the United States.

Part V

Do Differing Democratic Visions Make a Difference?

Economics and Partisanship

Chapter 10

Politics and Markets in Latin America
A Distinctive View of the Role of the State in Service Provision?

Kenneth M. Coleman

Privatization of public enterprises has been a part of the policy prescription imposed on Latin America by the so-called Washington Consensus of the international financial institutions (IFIs) as of the late 1980s.[1] While there are other elements to that package of policy prescriptions, certainly the belief among the IFIs was that the shrinking of the state would work to dampen inflation and lessen local credit crunches by making the state less of a borrower, and that the private sector could provide many services more efficiently than could the public sector. Consequently, lending by the IFIs was often conditioned on privatizing parastatal enterprises.[2]

Given the tremendous growth of parastatal enterprises in post–World War II Latin America under the logic of import-substitution industrialization, movements toward selling off or privatizing such enterprises seem to be a dramatic shift in public policy. For example, in table 1 it will be noted that two of the three countries examined in this book have experienced truly dramatic declines in the number of state enterprises. In Mexico the number of parastatal enterprises decreased by 80 percent between 1983 and 1993. In Chile, over a 16-year period (1973–89), the decrease exceeded 92 percent. By way of contrast, the decrease in parastatal enterprises observable in Costa Rica appears to be less—perhaps 35 percent in a decade.

One might think that such dramatic reorientations of the state role in the economy as occurred in Chile and Mexico would produce a severe disorientation in public opinion. Indeed, most analysts of the role of the state in Latin America writing in 1970 would have emphasized the existence of a different cultural tradition—one in which

TABLE 1 *Number of Parastatal Enterprises in Mexico, Chile, and Costa Rica*

	Mexico	Chile	Costa Rica
1973	—	596	—
1980	—	—	77
1983	1,058	98	—
1988	449	—	—
1989	—	45	50
1993	209	—	—

Sources: For Mexico, see Judith Teichman, *Privatization and Political Change in Mexico* (Pittsburgh: University of Pittsburgh Press, 1996), 131; for Chile, see Dominique Hachette, Rolf Lüders, and Guillermo Tagle, "Five Cases of Privatization in Chile," in *Privatization in Latin America*, ed. Manuel Sánchez and Rosanna Corona (Washington, D.C.: Interamerican Development Bank, 1993), 42; and for Costa Rica, see John Booth, *Costa Rica: Quest for Democracy* (Boulder, Colo.: Westview Press, 1998), nn. 5 and 17, p. 175; and from John Booth / personal communication, October 6, 1998. Note that for 1983 Hachette, Lüders, and Tagle disaggregated 48 cases of "genuine public enterprises" and 50 "peculiar" cases of enterprises on the verge of bankruptcy that the Chilean state took over on a short-term basis, i.e., up to 15 years. Since many public enterprises in Mexico had similar origins, I have aggregated the 50 "peculiar" cases with the others in Chile.

public support for a "developmental state" was an outgrowth of a long-standing orientation dating back to colonial experiences.[3] However, other insightful authors, such as Charles W. Anderson, have argued that the cultural orientation was always a bit more ambivalent than it seemed on the surface:

Despite the assumed "interventionist" tradition of the Hispanic state, there has been in fact in Latin America a historic bias toward the substantial delimitation of government's capacity to mobilize the resources of society. This is in part due to the prevalence of classical liberal ideas among many prominent in the economy, to the persistence of peasant and latifundia agriculture and to the general irrelevance and nonresponsibility of government to the concerns of the citizen. . . .[4] The formal norms governing the distribution of resources between the public and private parties have never been as straightforward or clear-cut in Latin America as they have been in some Western nations. The residues of the Spanish conception of the absolute state (particularly with regard to property rights), eclectic borrowings from a variety of foreign ideologies, and the heritage of such indigenous experiences as the Mexican Revolution, have given a cast of ambiguity to the question and made more plausible heterodox formulations of the way resources are to be divided between the state and private society than are possible in nations where a readier answer to the problem is contained in the political culture.[5] However, the absence of a cultural commitment on this matter complicates, rather than simplifies, the task of governance. Cultural ambivalence here often implies not so much tolerance or indifference as dissensus.[6]

Anderson's observations do suggest various intriguing interpretations of the present historical moment (the late 1990s). First, if there has been an "historic dissensus" in

Latin American societies on the role of the state, it might have been possible that
(*a*) the post–World War II movement (up through 1973 in Chile and 1982 in Mexico)
to create vast numbers of parastatal enterprises exceeded the actual public support
for such institutions (and has generated intense dissent from some citizens), but that
(*b*) the dramatic countermovement to privatize parastatal enterprises also exceeded
actual public support for such action (and, similarly, has generated intense dissent
from other citizens). Second, it is possible that citizens in Latin American states might
have a reasonably well defined sense of what services are appropriate for public provision and what services are most appropriate for private provision—and that such a
consensus might differ from those reached in other societies, such as the United States
or Western European states. Third, it is possible that the perception of an appropriate
balance between the private and the public might vary across Latin American states.
Indeed, one simple hypotheses would be that a nation's proximity to the United States
(in 1998, an age of strong cable television penetration and other mechanisms of cultural diffusion) might be correlated with greater affinity for the bias of North American
political culture. These hypotheses about political culture concern Alan Knight.

Knight raises the larger issue of defining political culture in his chapter in this volume. While he questions the utility of the concept of political culture, he stops short of
the radically nomothetic view of culture presented by Adam Przeworski and Henry
Teune as "that which is left over after explanation fails."[7] I use the phrase in two ways in
this chapter. The first is the conventional usage (among political scientists) of "a particular distributional pattern" of a given array of traits held to be central to identifying
and distinguishing between human cultures, or, in this case, human polities. In such
usage, the analyst wishes to identify both the central tendency, if there is one, and the
dispersion around that central tendency (be it a mean, median, or mode). Knight's
comments about Mexico, for example, suggest that whatever the "national" mean
might be on given indicators, there is considerable dispersion among the regions and
subregions of Mexico, and across time. I would concur with those caveats but hold
that, whatever the dispersion, there is some kind of central tendency at any given point
in time, and that comparisons across countries as to central tendencies and patterns of
dispersion are still stimulating. The greater problem with this usage of the concept of
political culture is theoretical—how is it that we select the dimensions across which we
compare?

However, my chapter also employs the "radically nomothetic" view of Przeworski
and Teune when it observes that, with regard to the provision of potable water and
schooling, once one takes out all the other impacts of demographic variables and atti-

tudes, what matters most is that one is a Costa Rican or Chilean or Mexican. Despite my best efforts to explain, by recourse to other variables, variation in attitudes about citizen preferences for providing services by public or private entities, I have failed to do so fully. And so when, after such efforts have failed, the dummy variables (explained below) for Costa Rica and Chile remain statistically significant, then I invoke the concept of distinctively national "cultures." But in so doing, I am confessing the "failure of explanation." The radically nomothetic perspective says: "Culture does not exist; to invoke the concept of culture is to confess that one has failed to explain variation." I feel comfortable with such an intellectual posture. That is because my intellectual training comes from that portion of political science grounded in the nomothetic tradition of inquiry.

Knight's interpretation of the deficiencies of the concept of culture is quite different. He wishes to "disaggregate" the concept of national culture and to generate descriptions of temporally and spatially constrained subcultures. But while unconvinced about the utility of the notion of culture, he does seem to believe that the job of the scholar is to identify a tapestry of interrelated variables unique to a given place and time. As such, his views are typical of the idiographic tradition of inquiry of which his discipline, history, is an important part.

So how *do* respondents in these three countries feel about the provision of services by the public or private sectors? The Hewlett data set afforded the opportunity to analyze responses to four items for which response alternatives were structured identically. The items are listed below.

Please tell me which activities should be state-owned and which should be private (rotation of the placement of the four attitude objects)?

	State	Private	Both	Don't Know
Airlines				
Schools				
Water				
Television				

While the text of the item mentioned only private or public ownership, interviewers accepted responses of "both" or mixed, and roughly one-fifth of respondents provided such answers on all four items. While the question of the proper boundaries of the public versus private sphere in economic activity was in actuality fought out over a much wider array of domains (as indicated by the 596 state enterprises that once existed in Chile and the 1,023 that existed in Mexico), this set of items gives us a range of areas through which to engage in preliminary analysis.

TABLE 2 *Preferences for Service Provision by Private or Public Entities* (percent)

Preferred Provider	Airlines				Schools				Water				Television			
	Mexico	Costa Rica	Chile	Ave.	Mexico	Costa Rica	Chile	Ave.	Mexico	Costa Rica	Chile	Ave.	Mexico	Costa Rica	Chile	Ave.
Government	28	36	30	31	51	71	68	61	57	66	75	66	27	26	30	28
Mixed	21	18	24	21	29	20	20	23	21	14	11	16	28	20	23	24
Private sector	51	47	46	48	21	9	13	15	22	20	13	18	45	54	47	49
Chi-Squared	24.3				119.4				96.1				29.5			
p	.001				.001				.001				.001			
N	3,396				3,396				3,396				3,396			

As table 2 indicates,[8] overall the consensus is that schools and water systems are best provided by government, with over 60 percent of all respondents favoring the public provision of such services and another 16 to 23 percent believing that there should be some role for the public sector in providing them. By contrast, there is a modal posture, although not as strong, that airlines and television networks ought to be private. In this case, the aggregated averages reveal that 48 percent of all respondents believe that airlines ought to be in private hands, 49 percent believe that television networks ought to be in private hands, and another 21 to 24 percent believe that there should be public and private activity in these two realms of service provision.[9]

But what about individual countries? Do respondents vary across our three research settings in their preferences for public versus private activity? The short answer is yes—Costa Ricans and Chileans appear somewhat more statist in their orientations than do the Mexicans.[10] The remaining data in table 2 illustrate that fewer Mexicans generally endorse the public provision of these services than do *ticos* (Costa Ricans) or *chilenos* (Chileans). Sometimes the difference is as little as 3.5 percent (for services where all respondents in all countries favor private provision), but it can be as large as 20 percent (for services where the statist orientation prevails in all countries). The one exception is with regard to the television industry, where Mexicans and Chileans are slightly less likely than Costa Ricans to favor "private-only" service provision (54 percent of *ticos* fall into the latter category, versus only 45 percent of Mexicans and 47 percent of Chileans). But on balance, across all four dimensions of service provision, 40 percent of Mexicans would favor the public provision of an "average service," whereas the mean preference for public service provision is 50 percent for Costa Ricans and 52 percent for Chileans.[11] The differences in the cross-national distribution of preferences are statistically significant in all four domains of service provision.

TABLE 3 *Mexicans, Costa Ricans, and Chileans: How "Latin American"
Are Their Views about Who Should Provide Services?*

| | Percentage preferring government ownership of: | | | |
	Airlines	Schools	Water	Television
Hewlett data sets				
Mexico (*N* = 1,200)	28	51	57	27
Costa Rica (*N* = 1,002)	36	71	66	26
Chile (*N* = 1,194)	30	68	75	30
Mean (*N* = 3,396)	31	61	66	28
Wall Street Journal Americas data sets				
Argentina (*N* = 1,001)	43	72	56	26
Bolivia (*N* = 751)	34	66	38	19
Brazil (*N* = 993)	29	72	62	27
Colombia (*N* = 1,000)	28	62	42	27
Dominican Republic (*N* = 757)	49	84	76	39
Ecuador (*N* = 500)	29	59	46	16
Guatemala (*N* = 752)	19	74	65	27
Panama (*N* = 754)	22	75	79	27
Paraguay (*N* = 478)	23	66	45	16
Peru (*N* = 1,029)	31	70	68	27
Venezuela (*N* = 1,000)	33	59	53	24
Mean of 14 countries[a]	31	69	61	26
USA	27	42	41	10

a. Unweighted, but including independent estimates (not those of the Hewlett study) for Chile
(*N* = 1,000), Costa Rica (*N* = 750), and Mexico (*N* = 1,199).

How would such attitudes compare with those found in the United States and elsewhere in the Americas? Results from an early 1998 hemisphere-wide survey sponsored
by the *Wall Street Journal* and major newspapers in 14 different countries are presented
in table 3.[12]

According to the *Wall Street Journal Americas* data, the regional average preference[13]
for government-owned schools is 69 percent; for government-owned water systems, 61
percent; for government-owned airlines, 31 percent; and for government-owned television networks, 26 percent. In sum, the three cases we are examining are very typically
Latin American. The preferences found in Mexico, Costa Rica, and Chile fall within the
Latin American range—with Mexico falling toward the low end. By way of contrast,
the percentages favoring public ownership are strikingly lower in the United States: 42
percent for schools, 41 percent for water systems, 27 percent for airlines, and a mere 10
percent for television. These differences would surely be significantly different in statistical terms.[14]

An equally interesting question may be, Is there an underlying structure to attitudes about the provision of services? And if so, is it a comparable structure in all three countries, or does it vary across countries? Appendix B indicates that Mexico differs from the other two countries. Mexicans have an underlying attitudinal structure in which certain services are seen as "more clearly public" (water and schools) and others as "more clearly private" (airlines and television). This can be observed via a factor analysis that produces two distinct factors (or underlying structures of covariation) in Mexico. In Costa Rica and Chile, by contrast, only one factor emerges from a factor analysis of these four items, indicating that while respondents in both countries prefer state intervention to varying degrees, there are no clear clusters of services in the minds of respondents. "More clearly private" services are not distinguished from "more clearly public" services among *ticos* and *chilenos,* perhaps because both national communities are more inclined to support public provision of services than is the body politic *mexicano.*

Yet in reality, a similar tendency exists in all four of the Hewlett data sets (aggregated, Mexico, Costa Rica, and Chile). That is, attitudes about water and schools covary strongly, while attitudes about airlines and television covary strongly. For example, the overall gamma (a coefficient of correlation for ordinal level variables) for attitudes about public versus private provision of schools and water services is +.58, and the overall gamma for the covariation of attitudes about who should manage airlines and television networks is +.49 (see appendix A). Those figures are strong across Mexico, Costa Rica, and Chile (schools/water = +.55, +.51, and +.68, respectively; airlines/television = +.46, +.52, and +.52, respectively).

By way of contrast, the overall gammas for schools and airlines (+.27), water and airlines (+.26), schools and television (+.24), and water and television (+.25) are much lower. Those values are especially low in Mexico (ranging from +.11 to +.17). Generally, the latter figures are higher in Costa Rica (ranging from +.18 to +.32) and in Chile (from +.36 to +.45). To reiterate, then, Mexicans distinguish between "more public" services (water and schools) and "more private" services (airlines and television), while Chileans in particular have a bias toward public provision of all services,[15] and Costa Ricans come in a close second in terms of their statist orientations. Yet the degree of support for public provision of airline and television services is lower in these countries, too. Hence, two factors emerge in the aggregated analysis.

SCALING DECISIONS

The fact that attitudes about who should provide services are divided into two underlying structures in Mexico and one in Costa Rica and Chile presents a challenge for analysis. My solution first involves assigning numerical values to the preference for service provision such that a preference for public service provision = 1, a preference for mixed service provision (some public, some private) = 2, and a preference for private service provision = 3. Thereafter, I analyze all respondents together and build two additive factor scales for use as dependent variables.[16] Finally, I will develop explanatory models of which kinds of Latin Americans favor private versus public provision of traditional state-provided services (schools and water, denoted as *pubserve*) and which favor private versus public provision of transport and communication services (airlines and television, denoted as *priserve*), which have for a longer period of time been provided in the private sector. Country will be used, along with many other variables, as an explanatory variable. Costa Ricans and (especially) Chileans will be expected to display a general bias toward the provision of all kinds of services by the state.[17] Readers should note that the coding of variables is such that those who score high on either *pubserve* or *priserve* favor private provision of those services.

THEORETICAL ASSUMPTIONS

Often, analysts of public opinion examine demographic correlates of public opinion such as income, education, age, religion, and gender. While the theoretically expected relationship of such variables to attitudinal or behavioral outcomes may vary with the context,[18] in general certain suppositions could be made.

For example, one might hypothesize that as income levels increase, support for privatization might also increase. However, this relationship might well be mediated by the nature of one's employer. Those employed by government, even if higher-paid individuals, might be less enthusiastic about privatization than would equally well paid individuals from the private sector. Regrettably, the data set provides a better test of the income hypothesis than of the employment hypothesis. We will test the income hypothesis and a weak variant of the public/private employment hypothesis.[19]

As to a hypothesis for education, making inferences is difficult precisely because of what appears to be a sea change in intellectual currents. Prior to 1973 in Chile and 1982 elsewhere, one might have assumed that many of those with higher education were likely to be statist in their orientations, favoring the public provision of services. That was the reigning intellectual orientation in much of the postwar era. After the politico-economic crises of 1973 (Chile) and 1982 (Costa Rica and Mexico), however, one might have expected support for privatization to grow, if only because intellectual currents had changed. Moreover, the percentage of Latin Americans attending institutions of higher education who attend private institutions has grown from 14 percent of all enrollees in 1955 to 38 percent in 1994.[20] One might suppose that those who have chosen private education might also prefer the private provision of additional services. So I will hypothesize that the more recent tendency would prevail—that those with higher education would prefer privatization.

The logic adduced to make the prior inference, however, suggests that older respondents will be more likely to prefer the public provision of services and to oppose privatization. There should be a significant generational effect observable in these data.

I see no reason to believe that men should differ from women in their attitudes about whether government or the private sector should provide services. The most striking pattern about gender differences in the political behavior of Latin Americans is that, in the aggregate, there is little difference. With regard to this particular set of attitudes, we also expect little difference.

With regard to religious preference, one striking phenomenon in Chile, Costa Rica, and Mexico is the diffusion of Protestantism. The Hewlett data set reveals 5 percent of the Mexican population, 10 percent of Costa Ricans, and 16 percent of the Chilean population to be Protestant. While there is a general supposition that Protestants will be politically conservative (largely because *evangelical* Protestantism has been the source of much growth), recent empirical analyses reveal a more complex picture.[21] Indeed, in a few regards, Latin American Protestants appear more progressive than Catholics or others. Consequently, I hypothesize no aggregate relationship between religious identification (Protestantism versus Catholicism and others) and preference for private or public provision of services.

In addition to demographic variables, there are some attitudes that might conceivably be construed as *causes* of preferences for the public or private provision of services. Such attitudes could include (1) self-placement on an ideology scale, (2) philosophical orientation to personal responsibility versus public responsibility for one's welfare, (3) degree of satisfaction with the existing democratic structures, (4) one's assessment of one's personal economic situation at the moment, and (5) the respondent's projected personal economic situation in a year.

Basically, one would expect that (1) rightists, (2) those who favor personal responsibility over state guarantees of welfare, and (3) those who do not believe existing democratic institutions to be working well might be more favorable toward the private provision of services. With regard to personal economic situations, both actual and projected, one might assume that in an era of privatization, those whose personal economic situations are most favorable would be most supportive of the private provision of services. That hypothesis, therefore, would have two variants—pertaining to the relationship between current perceived financial situation and preference for private services, as well as between one's projected financial situation in 12 months and the private provision of services. In each case, the expected relationship would be positive.

DATA ANALYSIS AND INTERPRETATION

A multiple regression analysis was done with each factor scale as a dependent variable and including all of the variables mentioned above. For specific measurement procedures on the independent variables, see appendix C. The two dependent variables, *pubserve* (pertaining to schools and water) and *priserve* (pertaining to airline service and television), are each coded so that a high score indicates a preference for private provision of services. Therefore, the names refer to traditional expectations about who should provide such services. And those traditional expectations differ.

With regard to variation in attitudes about services traditionally construed as public (schooling and the provision of water), table 4 reveals eight variables to be statistically significant predictors. First, note that the dummy variables for Costa Rica and Chile are each statistically significant and that the standardized Beta weights (adjusted to put all independent variables on a comparably measured scale)[22] for these variables are the strongest in the equation. This is a striking finding. It implies that once one takes out all the other impacts of demographic variables and attitudes, what matters most is that one is a Costa Rican or a Chilean or a Mexican. Since the coefficients are negative, this implies that being a *tico* or a *chileno* makes one significantly less likely to favor the private provision of schooling or water than if one were a Mexican.

Other findings about *pubserve* reported in table 4 also deserve emphasis. First, note that only one demographic variable predicts attitudes about who should provide schooling and water: age. The older the respondent, the more likely he or she is to oppose private provision of schooling and water ($p = .015$; Beta $= -.05$). However, three attitudinal variables and two assessments of personal economic conditions also predict attitudes about the provision of schooling and water.

Both the belief that democracy is working well and a general orientation as to whether the state or individuals should be primarily responsible for human welfare are significant predictors. Those who believe that "democracy is working well" are likely to endorse the private provision of services—perhaps because the neoliberal thrust of public policy in the 1990s is toward privatization. Those who evaluate current democ-

TABLE 4 *Determinants of Preferences for Private Provision of Services*

Independent Variables	Pubserve: *services that were traditionally public (schooling, water)*				Priserve: *newer and more frequently private services (airline travel, television)*				No. of times stat. significant
	b	Std. error	Stat. sig.	B	b	Std. error	Stat. sig.	B	
Constant	−.09	.15	NS		−.76	.16	.000		
Demographic									
Income (light bulbs)	.01	.02	NS	.01	.06	.02	.010	.06	1
Private-sector employment	.01	.01	NS	.00	.05	.05	NS	.02	0
Education (no. of years)	.00	.01	NS	−.02	.02	.01	.005	.07	1
Age (grouped)	−.07	.03	.015	−.05	−.01	.03	NS	−.00	1
Gender (female = high)	−.04	.04	NS	−.02	−.02	.04	NS	−.01	0
Protestant	−.02	.07	NS	−.01	−.24	.07	.000	−.07	1
Attitudinal									
Ideology (1 = left; 10 = right)	.04	.01	.000	.10	.04	.01	.000	.08	2
State responsible for indiv. welfare	−.08	.03	.002	−.06	.02	.03	NS	.01	1
Democracy working well	.03	.02	.042	.04	.01	.02	NS	.01	1
Economic assessments									
Current situation	.10	.02	.000	.11	.07	.02	.000	.08	2
In a year	.04	.02	.030	.05	.02	.02	NS	.02	1
Country dummy variables									
Costa Rica	−.47	.05	.000	−.21	−.01	.01	NS	−.01	1
Chile	−.37	.05	.000	−.18	.01	.01	NS	.00	1
R (R^2)	.27 (.07)				.20 (.03)				
F (significance)	15.2 (.000)				7.7 (.000)				
N	2,477				2,477				

racies favorably may be evaluating "neoliberal democracy." This relationship is just barely significant, however (p = .042). Those who believe that the state should work to guarantee the welfare of citizens are, not surprisingly, likely to oppose the private provision of schooling and water (p = .002; Beta = −.06). But the strongest attitudinal orientation in predicting attitudes about who should provide schooling and water is a 10-point ideology scale (where 1 = left and 10 = right). This scale is strongly predictive, with rightists significantly more likely (p < .001, Beta = +.10) to favor the private provision of these services than are leftists.

The two variables assessing the economic situation of the respondent also predict attitudes toward the provision of "public" services (schooling and water). The respondent's assessment of her or his current economic circumstance is another reasonably strong predictor (p < .001; Beta = +.11), with those who find their current economic circumstances to be favorable most likely to endorse the private provision of schooling and water and those less favorably situated economically (in their own minds) tending to be less enthusiastic about privatization of these services. Similarly, those who expect personal economic improvement over the next 12 months tend to be favorable to the private provision of traditional public services (p = .03; Beta = +.05).

Overall, the regression equation yields a coefficient of multiple correlation of .27, which would statistically explain a mere 7 percent of the overall variation—a total not uncommon in survey research. Perhaps more meaningful is the pattern of results in which, *(a)* after country of the respondent is considered, *(b)* age, *(c)* assessments of personal economic circumstances, and *(d)* general ideological and attitudinal orientations seem to be driving assessments of whether traditional public services should be privatized. As we shall see, this pattern differs partially from that found for determinants of attitudes about the private provision of airline service and television service.

Table 4 also includes the same variables used in a prediction equation for *priserve*, attitudes regarding the private provision of airline and television service. As we recall, the overall distribution of attitudes favorable to privatization was greater for these two services. The first and most striking finding with regard to *priserve* is that country does not matter. Once the effects of personal economic assessments as well as demographic and attitudinal variables are accounted for, no statistically significant difference remains here between Mexicans, Chileans, and Costa Ricans.

However, with regard to this dependent variable, three demographic items do prove to be significant predictors—income, education, and Protestantism. Income works as one might expect: those with high income favor the private provision of airline travel and television service (p = .01; Beta = .06). Education also works as we hypothesized; those with the most education do tend to be most favorable toward the private provision of airline and television service (p = .005; Beta = .07). The relationship of Protestantism to this dependent variable, however, provides another of the surprises that have been emerging from recent research about religion in Latin America. Protestants are *less likely* to favor the private provision of airline and television service than are Catholics or others.

The two strongest determinants of attitudes about the private provision of airline and television service are ideology (p < .001; Beta = .08) and assessments of one's current economic circumstance (p < .001; Beta = .08). Again, those whose current economic situation is self-assessed as favorable are most positively inclined to the private provision of services. And those who describe themselves as rightist (or toward the upper end of a 10-point scale where 10 equals right-wing) are also those most inclined toward private airlines and private television companies.

Overall, however, the ability to predict variation in who favors private provision of air and television service is more restricted. In this equation, the R reaches only .20, yielding a paltry "explained variation" of 3 percent. The biggest contrast is that country accounts for no difference. So, while it appeared back in table 2 that the bivariate relationships between country and preferences for provision of air travel and television services were statistically significant, those relationships washed out in multivariate analysis. However, ideology and self-assessments of one's economic circumstances determine attitudes about service provision in the cases of air travel and television services *(priserve)* as well as for schooling and water provision *(pubserve)*.

CONCLUSION

The purpose of this volume is to assess the extent to which a distinctively Latin American vision of democracy might exist. The *Wall Street Journal Americas* survey suggests that on the issue of private versus public provision of services, Latin Americans are substantially different from North Americans. However, the analysis in this chapter suggests one possible caveat to that generalization. With respect to the relationship between democracy and markets, there appear potentially to be two Latin American political cultures.

Mexicans seem significantly different from Costa Ricans and Chileans with regard to their willingness to consider the private provision of schooling and potable water systems, given the Hewlett data set.[23] It should be reiterated that this is a matter of degree, not of kind (see table 3). In Mexico, those who favor public provision of such services still exceed 50 percent, but fall 10 to 20 percent below the comparable figures in Costa Rica and Chile.

As a caveat, note that in all three countries the percentage who favor publicly owned airlines and television companies is considerably lower (in the range of 26 to 50 percent, depending on whether one focuses on those who favor "only government-owned entities" or adds in those who favor "some publicly owned corporations and some private ownership"). By contrast, in a political culture such as the United States, history suggests that support for public ownership of airlines or television companies would be even lower,[24] and the *Wall Street Journal Americas* data confirm that expectation (the figures are 27 percent and 10 percent, respectively). So, within a general range of attitudes more favorable to public ownership than would be found in the United States, these three Latin American publics exhibit two subsets of opinions.

Mexicans have evolved views that seem closer to those found in the United States on the issues of privatization—seen most notably in the case of those services traditionally provided by public entities, schooling and potable water. As intimated earlier, there is a double irony here: Mexico was long the most nationalist of Latin American states, precisely because of its proximity to "the hovering giant" to its north—a giant long disposed to intervene in Mexican policy debates.[25] Chile, by way of contrast, had the most assertively privatizing government of the period between 1973 and 1990, yet public opinion in Chile is today no more favorable toward privatization than is the case in other Latin American states.[26] The best post hoc explanation for both findings might well be the impact of Mexico's proximity to the United States in an era of globalization, entailing both an integration of communication systems (with their embedded ideological messages) and the extraordinary fluidity of capital flows. Mexicans are under considerable pressure to buy into "integrationist" postures, under terms suggested by the capitalist center through the international financial institutions. Chile is distant from the United States geographically and seemingly also in terms of underlying economic culture.[27] Chile has long exhibited cultural dissensus on the proper role of the state in the economy, but it is a dissensus centered on the notion of a mixed economy.[28]

Another way to approach the issue of whether there is a peculiarly Latin American vision of democracy would be to ask about the *determinants* of attitudes about the public and private provision of services. In table 4, the column on the right indicates the number of times specific independent variables proved to be significant predictors of attitudes. Only two variables were significant predictors in both equations—ideology and one's assessment of one's current economic circumstance. Right-wingers who found themselves in particularly comfortable economic circumstances are especially likely to favor the private provision of services—be they services traditionally provided by the state or those more frequently provided by the private sector. Gender and private employment do not seem to have any impact. Other variables influence one set of attitudes but not the other. In this regard, the determinants of attitudes about privatization do not seem unique to Latin America. One would expect such relationships to exist as well in the United States, Western Europe, or elsewhere.

In a recent article, Jorge Domínguez makes the novel argument that democracy may well strengthen the propensity to choose markets.[29] Turning a classic argument on its head, Domínguez argues that, rather than free markets' making democracy more likely, perhaps adopting democratic forms of government makes the opening of economies and the deepening of market mechanisms more probable. The current results can in no way provide a definitive assessment of the Domínguez thesis, which is argued convincingly. But these results do provide a note of caution. If the extent of democratization were *the major determinant* of public opinion supportive of market solutions, then we might expect Mexicans to exhibit the least support for market mechanisms and Chileans and Costa Ricans to exhibit the most. Mexico has clearly progressed the most slowly along the road toward democracy, although accelerating greatly with the 2000 presidential election. Chile had a well-established democracy, although it was interrupted by dictatorship for 17 years, while Costa Rica's current tradition of democracy has survived 50 years, since 1948. Hence, the extent of democratic consolidation is not correlated with public preferences for market mechanisms in those three countries. Perhaps other factors, such as those noted above, also play a role in reorienting public opinion, or more cases would be needed to see the relationship Domínguez expects.

The relationship between democracy and markets is complex, as indicated by the lack of scholarly consensus on just what the apparent correlation means. Elite actors play a major role in defining the structures that mediate between markets and democratic institutions. Those elites operate increasingly in an international context in which choices are constrained. But public opinion is also formed in such a context. And that context is subject to change.[30] That being the case, the reading that we have taken in 1998 of the views of Latin Americans toward the proper mix of public and private service provision should be reexamined periodically. As Anderson noted long ago, the "absence of a cultural consensus" on norms about the proper division of resources and service provision between the public and private sectors may be the distinguishing trait about Latin America. Disputes about precisely such issues have led to the downfall of democracy—notably in Chile. If Domínguez is correct, the current wave of democratization may be permanent and may lead to a final resolution of such historic ambivalence. A hopeful sign is that the international environment seems to be evolving in a way that may put less pressure on Latin American governments to totally abandon historic orientations toward public service provision. However, it would be excessively sanguine to expect that a "historic consensus" will suddenly emerge where one has never existed.

People disagree over the public and private sectors precisely because there are cases to be made *both* for efficiency and for equity. The tension between those who put priority on efficiency and those who put priority on equity will always be reflected in public opinion, in Latin America and elsewhere. The Latin American tradition has emphasized the role of the state in pursuing equity. Those who favor privatization in the Americas will be able to modify public opinion when they convince their fellow citizens that the private sector can attain both ends more effectively than can the state. Until such time as they make such an argument persuasively, public opinion may be resistant to change, as it appears to be in Costa Rica and Chile. Indeed, Edward Schumacher, writing in the *Wall Street Journal Americas,* says, "much of the privatization sweeping Latin America is being done without public support . . . raising questions about eventual backlash."[31] I would concur.

While Domínguez may be correct that democracy can make market systems more sustainable, the leaders of democratic governments will eventually have to produce economic results visible to citizens in order to consolidate both democracies and markets.[32] Given historic distributional inequalities endemic to the Americas, the challenge will be substantial to use newly privatized activities to provide benefits that citizens find palpable.[33]

In summarizing what these data and recent historical events suggest about the relationship between democracy and markets, I would make four basic points. The first is that the consensus of international financial institutions is that democracy is best supported by markets, but Latin American populations are less certain. Second, the large numbers of Latin Americans who live at the margins of economic viability may prove willing to abandon either democracy or markets for leaders who promise to attain visible economic results. These persons see both markets and democracy as instruments for the attainment of yet-to-be-achieved minimum standards of human welfare. For many, democracy and markets are means, not ends. They will remain such until people "have enough to be more."[34] Third, there is a potential for conflict between the international financial institutions and governments in the Americas over issues of privatization. Finally, there is a potential for conflict within Latin American countries over such issues as well. The lessons of the collapse of democracy in Chile should not be forgotten. Just as the Chilean left misread the actual degree of support for nationalizations in 1970–73, so too may governments and international institutions today misread the actual degree of support for privatizations. Imposing a solution—either for nationalization or for privatization—may do little to consolidate democracy in the region.

APPENDIX A: INTERCORRELATIONS OF ITEMS PERTAINING TO THE PROVISION OF SERVICES

Overall Intercorrelations: 3 Countries*

	Airlines	Schools	Water	Television
Airlines	—	.271	.257	.492
Schools		—	.597	.240
Water			—	.248
Television				—

* Entry = gamma. All correlations are positive and significant at the p = .001 level. Number of cases ranges from 3,181 to 3,284 in separate analyses.

Mean inter-item gamma = .351.

Mexican Intercorrelations*

	Airlines	Schools	Water	Television
Airlines	—	.172	.111**	.455
Schools		—	.553	.130***
Water			—	.140
Television				—

* Entry = gamma. All correlations are positive and significant at the p = .001 level unless otherwise noted. Number of cases ranges from 1,130 to 1,163 in separate analyses.

** Significant at .01 level.   *** Significant at .003 level.

Mean inter-item gamma = .260.

Costa Rican Intercorrelations*

	Airlines	Schools	Water	Television
Airlines	—	.235	.321	.523
Schools		—	.509	.184
Water			—	.286
Television				—

* Entry = gamma. All correlations are positive and significant at the p = .001 level. Number of cases ranges from 931 to 965 in separate analyses.

Mean inter-item gamma = .343.

Chilean Intercorrelations*

	Airlines	Schools	Water	Television
Airlines	—	.381	.373	.517
Schools		—	.681	.449
Water			—	.361
Television				—

* Entry = gamma. All correlations are positive and significant at the p = .001 level. Number of cases ranges from 1,130 to 1,164 in separate analyses.

Mean inter-item gamma = .460.

APPENDIX B: FACTOR ANALYSIS AND
SCALING PROCEDURES

A factor analysis of the four service provision items was performed with orthogonal rotation. The analysis was performed on the aggregated data set, as well as on each national data set.

Factor Analyses of Preferences for Service Provision: Aggregated and by Country

| | Factor Loadings* for: | | | | | |
| Service | All Respondents | | Mexico | | Costa Rica | Chile |
	Factor 1	Factor 2	Factor 1	Factor 2	Factor 1	Factor 1
Airlines	.11	.82	.07	.82	.69	.66
Schools	.82	.10	.82	.08	.56	.72
Water	.82	.11	.83	.05	.65	.67
Television	.11	.82	.06	.82	.69	.70
% Variance explained	34	34	34	34	42	47
N	3,160		1,127		922	1,110

Orthogonal rotation is a procedure designed to maximize the unique identifiability of factors, once it has been established that multiple factors exist. See Jae-On Kim, "Factor Analysis," chap. 24 in Norman H. Nie, C. Hadlai Hull, Jean G. Jenkins, Karin Steinbrenner, and Dale H. Bent, *Statistical Package for the Social Sciences,* 2d ed. (New York: McGraw-Hill, 1970), 482–86. The results of the factor analysis are presented in the table.

The next step was to build two scales combining two items each. Factor scale coefficients (which are roughly proportionate to, but not identical with, factor loadings) were used to weight the standardized value of each item. A factor scale coefficient represents the extent of participation of each item in an underlying structure of covariation. Standardized variables are adjusted so that the variable has a mean of zero and a standard deviation of approximately 1.0; factor scales, being the sum of standardized variables weighted to account for the underlying structure of covariation, also have the properties of a mean of zero and a standard deviation that approaches 1.0.

The specific equations used to create the scales analyzed in this study follow.

Total sample:

$Pubserve = -.09*(airlines - 2.18)/.87 + .62*(schools - 1.53)/.74 + .62*(water - 1.53)/.78 - .07*(television - 2.21)/.85$

$Priserve = .62*(airlines - 2.18)/.87 - .08*(schools - 1.53)/.74 - .08*(water - 1.53)/.78 + .62*(television - 2.21)/.85$

Note that the entry before each parenthetical expression varies between the two equations, but that the parenthetical expressions remain the same. The entry that varies is the factor score coefficient (the weight representing the participation of the item in the underlying structure of covariation). The expressions that remain the same between the two equations are a standardization of each item, that is, giving the distribution of preferences a mean of zero and a standard deviation of 1.0.

For a comprehensible short discussion of factor scaling, see Kim, "Factor Analysis," especially pp. 487–89.

APPENDIX C: MEASUREMENT OF INDEPENDENT VARIABLES

Income: Number of light bulbs in the dwelling one occupies, recoded by MORI into four groups: 1 to 5, 6 or 7, 8 to 12, and 13 or more.

Private-sector employment: A dummy variable coded as 1 if respondent indicated employment as an independent professional or in private business. Nineteen percent of all respondents received this code. All other respondents received a zero. This measure provides a "weak test" of the hypothesis because it clearly entails measurement error. Certain other employment categories entail occupations that may have either public or private manifestations. Hence, this dummy variable does not capture all of those employed in the private sector, just a subset.

Education: Number of years up through 12 years, then the codes 13 (some university), 14 (university degree holder), 15 (some graduate training), and 16 (graduate degree holder) were employed.

Age: Grouped by MORI into the following categories: 18 to 29, 30 to 49, and 50 or more.

Gender: 1 = male, 2 = female.

Protestant: Dummy variable coded such that Protestants = 1; Catholics, others, no religion = 0.

Ideology: Ten-point scale for self-placement, with 1 identified as left and 10 as right. Item P27.

State responsible for individual welfare: Item P28 recoded such that 3 = state should be responsible for the welfare of individuals, 2 = both state and individuals should be responsible, 1 = individuals should be responsible for their own welfare.

Democracy working well: Individuals asked to rate the functioning of democracy in their country via item P7. Ratings recoded such that 5 = very satisfied, 4 = somewhat satisfied, 3 = neither satisfied nor dissatisfied, 2 = somewhat dissatisfied, and 1 = very dissatisfied.

Assessment of current personal economic situation: Item P42 recoded such that 5 = very good, 4 = somewhat good, 3 = neither good nor bad, 2 = somewhat bad, and 1 = very bad.

Projective assessment of personal economic situation in 12 months: Item P43 recoded such that 5 = much better, 4 = somewhat better, 3 = same, 2 = somewhat worse, and 1 = much worse.

Costa Rica: Dummy variable, coded such that Costa Rica = 1, other countries = 0.

Chile: Dummy variable, coded such that Chile = 1, other countries = 0.

APPENDIX D: CHOOSING BETWEEN THE HEWLETT AND *WALL STREET JOURNAL AMERICAS* DATA SETS

The Hewlett and *Wall Street Journal Americas* data sets were both generated by Market and Opinion Research International (MORI), but they produce different estimates of the preferences for public versus private provision of services (see table). Those differences are troublesome in the case of Mexico and in the case of the *priserve* variable for Costa Rica.

The net effect of these differences is to make it more likely in the Hewlett data set than in the *Wall Street Journal Americas* data set that two separate factors would emerge in Mexico, as has been described in the text. Also, the differences make it more likely that two separate factors

Percentage Preferring Government Ownership

	Hewlett Study (July 1998)	WSJ Americas Study (January–February 1998)	Interpretation
Mexico—Schools	51	75	Mean difference for
Mexico—Water	57	68	*pubserve* items: −17.5%
Mexico—Airlines	28	41	Mean difference for
Mexico—Television	27	32	*priserve* items: −8%
Chile—Schools	68	65	Mean difference for
Chile—Water	75	70	*pubserve* items: +4%
Chile—Airlines	30	26	Mean difference for
Chile—Television	30	31	*priserve* items: +1.5%
Costa Rica—Schools	71	60	Mean difference for
Costa Rica—Water	66	74	*pubserve* items: +1.5%
Costa Rica—Airlines	36	19	Mean difference for
Costa Rica—Television	26	21	*priserve* items: +11%

would *not* emerge in Costa Rica (from the Hewlett data set), whereas in the *Wall Street Journal Americas* data set, two factors might have emerged. These expectations remain speculative, because the *Wall Street Journal Americas* data set is not available to be analyzed.

What might produce these discrepancies between the two data sets? For Mexico, one good hypothesis, offered by Roderic Camp, is that the two data sets differ in their rural-urban composition. That appears to be the case, as indicated in the table.

In fact, the Hewlett data set represents the large urban environments very well, while the *Wall Street Journal Americas* data set captures the rural end of the spectrum well. Both data sets are somewhat misleading, although if they are properly weighted, the distorting effects will be minimal.

If unweighted, slight distorting effects could occur. An analysis of the Hewlett data set reveals correlations (gamma) in Mexico of −.07 and −.11 between size of locale where the respon-

Rural-Urban Composition of Data Sets (percent)

	Hewlett Study (July 1998)	Mexican Census of 1995	WSJ Americas Study (January–February 1998)
Metropoli (> 1 million)	19	20[a]	11
Large cities (100,000–1 million)	36	36	45
Medium cities (50,000–100,000)	11	5	11
Small cities (15,000–50,000)	22	9	4
Rural (less than 15,000)	12	31	32

Source: Visión latinoamericana codebook, section C, p. 16; *Wall Street Journal Americas* Mirror on the Americas report, p. 8; and data files from the *Conteo Nacional de Población y Vivienda de 1995*, Instituto Nacional de Estadística, Geografía e Informática (INEGI), República de México, provided by Sta. Rita Palacio, after an inquiry at the INEGI website, December 1998. Web site: http://ags.inegi.gob.mx/ homepara/estadistica/.

a. Counting only Mexico City's 8,500,000 population in the Federal District (D.F.), plus all municipalities of over 1,000,000, four of which are in the greater Mexico City area (Netzahualcoyotl, Edo. de México; Gustavo Madero, D.F.; Ecatepec de Morelos, Edo de México; and Iztapalapa, D.F.). The remaining three cities of over a million are Monterrey, Puebla, and Guadalajara. Ciudad Juárez falls just short at 995,000.

dent resides and preference for statist solutions on television and airline service, both significant at the p = .05 level. That is, residents of small cities and rural locales tend to prefer state provision of television and airline services. However, no significant correlations exist between size of locale of the respondent and preference for public or private provision of schooling or potable water.

The weighting procedure employed by MORI with the Hewlett data set does not appear to shift the distribution substantially toward smaller locales (see *Visión Latinoamericana* codebook, section F, page 2). Nonetheless, since the size of locale of the residence of respondents is related *in different ways* to these four indicators in Mexico, I infer that the Hewlett findings of two separate dimensions of attitudes about service provision would tend to hold up in other surveys. The total distributional profile might be more heavily weighted toward statist solutions in Mexico than this data set reveals to be the case. However, urban Mexicans will likely remain more disposed toward privatization (in the provision of certain services) than will rural or small-town Mexicans.

Chapter 11

Chilean Citizens and Chilean Democracy
The Management of Fear, Division, and Alienation

Louis W. Goodman

In the fall of 1967 I began living in a "popular" neighborhood in the south-Santiago *comuna* of La Cisterna to carry out a participant observation study of the lives of blue-collar workers there. One of my first acquaintances was a construction worker active in a local Christian Democratic community organization. We had become friends, and I asked for his help with my study. He agreed and I led off with the question, "What do you think is the greatest problem confronting Chilean workers today?" Based on our earlier conversations, I fully expected him to say something like, "A lack of class consciousness prevents Chilean workers from uniting politically to improve their personal circumstances." His answer surprised me. It was "The dental problem." After I recovered I asked him, "What dental problem . . . what do you mean?" Patiently he explained that many Chilean male workers begin to lose their front teeth in their mid-thirties. This, he told me, had numerous personal consequences, ranging from not being seen as fit for employment in job lineups to difficulties making oneself attractive to women in social circumstances. "If the government could only begin a program of providing free dental plates to all citizens," he opined, "then we could all be much more productive and happy."

This was a citizen's (albeit sexist) view on an important social issue. The citizen was active in his community, a party militant, and had voted whenever he had the opportunity. Despite his political activism, given the chance to voice his concerns, he focused on an issue that was very personal and very specific. At the time of our conversation, this man's political party held Chile's presidency and commanded the largest bloc in congress, yet it was meeting increasing opposition to its political initiatives. This man had strong opinions on the issue of expansion of voting rights to the poor as well as issues of income distribution and labor rights. Nevertheless, when given an opportunity to talk about issues that affected people like himself, he chose to discuss a subject of personal import rather than an abstract political or social structural matter.

DEMOCRACY THE CONCEPT

Much of the data that are the subject of this book are similarly informed, since the respondents, like my friend, were all city dwellers. The questions that generated the data are broad-ranging and gave respondents opportunities to reveal personal concerns. They also gave the respondents the opportunity to reflect on their personal circumstances in a larger context. Their answers show both the promise and the limitations of citizen surveys for addressing abstract issues such as political culture and democracy in a particular country.

The very first question is an excellent example of the promise and limitations of such surveys: "In one word, could you tell me what democracy means to you?" Among the 1,194 Chilean respondents, 25 percent said that it meant "freedom," 18 percent "equality," 12 percent "a form of government," 10 percent "the vote," 10 percent "legality," and 8 percent "welfare." Only 25 percent of the respondents gave a response that unambiguously indicated that they felt that democracy meant they had freedom—that they were free to pursue their personal interests. The great majority of the respondents gave answers that stressed systemwide aspects of democracy, belying, I would argue, a concern that the political system might not give them adequate protection to exercise the freedom to pursue individual interests.

These one-word definitions barely capture the complexity of Western understandings of democracy. Most simply stated, democracy is commonly understood to be a system of government in which ultimate political authority is vested in the people. In a modern pluralistic democratic political system, people-vested power typically is exercised by groups or institutions through complex bargaining and compromise. Democracy is consolidated through respect for the concepts of individualism, liberty, equality, and fraternity.[1] Making these concepts concrete means that the basic task of government is to allow each individual to develop to his or her highest potential; each individual is allowed the greatest amount of freedom consistent with public order; all individuals have equal rights and opportunities; and individuals strive to cooperate to build a wholesome society.

Simple definitions hardly capture the complexity of Robert Dahl's term *polyarchy,* his name for actual political systems that attempt to approximate ideal democracy and in which governments provide the following seven institutions to their citizens:

1. Elected officials
2. Free and fair elections
3. Inclusive suffrage
4. The right to run for office
5. Freedom of expression
6. Alternative information
7. Associational autonomy[2]

Similarly, the definitions do not capture Diamond, Linz, and Lipset's more concise definition of political democracy, in which a system of government must have:

1. Meaningful and extensive *competition* among individuals and organized groups (especially political parties) for all effective positions of government power, at regular intervals, and excluding the use of force.

2. A highly inclusive level of *political participation* in the selection of leaders and policies through regular and fair elections in which no adult social group is excluded.

3. *Civil and political liberties* such as freedom of the press, freedom of expression, and freedom to form and join associations, sufficient to ensure the integrity of political competition and participation.[3]

The questions on which this analysis is based, simple as they may be, attempt to depict important aspects of Chile's 1998 political culture. While many authors (such as Knight in this volume) correctly argue that political culture characteristics can be ephemeral or trivial, with ambiguous connections to the workings of a nation's political system, few would argue that knowledge of political culture cannot help one to understand the workings of such systems' small institutions (civil society) or its big institutions (the elements of the state).

Thus, if one wishes to strengthen or deepen any or all of the aspects of Dahlian polyarchy or Diamond/Linz/Lipset democracy, knowledge of the political culture of the country in question is essential. This has been argued recently in Francis Fukuyama's popular book *The Great Disruption*[4] and in many classic works discussing how political culture influences the formal elements of a nation's political system. The way it works, in theory, is that loosely shared cultural understandings impact individual attitudes and behaviors. This, in turn, affects the various elements of the political system—the state, political society, and civil society, to use Antonio Gramsci's terms.[5] Thus, both for understanding how individuals experience their political systems and for attempting to change a given system, knowledge of the culture that influences it can be essential.

The remaining sections of this essay will first quickly review the nearly 200 years of Chile's post-independence history and will highlight the "critical junctures" that forged the political culture of Chile in 1998. I will then look at three elements of the country's political culture reflected in the survey data: division, alienation, and fear. Finally, I will discuss approaches that might help Chile's political society to deepen democracy in its political system.

THE HISTORY OF CHILEAN DEMOCRACY

Democracy, of course, can only be understood concretely in the context of particular nations' political systems, and each has its own unique history and culture. Chilean democracy is no exception. Chile gained its independence in 1810 when Spain's domination of its Latin American colonies was loosened by Napoleonic France. The war of independence in Chile, as in most of these colonies, was in reality a civil war among local factions. From independence through the 1830s the Chilean political system was disorganized and anarchic, although it moved more quickly to republican rule than other former Spanish American colonies.[6] This transition was eased by the imposing presence of some 200 close-knit Chilean Creole families who regarded themselves as nobles and who had been prominent prior to independence. Disputes between conservatives and liberals were fierce during the post-independence period, both for the office of the presidency and for the patronage it controlled. These conflicts were essentially intra-elite until the late 1850s, when a bitter dispute erupted over the authority of the Catholic Church in Chile. For the first time, formally organized political parties appeared in Chile, crystallizing (to use Lipset and Rokkan's words) around a clerical/anticlerical cleavage.[7] In response to a relatively minor incident in 1856, Catholic Archbishop Rafael Valdivieso attempted to mobilize important segments of Chile's Catholic population. At that time the Conservative Party was formed to defend the interests of the church and to protect it from state interference; the Liberal Party was formed by Catholic loyalists seeking to oppose the government of President Manuel Montt; and the Radical Party was constituted to defend secular and relatively anticlerical principals in the wake of an alliance between the Conservatives and Liberals.

This institutionalized division among three political parties was the first of three "critical junctures"[8] that formed the volatile Chilean political system, which in 1969 elected as president the Marxist Salvador Allende (overthrown in 1973 by a military coup headed by Augusto Pinochet). The two other critical junctures occurred in the 1920s and the 1950s. The former was sparked by social conflict in Chile's cities and mining communities. Between 1920 and 1932, demands by worker and middle-class groups forced Chilean party elites to respond by granting these groups increased social power. The result was the emergence of the Socialist and Communist parties on the left, with the Radical Party moving to the center of Chile's political spectrum. The third "critical juncture" was caused by the spread of popular politics to Chile's countryside, sparked by the Catholic Church's support for broadened suffrage. The result was that from 1963 onward, the Christian Democratic Party dominated the center of Chilean politics.

Even with its deeply divided, multiparty political system, up until 1973 Chile was widely described as Latin America's most stable democracy. Chileans even referred to themselves as "the English of Latin America." This was because Chile had experienced only one institutional rupture (the Civil War of 1891) in more than 150 years of independence. Despite this apparent order, the political system was profoundly divided among adherents of leftist, centrist, and conservative ideologies. This was particularly apparent in the Cold War years and was consistently evident in public opinion polls and electoral results. Pollsters Eduardo Hamuy and Carlos Huneeus, for example, reported the ideological distribution of the Chilean electorate between 1958 and 1986 (shown in table 1) in response to the questions "Do you feel closer to the right, center, or left?"[9] Data from this book's questionnaire extend that time series to the 1990s.[10]

These divisions were consistently manifested in electoral results. Between 1937 and 1973 Chile's parties of the right received less than 20 percent of the vote in congressional elections in only one year (1965, the year after they failed to field a presidential candidate for the 1964 elections); the center parties received votes ranging from 28.1 percent of the electorate in 1937 to a high of 55.6 percent in 1965; and the left vote, which was 15.4 percent in 1937, grew to 34.9 percent in 1973.[11] The volatile nature of this polariza-

TABLE 1 *Ideological Distribution of the Chilean Electorate, 1958–98* (percent)

	1958	1961	1964	1970	1973	1986	1998
Right	31.4	23.8	17.4	26.6	21.9	16.6	15.8
Center	17.8	28.2	29.0	24.2	26.8	41.2	48.7
Left	24.5	26.5	32.0	26.0	42.9	14.2	11.4
No response	26.3	21.5	21.6	23.2	8.4	28.0	24.1

Source: 1958 to 1986 data from Carlos Huneeus, *Los chilenos y la política* (Santiago: CERC, 1987). 1998 data from question 27 in this volume's appendix 2.

TABLE 2 *Results of Chile's 1958, 1964, and 1970 Presidential Elections*

	1958		1964		1970	
	Candidate	%	*Candidate*	%	*Candidate*	%
Right	Alessandri	31.2	Duran	4.9	Alessandri	34.9
Center	Bossay	15.2	Frei	55.7	Tomic	27.8
	Frei	20.5				
Left	Allende	28.6	Allende	38.6	Allende	36.2
Blank/void		1.2		.8		1.1

Source: Direccion General del Registro Electoral, Santiago, Chile, reported in Timothy R. Scully, *Rethinking the Cener: Party Politics in Nineteenth and Twentieth Century Chile* (Stanford: Stanford University Press, 1992), 164.

tion is even more evident in the results of the last three pre-coup presidential elections, in 1958, 1964, and 1970 (see table 2).

This political division, combined with the Chilean constitution of 1925 allowing the highest vote-getter to become president, meant that small shifts in voters could produce drastically different political outcomes. Thus the 1970 victory of perennial left-wing coalition candidate Salvador Allende represented a break from the right-wing and center administrations that had occupied Chile's executive throughout its previous history. The election of the Marxist Allende was accomplished with only 36.2 percent of the vote—1.3 percent more than was won by the conservative Jorge Alessandri (who, ironically, received a higher percentage of the vote in 1970 than he had in 1958, when he won the presidency) and 2.4 percent less than in Allende's own unsuccessful bid for the presidency in 1964.

The Allende government's efforts at reactivating Chile's stagnating economy, redistributing income, and taking steps to create a socialist economy met with initial success. Soon, however, the government faced strong reaction from internal and external forces whose position and privileges were threatened. Many of the government's programs were stalled by its inability to forge alliances in congress, especially with the centrist Christian Democratic Party. These efforts also were hobbled by polarizing disagreements within the president's coalition, which made efforts at compromise all the more difficult. When Allende's coalition made unprecedented gains in the 1973 off-year congressional election, the political climate became dominated by confrontation. There were political skirmishes in Chile's streets; many essential services were interrupted by sabotage or disorganization; professional groups went on strike demanding Allende's resignation; and citizens hoarded goods and mobilized on the left and right in fear of attack or civil war.

This charged climate was interrupted on September 11, 1973, by a bloody military coup that installed a junta government led by the army commander, Augusto Pinochet. While the Allende government's attempt to create a socialist economy had represented a break with Chile's political past, the actions of the Pinochet regime were far more extreme. Convinced that only fundamental change and a long period of tutelary military rule could purge Chile of what he saw as political demons, Pinochet persecuted politicians, labor leaders, students, journalists, intellectuals, and all who had been part of Allende's Popular Unity government. He particularly struck out at less privileged groups, which he saw as prime breeding grounds for Marxist politics. He rewrote Chile's constitution, designating himself president and having the new constitution approved by plebiscite in 1980. He led Chile on an economic roller coaster, restructuring the nation's economy and quickly leading it into a profound recession. In the early 1980s, adopting policies suggested by the World Bank and using University of Chicago–trained neoclassical economists to implement them, Chile began to revive its economy, with increasing growth and dampened inflation. Still, despite more than 15 years of economic progress, at the end of the twentieth century Chilean society is among the most divided in the hemisphere. One-third of the population lives in poverty despite glittering middle- and upper-class neighborhoods and urban skyscrapers.

In 1988 Chile's voters surprised Pinochet by choosing in a plebiscite to hold democratic presidential elections rather than extend his mandate for another eight years. Patricio Aylwin, a Christian Democrat and the candidate of a center-left coalition, was elected president in 1990; in 1996 Eduardo Frei, another Christian Democrat supported by the center-left, was elected to Chile's highest office. Despite the return of democratic presidential politics in Chile, the country remained "safeguarded" by a set of institutional reforms that were included in the constitution of 1980. Chief among them is a bloc of nine designated senators who, combined with the Chilean right, effectively veto any constitutional reforms. In addition, Chile's military dominates a number of the nation's key constitutionally designated bodies, including the National Security Council and the Constitutional Tribunal. The military, in turn, is safeguarded by a constitutional guarantee of 10 percent of the profits of the state copper corporation, with a minimum of $180 million per year.

Augusto Pinochet left the Chilean presidency in 1990 but continued until 1998 as commander-in-chief of the armed forces, when—according to the terms of the 1980 constitution—he took a seat in Chile's congress as "Senator for Life." His moving to the Senate reminded Chileans of the polarized politics of the past. Victims of his regime's persecution and left-wing legislators protested his transfer, since the immunity from prosecution granted Chilean senators would prevent Pinochet's actions while head of state from being judged in a Chilean court of law. While this sparked nasty exchanges with Pinochet supporters when he was installed in the Senate, even more political polarization was threatened when Spanish judge Baltazar Garzon requested that the British government extradite the Senator for Life from Britain (where he had undergone medical treatment) to Spain to be judged for crimes against Spanish citizens during his presidency. The reaction in Chile has sparked renewed confrontation. Polls indicate that Pinochet continues to have the uncompromising support of 25 percent of Chile's population, 80 percent of whom are from higher economic groups and from the military.[12] Although another poll indicates that 70 percent of the population are apathetic about Pinochet's fate, many argue that Chile is still reeling from the terror of his regime. Writer Isabel Allende, niece of its most prominent victim, describes her country as follows:

[Chile] is traumatized, like an abused child that is always expecting the next blow. The right is afraid of losing its privileges . . . The left fears the possibility of another coup and the horrific repression of the past. The Government fears the military and a polarization that would bring unrest and instability. And the rest of the people fear the truth . . . the heritage of [Pinochet is] a nation in fear. Although we have a long way to go, it is refreshing to see the beginning of the end of the reign of fear.[13]

What do the data provided by the 1,194 Chileans interviewed about democracy in July of 1998 tell us about Chile's political culture and its political system? To what extent do the data then manifest the characteristics of Chile's more than one hundred years of history, of the authoritarian regime in place from 1973 to 1990, or the change suggested by Isabel Allende? To these questions we now turn.

THE DATA

The questionnaire (presented in appendix 2 at the end of this book) data show that in July of 1998 the wounds of the politically divided Chileans continued to fester, even if they were healing. In question after question the data show a population that is divided, alienated from politics, and afraid to take political action. The questionnaire's opening item, asking for a definition of democracy in a single word, generated relatively little enthusiasm for the concept of liberty, the hallmark of a fear-free political system. The second question evoked additional alienation from politics, with only 11 percent of the respondents indicating that they thought there was "much democracy" in their country. Question 4, asking if democracy is preferable to authoritarianism, generated only a 50 percent positive response, which is especially low in the context of

Chile's relatively smooth post-1990 democratic political process and its improved economy. Based on responses such as these, I suspect that my worker-friend of 1967 would be less eager to engage in political issues today than he was 31 years ago.

POLITICAL DIVISION

While evidence of a divided polity is present in most of the questionnaire responses, a few stand out. The answers to question 27 define Chile's political topography from a left-center-right perspective. When asked to locate themselves politically, Chileans gave responses that yielded a distribution consistent with the country's past political divisions (see table 1). Although the percentage defining themselves as centrist has increased over the years, sizable portions of Chile's electorate continue to identify themselves politically as being on the left or on the right.

Chile's divided politics are further underscored by the answers to question 31, which asked, "With which political party do you most sympathize?" Only 23 percent indicated sympathy for the top party in the Chilean congress, the Christian Democratic Party; only an additional 37 percent reported sympathy for any other political party; and a whopping 40 percent reported no political party allegiance. Chile's political party system has been divided since independence. While parties have been arrayed along a left-center-right continuum, at times the division has verged on fragmentation. Both the party composition of the contemporary Chilean congress and the questionnaire data show that political division continues to be a salient feature of Chilean politics.

While political division is most easily indicated by party membership, divergences in political attitudes can show the underlying preferences that create those divisions. An important basis for the division is indicated by question 32, which asked, "What has been the principal obstacle for democracy in Chile?" No clear answer appeared in the sample, of which only 11 percent had opined that Chile has much democracy. Poverty was seen as the principal obstacle by 20 percent of the respondents; government by another 20 percent; political parties by 16 percent; lack of education by 13 percent; social passivity by 7 percent; and corruption by 6 percent. A sizable portion of the sample identified social causes for democracy's flaws—maladies to which Chile's sometimes-large state apparatus has responded with variable enthusiasm over its history. Another considerable portion saw the government and elements of the political system as the cause—motivations that have led to calls for state shrinkage in many countries, including Chile, in recent years.

Another question that reflected a component of traditional Chilean political division was question 11, which asked, "Which is most important: maintaining order, increasing political participation, combating inflation, or protecting freedom of expression?" Maintaining order was the preference of 38 percent of the respondents, with 30 percent choosing political participation and 15 percent choosing each of the other alternatives. The divisions reflected in these answers, I would argue, derive directly from the 180 years of post-independence history that formed Chile's 1998 political culture.

POLITICAL ALIENATION

That a sizable portion of the Chilean electorate has been alienated from politics is reflected in table 1. With the exception of 1973, the last year of the Allende presidency, more than 20 percent of the population consistently refused to identify their political tendency as left, center, or right. In some other countries, such responses might rather indicate ignorance or, at most, indifference. However, most "non-identifiers" I knew in 1967 in La Cisterna were very aware of the political alternatives and actively sought ways not to be involved, often under strong pressure from friends and neighbors.

More telling, however, are three of the questionnaire's items that probe attitudes about elements of Chile's political system. In response to question 31, which asked, "With which political party do you most sympathize?" 40 percent of the respondents answered "none." In response to question 33, which asked, "How important is politics?" only 19 percent indicated that it was very important, and 14 percent indicated that it was of no importance at all. In response to question 35, which asked, "What party would you vote for if there were elections today?" 29 percent indicated that they would not vote. These large percentages of the sample reporting disdain or indifference toward politics in Chile indicate that, even though the country has a long history of electoral politics—a history that has been successfully revived for nearly 10 years—in 1998 many Chilean citizens were alienated from national politics.

This alienation is also reflected in responses to question 36, which measured the amount of trust individuals had in a range of national institutions. In general, public institutions associated with politics were least trusted, and private institutions were the most trusted. The most trusted institution was the family, with 94 percent of the sample reporting much or some trust. It was followed by, in order, schools (89 percent), the church (80), small business (73), television (65), the police (61), the press (57), the army (53), the executive branch of government (51), congress (43), unions (41), the courts (37), and political parties (27). While this is a familiar pattern in other countries, including the two others analyzed in this volume—Costa Rica and Mexico—it reflects the institutional preferential underpinnings of the large proportion of Chileans who are alienated from national politics. This Chilean focus on things other than politics is also reflected in question 13, in which respondents were asked whether it is more important for democracy to improve or for the economy to improve. Improving the economy was chosen by 68 percent of the sample; only 13 percent said improving democracy, with another 13 percent choosing both. The level of disappointment with Chilean democracy was indicated by responses to question 7, in which 55 percent of the sample indicated that they were not satisfied with the functioning of democracy in Chile and another 8 percent refused to answer the question.

That such a large portion of Chile's population is disappointed with and alienated from the functioning of its political system is not surprising in the context of the country's political history. The current government far from satisfies the traditional ideals of Chile's right or left, both of which continue to have sizable bases of support. The militance of partisans at both political extremes has further alienated many Chileans from democratic politics, as has the inability of the political system to deal with the nation's persistent poverty and other social problems. Furthermore, despite the relative stability of Chile's political party system and the relative strength of its economy, the performance through 1998 fell short of the hopes some had for a redemocratized political system.

FEAR OF POLITICAL INVOLVEMENT

In advanced industrial societies, fear is largely seen as an individual, personal emotion. Citizens of countries such as the United States have not directly experienced generalized violence, the erosion of legal protections and public values, or the loss of collective or even primary social connections. Much of Chile's monied elite felt they had such experiences during the presidency of Salvador Allende, and Allende's supporters and many of Chile's poor felt similarly abused as a result of the coup that brought Augusto Pinochet to power. The personal result of such experience is uncertainty, insecurity, and self-doubt, as individuals cannot predict the consequences of social action when public authority is arbitrarily and brutishly exercised.[14]

It is not surprising that a residue of a culture of fear could exist in 1998 Chile, less than 10 years after the return to democratic rule. While items focusing on fear of political involvement were not an explicit part of the questionnaire upon which this analysis is based, evidence of it is present in a number of responses. The meager focus on liberty (25 percent) in question 1 when respondents were asked to define democracy can be seen as fear of the unpredictable consequences of individual action in Chilean politics and a focus on other values, such as equality, legality, and stability.

Three questions focusing on political institutions reflect a fear of the consequences of political competition in Chile. Only 35 percent of the sample saw any value in Chile's president "at times being from one party and at times another" (question 15). Only 31 percent saw a value in "the president of the republic being from one party and the majority of congress from another" (question 19). Only 18 percent saw a value in a balance of power between Chile's president and its congress, with 28 percent preferring a more powerful congress and an overwhelming 50 percent in favor of a more powerful presidency.

Fear of consequences of actions by the press was evident in answers to question 9. Sixty-nine percent of the respondents indicated that the media should restrict its powers of investigation and particularly not examine details of individuals' private lives. Finally, when asked (in question 29) whether people in general can be trusted, 76 percent of the sample responded in the negative.

While these questions did not directly probe the existence of a culture of fear in Chilean politics, the responses indicate clear concerns about the consequences of political instability, of journalistic investigation, and of the level of trust Chileans have in other citizens. Combating such fear, whatever its source, is essential for political leaders and others who might hope for greater involvement of Chilean citizens in their nation's politics, consistent with democratic ideals.

MANAGING CHILEAN DEMOCRACY

Will Chile's political system be able to build trust among the nation's various political groups? General Pinochet's hope that years of military control would rid the country of its political divisions does not seem to have been fulfilled. The survey data show that, as individuals, Chile's citizens continue to be divided, and a sizable proportion are fearful of and alienated from politics. While some small new political parties have emerged, and some political interests have assumed new names (the parties of the right are no longer named "Conservative," "Liberal," or even "National"), the elements of Allende's Popular Unity coalition still make up the left, the Christian Democratic Party still occupies the center, and the parties of the right command significant loyalties. As the data reported in table 1 indicate, political self-identification in 1998 was not that much different from that of pre-coup 1973. Different is the fact that the political center and much of the political left have, since 1990, formed a broad coalition that has been able to prevent the political right, including Pinochet partisans, from controlling Chile's executive branch. Whether this broad coalition can hold or whether it will dissolve due to turmoil surrounding Pinochet's status or for some other reason is a key question for Chile's divided and fearful polity. This is a very real question, since the individual nominated in 1999 as the coalition presidential candidate, Ricardo Lagos, is a Socialist. Questions have been raised about whether members of Chile's largest party, the Christian Democrats, could accept a member of a party of the left to lead their coalition or whether this would cause some center-right voters to abandon the coalition and vote for the candidate of the right.

While these are important questions, scholar-analysts have suggested that such political maneuvering is trivial compared with the basic structural change needed to stabilize democracy in Chile. Timothy R. Scully argues that Chile's political system was unstable and divided after World War II because the party occupying the center (the Christian Democrats) was "programmatic" rather than "positional." Scully describes a programmatic center as having a specific program in between right and left on which it may not be willing to compromise; he describes a positional center as viewing its role as "winning control of the government and then keeping it."[15] He attributes the extraordinary longevity and stability of the Chilean party system to the crucial role of political broker played by a positional center made up largely of the Liberals and then the Radicals until the late 1950s. Since the long-standing tripartite division of Chile's electorate has apparently survived Pinochet's attempts to restructure the party system, Scully suggests that the trauma of military rule may have caused Chile's politicians to "reappraise both the value and the very fragility of the give and take required of democracy."[16] The role of the Christian Democratic Party in the broad coalition in the two post-Pinochet elections and the terms of the Christian Democratic presidents suggest that a solution may have been found for managing Chile's divisions by the political parties themselves.

For Arturo Valenzuela, changing the nature of Chile's political center would likely not be sufficient to stabilize Chilean democracy.[17] Valenzuela argues that institutional capacities for political accommodation among Chile's three strong political currents must be strengthened in order "to bridge the centrifugal realities of Chilean politics and to achieve a minimum consensus on the rules of the game and the policies required to govern the country."[18] Valenzuela points out that Chile has experienced a "continuous crisis of presidentialism," with all elected Chilean presidents since the 1920s chosen by minorities or fragile coalitions and experiencing great difficulty governing the country. He also suggests that the success of the post-Pinochet governments is based on cooperation fueled by fear of "authoritarian reversal."

The institutional change that Valenzuela recommends for Chile is the transformation of its political system from presidential to parliamentary democracy. He states that it would diffuse the enormous pressures for structuring high-stakes coalitions around a winner-take-all presidential option, eliminate the paralyzing stalemate and confrontation that have characterized executive-legislative relations in twentieth-century Chile, and contribute to the further moderation of Chilean politics. Having the chief executive elected by parliament, he argues, would encourage centrist tendencies because a coalition would have to be formed and sustained among the legislators to select and maintain the executive in office. The need to maintain this coalition would prevent the executive from unilaterally adopting political strategies supported by limited political groups. This would be the case because such moves would require broad support, thus strengthening moderate tendencies of both the right and the left. Furthermore, Valenzuela suggests that members of congress faced with the possibility of losing their seats in a new election would have an added incentive to find ways to structure working coalitions.

DEMOCRACY IN CHILE: CONCLUSIONS

Democracy in Chile, or in any other country, is both an individual and a collective phenomenon. The questionnaire whose results are presented above and in an appendix to this book describes a divided political culture with substantial political alienation. A review of Chile's political history shows that this division has existed for nearly 200 years and that political participation was substantially limited over much of that history. The questionnaire results also show a phenomenon that is relatively new to Chile: political fear. This fear was probably generated by the extreme trauma experienced by Chileans of all political persuasions during the turbulent Allende years and then during the extremely repressive government headed by Augusto Pinochet.

A key question is whether this fear can be exorcised and whether the alienation and division can be managed. Chile's history points to a time when the divisions were managed by what Scully would call a "positional" political center. The amount of time required to heal Chile's political wounds is difficult to estimate. And time, as has been seen in late-twentieth-century Yugoslavia and elsewhere, may not be enough, because willful leaders can reopen wounds for particular purposes. More structural institutional change such as that suggested by Arturo Valenzuela may offer promise for creating the stabilizing and consensus-building mechanisms required to further consolidate and deepen Chilean democracy.

Part VI

Is Culture a False Variable in Democratic Theorizing?

A Doubter's View

Chapter 12

Polls, Political Culture, and Democracy
A Heretical Historical Look

Alan Knight

I

I am not a political scientist, still less a psychologist, so my contribution to this volume is untypical. I will try to bring to bear my historical knowledge of Mexico, commenting—sometimes from a methodologically inexpert stance—on the several case studies and the survey data that inform them. The common theme we are addressing is Mexican political culture and its relationship to democratization. Both concepts, as I shall suggest, are problematic, but "political culture" is especially problematic. I admit to having used it and I would not wish to deny its occasional utility, so long as it is used in quasi-behavioral terms (whereby "political culture" becomes a descriptive term, a shorthand summation of the way in which politics is "done" in certain countries, regions, or sectors).[1] But I also think it is vague, easily overworked, and often unable to carry the explanatory weight that is placed upon it. This generalization, incidentally, is just as valid for historiography as it is for political science. Indeed, given the current vogue for the "new cultural history," which often makes a virtue of semantic vagueness and methodological bumbling, it is likely that history is much more culpable than political science.

This does not prevent "culture" from being extensively used. (Is there any rule that says that conceptual use reflects conceptual utility? I would doubt it. The survival of the fittest [concept] is a less ruthless and certain process in the social sciences than in the natural sciences.) Distinguished Mexican thinkers—Paz, Fuentes, Ramos (who is in turn cited by Kahl)—have explored, in somewhat navel-gazing fashion, the supposed psyche or culture of their compatriots.[2] By way of example: according to Paz, Mexicans display a macho "willingness to contemplate death," a "fondness for self-destruction," and a "servility towards the strong . . . and devotion to personalities rather than to principles."[3] Outsiders have seen Latin America as possessing a common culture, indelibly stamped by its Iberian, Catholic, corporatist, and sometimes indigenous past.[4] This common past, however, is shared by countries as historically diverse as Argentina and Costa Rica, Uruguay and Mexico.[5] Even neighboring countries of comparable size display quite different historical trajectories: Costa Rica and Guatemala, Deborah Yashar observes, "represent Latin America's most divergent regimes"; Costa Rica and Nicaragua, in the words of Booth and Seligson, "have long been virtually opposite in regime types."[6] Indeed, the plot thickens when we learn that, on a scale that purports to measure preference for democracy over other systems, Panama comes close on Costa Rica's heels (77.5 percent as against 84.5 percent): a conclusion that, to say the least, is historically counterintuitive.[7]

As regards Mexico, the powerful Mexican president has been seen as a reincarnation of the Mexican *tlatoani,* notwithstanding the long hiatus of the colony (when, especially c. 1521–c. 1750, centralized authority was constrained); the post-independence hiatus from 1821 to 1876, when presidents came and went in bewildering and ineffectual succession; and the short hiatus of the Maximato (1928–34). So the Aztec legacy presumably remained dormant for the best part of 400 years until it finally welled up from the Mexican psyche—the racial unconscious?—and gave us the PRI. (Readers who suspect that my "Mexican psyche/racial unconscious" is an outdated straw man might consult Fuentes, who ponders the country's "deep subconscious decision" to maintain multiple historical levels, whatever that might mean.)[8] I do not deny that certain "colonial legacies" are significant for postcolonial Latin America: specifically, a distinctive land tenure system and an ethnically stratified society.[9] But even these "legacies" varied greatly from place to place, and were capable of radical transformation in the years after independence.

An additional factor deserves preliminary mention: "from place to place" need not imply national causality or homogeneity. Survey data are often presented in national terms, and, indeed, nationality appears to be a key predictor of respondents' answers, therefore of presumed cultural characteristics: it is a "striking finding" that "once one takes out all the other impacts of demographic variables and attitudes, what matters most is that one is a Costa Rican or a Chilean or a Mexican."[10] Insofar as this finding relates to policy preferences (roughly, public as against private provision of services), this is both significant and convincing. Government policies in respect of services are implemented nationally, hence have impacts throughout the national territory, and they may well contrast with comparable policies and impacts in other national territories. British and American attitudes toward health provision would no doubt vary in similar fashion. Does this reflect "cultural" differences, especially "cultural" difference with respect to democracy? Not necessarily. My point is not just that public opinion about certain national policies can be genuinely and distinctively national (i.e., can demarcate Mexicans from Chileans), without that telling us much about contrasting political cultures; it is also that the use of national as against subnational units may be arbitrary and at times unhelpful.

For one thing, some countries are more homogeneous than others: Costa Rica has historically displayed an ethnic, political, and cultural homogeneity that—even if in some respects it is patently subjective, "discursive," and even unreal—generates a certain homogeneity of response.[11] One key element has been the *ticos'* calculated indifference to the black Atlantic coast.[12] In that sense, Costa Rica can be said to have a relatively homogeneous (if somewhat contrived) political culture. The same cannot be said of Mexico, whose size, complexity, regional and ethnic differentiation, and extreme social stratification—stressed by Humboldt in the 1800s and still apparent today—make the notion of a common culture hard to sustain.[13] Shared responses to national policies are one thing: whether it is privatization in the 1980s, agrarian reform in the 1930s, or anticlericalism in the 1920s, Mexicans from Tijuana to Tapachula had to respond to government initiatives, hence they shared a common political fate as Mexicans under a Mexican government. No doubt it would have been possible—if a little dangerous—to collect survey data relating to agrarian reform and anticlericalism, and to calibrate who favored what. But if we are seeking to understand values, attitudes, or mentalities, we would have to disaggregate, down to the regional, municipal, and even local level. We know that Mexican communities have, over the long term, displayed contrasting political allegiances; we might, if we wished, consider these to be contrasting "(micro-) political cultures."[14] Often, such micropolitical cultures feed on dyadic antagonisms, which link neighboring communities in ancient rivalries; furthermore, while these rivalries are often "value-free" (they are Hobbesian conflicts over power and resources, lacking ideological consistency), some do display a consistent radical/conservative inflection: radical Juchitán against conservative Tehuantepec; Mazamitla against San José de Gracia; Naranja against Cherán.[15]

Broadly consistent allegiances can also be discerned at the regional level, although they are subject to interesting—and often little-understood—processes of transformation. In 1810 the Bajío was the focus of popular protest, while central Mexico (including

Morelos) was relatively quiet; a century later, with the Revolution, the roles were reversed. In the generation after independence, liberal mobilization was strongest in the "liberal crescent" that stretched from Guerrero through Jalisco to Zacatecas;[16] a century later, this region would nurture the Cristero rebellion against the anticlerical state. Chihuahua, liberal and revolutionary in the Revolution, became a bastion of the PAN in the 1980s (though it has since returned to the PRIísta fold: is Chihuahua becoming the classic "swing" state?). Some analysts would also posit a regional/ethnic breakdown: "unlike their Mixe neighbors who have evolved more authoritarian structures and who in recent times have frequently reported to caciques (political bosses), the Zapotec are intensely egalitarian about governance."[17]

Note that none of these allegiances or transformations has anything to do with ineluctable "modernizing" trends, as I understand them. We are not dealing with uni-linear "modernization," but with processes of historical change—regional, municipal, and local—that are amenable to particular explanations, related especially to distinct historical experiences: wars, invasions, revolts, land disputes, local rivalries, center-periphery tensions, clerical ambitions, industrialization, unionization, migration, ethnic conflicts. If recognizable "political cultures" can be discerned, recent historical research would suggest that they have to be discerned from the bottom up. Even supposedly homogenous ("Catholic-clerical") regions such as Jalisco, Michoacán, or the Bajío demand careful disaggregation and reveal sharp subregional contrasts.[18] As a result, the amalgamation of all these experiences, outcomes, and allegiances into a supposedly common Mexican national culture—and this would be true for 1810, 1910, or even 2010—seems to be highly problematic. Chihuahua is not Chiapas and never has been. Within Chiapas, San Cristóbal and Tuxtla Gutiérrez are both different and antagonistic. The lowest common denominator of any broad, encompassing national formula would be bathetic: it might distinguish the great amalgam of "Mexico" from the yet greater amalgam of, say, "the United States"; but in doing so, it would tend either to reiterate the obvious (e.g., Mexicans distrust their police more than Americans do) or to generate vague and speculative generalizations not far removed from the poetics of Octavio Paz (levels of "trust" are low in Mexico; Mexico is a macho culture; Mexico is more violent, etc.). What Geertz called "wall-sized culturescapes of the nation" are, in most cases, crude caricatures, and certainly not careful blueprints that can serve as a guide to understanding.[19]

I shall develop some of these points as I proceed: this initial demarche is designed to question the notion of a meaningful national culture (in particular, a national culture subject to shared processes of transformation, perhaps related to "modernization"), as opposed to a shifting, variegated, mosaic "culture" whose shifts may have little to do with modernization, and whose variegation is such that the search for useful, common, explanatory features proves frustrating and certainly offers no firm foundation for useful generalization, still less prediction.

II

If we are to relate culture to democratization, we need some agreement on what these terms mean. Democratization is somewhat more straightforward (though I am aware it is presumptuous of me to wade into definitional discussions that will be meat and drink to most of my colleagues in this collection). I take it that our concern is with procedural liberal democracy, rather than participatory, workers' or other sui generis forms of "democracy." (The point is relevant in the Mexican context, given the recurrence of such qualified forms, which led Enrique Krauze to call for a "democracy without adjectives.")[20] In particular, we may wish to conceptualize liberal democracy in Dahlian terms, thus embracing several facets: fair, free, and regular elections; mass participation and voter "efficacy"; free expression and association, backed by the rule of law.[21]

Two initial points may be worth noting: first, economic redistribution and well-being do not figure in this definition. Hence, the notion that democracy is intrinsically bound up with equality or *bienestar social* (social welfare) is misconceived. Respondents who infer as much have misunderstood democracy; and it may be questioned whether their "culture" (assuming one wishes to frame the argument in these terms) is, for this reason, genuinely democratic. (We may, of course, wish to speculate about the causal relationship that links democracy, thus defined in Dahlian/procedural terms, and economic development; this raises the familiar question of whether functioning liberal democracy requires—or at least closely correlates with—relatively rich, literate industrial societies.[22] But this does not, of course, imply an economic dimension to our definition of democracy. Democracy may benefit from economic development, but democracy need not involve economic development.)

Second, the several facets mentioned above are not always mutually supportive; indeed, they may pull in different directions. There is suggestive evidence that, in contemporary Mexico, increased participation and electoral competition have been accompanied by greater political violence (especially violence directed against opposition activists and journalists), hence a deterioration in respect for civil rights—which was far from perfect anyway.[23] "Have been accompanied by" is, of course, an evasive formulation, which suggests correlation but not necessarily causality. If—as seems quite probable—a causal link is involved, it most likely involves official or quasi-official repression of an ebullient opposition.[24] However, moves toward mass democracy and majoritarian rule can also generate conflict and the derogation of rights within civil society. It is a common dilemma of democracy—one that greatly exercised nineteenth-century liberal minds—that, as mass participation and mass democracy expand, so minority rights may be jeopardized.[25] Conversely, minority rights may be better protected in limited or partial democracies—in states (such as Austria-Hungary or Argentina c. 1900) that were to a degree liberal, but not fully democratic. In oligarchic Argentina, elections were narrow and fraudulent, but a fair measure of free speech and legal protection prevailed. Such cases may be anomalous, perhaps short-lived. But they are not uncommon. If we address the case of contemporary Mexico, we can certainly discern increased electoral participation and pluralism, hence more meaningful elections. But the rule of law still looks shaky. (Is it shakier than it was during the heyday of the Pax PRIísta in the 1960s? I am not sure; nor, it seems, are experts.)[26] Political violence certainly appears to be widespread and threatening: consider Chiapas, the EPR (Ejército Popular Revolucionario), high-level political assassinations, narcopolitical violence, and the fate of opposition activists and journalists already mentioned.

If "democracy" is a well-theorized and manageable concept, the same cannot be said of "culture." In one broad and scientific sense, the definition is straightforward: "people ache to believe that we human beings are vastly different from all other species—and they are right! We are the only species that has an extra medium of design preservation and design communication: culture."[27] In other words, we are not dependent on genetic transmission of information; language, in particular, makes possible the accumulation of information, hence the evolution and transmission of acquired characteristics, across generations. Though precise, this definition of "culture" is very broad; Kluckhohn supposedly produced 11 subdefinitions or glosses in 27 pages.[28] Hence social scientists—and others—make further distinctions: "high" and "low" culture;[29] "political," "religious," "material," "national" culture, etc. As I have already suggested, the notion of a national political culture—a set of beliefs, attitudes, and practices characteristic of a given country, such as Mexico—easily risks becoming a dangerously vague reification. Are there meaningful commonalties that link *regiomontanos, tapatíos,* and *yucatecos*—and that distinguish them, taken together, from Guatemalans, gringos, or *ticos?* In other words, is there "something out there" that, given the right methodology, we can "get at" (which being the case, our goal is to find the right methodology)? Or is the "something-out-there" a chimera, hence no basis for making meaningful explanations of politics?

We should recall that social scientists of the past have wasted a good deal of time and effort—and, sometimes, generated a good deal of grief and prejudice along the way—by imputing "racial" characteristics, which are now generally accepted to be mythical, or "national characteristics," which are not much better.[30] Hobbes lampooned scholastics who believed that the world consisted of "accidents" inhering in mysterious "quiddities"; we have to decide whether "political culture" is a quiddity, a false reification, or, rather, a "true" reflection of the world, which can be grasped and in turn used to aid our understanding of the process of democratization. (I have already made clear that I do not consider "democracy" to be a false reification or quiddity.)

My tentative answer to this question is that "culture"—specifically, "political culture"—is, at best, a grab bag of practices, opinions, and allegiances that, in the great majority of cases, needs to be unpacked if it is to be of any explanatory use. Invocations of "political culture" as a cause, an explanation, a primum mobile, are nearly always hollow and unconvincing, especially if these are pitched at the national level.[31] For, at best, "political culture" is an aggregative and descriptive concept; as Ernest Gellner put it, "culture is a shorthand term rather than a real explanation."[32] Often, it aggregates too much, hence needs to be disaggregated, by time, place, and social group. And by virtue of being descriptive, it cannot really explain political change. To say that an individual, group, or regime behaves in such and such a way because of their "political culture" is about as useful as Aristotle's explanation of gravity: things fall because it is in their nature to fall.

By way of disaggregation, it is worth noting that political culture has been defined as embracing the "subjective propensities, actual behavior, and the framework within which behavior takes place."[33] Now, "actual behavior" arguably falls within the realm of political and historical narrative, broadly defined. An account of the 1988 or 1994 elections that describes how and why Mexicans voted the way they did may help us understand Mexican "political behavior," but such a narrative need make no reference to "political culture" by way of explanation. Polls that mapped voting intentions, or that sought to understand how intentions were affected—by PRONASOL (National Solidarity Program), or the 1994 televised debate, or the *voto miedo* (the "fear vote")—are valid aids to narrative explanation that do not need to fall back on covering laws derived from political culture. To explain the (electoral) success of PRONASOL does not require a general affirmation of Mexican susceptibility to populism or clientelism; in other words, "subjective propensities" need not be invoked. Similarly, intelligent and well-crafted questionnaires can (I think) probe the phenomenon of the *voto miedo*, or voters' perceptions of electoral transparency, without the questioner having to propose an underlying Mexican propensity to fear, risk aversion, conservatism, or any other inherent attribute.[34]

Similarly, we can explore the "framework within which behavior takes place" by analyzing either formal politico-constitutional institutions or informal but patterned practices. Electoral laws are relevant in the first instance, *caciquismo* (political bossism) in the second. Changes in electoral law clearly affect political behavior—making it easier, for example, for opposition parties to gain registration and representation. *Caciquismo* is a durable phenomenon, which follows recognizable patterns, including, I would suggest, multitiered hierarchies from the local up to the national level.[35] Again, no "cultural" imputation is required to explain *caciquismo*. Mexicans may be familiar with the phenomenon—as they are familiar with tortillas and tequila—but it would be wrong to "explain" *caciquismo* in terms of some deeply rooted "subjective propensity" toward patrimonialism or boss politics. For where would that propensity reside, and how could it be isolated or investigated? And—a more practical question—how could it be extirpated? *Caciquismo*, in my view, derives from particular political, sectoral, class, and ethnic interests: that is where both research and reform should be focused.

Some would say that polls can indeed isolate and investigate "subjective propensities"—or, as some prefer, "orientations to action."[36] In my view, that depends a good deal on what is meant by "subjective propensities" or "orientations to action." The sort that are meant to underlie "political culture" are, in my view, elusive. Phenomenologically speaking (excuse my pretension), polls are brief verbal exchanges of fragmentary information.[37] Sometimes the information they yield is specific, concrete, and falsifiable. For example, if pollsters ask about voting intentions on the eve of an election, they are seeking specific information—how an individual will act in one narrow particular in the very near future. There are still problems and imponderables: is the sample appropriate, is the question correctly framed, is the respondent truthful? (They may "lie" for several reasons, of course: out of fear, misunderstanding, a desire to please—hence the "social desirability distortion."[38] I return to these questions later.) However, I am persuaded that such polls, when properly conducted, can be quite accurate and useful. Above all, they are falsifiable: if the actual election result mirrors the latest poll, this would seem to be strong (if not incontrovertible) evidence that the poll was accurate.

But a voting intention is not a "subjective propensity" or "orientation to action" of any great depth or duration. It may depend on short-term factors (in the case of floating voters). It is certainly not a causal explanation of anything (beyond the immediate election result). Of itself, it does not tell us why a given individual is going to vote PRI or PAN or PRD. It is a narrow, technical piece of descriptive information, a kind of min-imal political byte. Broader subjective propensities, of the kind that supposedly under-pin—or constitute—"political culture," are another matter. Opinions about democra-cy, levels of interpersonal trust, left-right ideological placement, or attitudes toward illegal, corrupt, or immoral behavior are much more fluid, nonspecific, and nonfalsifi-able. For example: why do 19 percent of Costa Ricans classify themselves as extremely right-wing, compared to only 3 percent of Mexicans?[39] Why, according to a different (1986) poll, do 35 percent of Mexicans consider themselves right-wing?[40] What—excuse more pretension—is the ontological status of such findings, which take one-off answers to complex quasi-philosophical questions (questions defying straightforward answers; compare "I will vote PRI/PAN/PRD tomorrow") and which optimistically assume a remarkable degree of common information and understanding about con-cepts ("left-wing/right-wing") that have baffled generations of scholars. Conclusions built upon such data risk being misleading, or irrelevant, or sometimes trivial.

Before presenting this critique in more detail, let me acknowledge some conclusions of the survey in question that seem to me to be valid, if unsurprising. Mexicans appear to be twice as concerned about inflation as Chileans or Costa Ricans.[41] This seems emi-nently plausible, given Mexico's recent economic history. (Mexico's more distant eco-nomic history might also be a factor: attempts have been made to establish how far memories of revolutionary violence still count in Mexican politics;[42] and, since Mexico also experienced a devastating revolutionary hyperinflation,[43] that experience, too, could have left a lasting legacy. However, it did not deter the administrations of the 1970s from pursuing inflationary policies.) The historical legacy of inflation is apparent in other contexts (Germany, perhaps Argentina); the statistical difference between Mexico and Chile/Costa Rica is striking; and "inflation" is a fairly straightforward con-cept, as culturally neutral as money itself. More speculatively, we might hypothesize that the electoral success of the PRI in 1994 (like that of Argentina's PJ in the same year) was in some measure due to its "conquest" of inflation. But can we elevate "fear of infla-tion" to the level of a keystone of national political culture? Not, I think, unless it dis-plays a distinct durability, linked to explanatory power. After all, there are plenty of short-term attitudes, moods, or opinions, the product of passing circumstances, which we would not wish to turn into keystones of "national political culture." Mexicans became very engaged with domestic Spanish politics between 1936 and 1939, but that engagement was a transient—and perfectly logical—phenomenon, produced by the Spanish civil war, which resonated with contemporary Mexican experience. Aligning oneself with Spanish political currents did not, however, become an enduring feature of Mexican political culture.[44] Fear of inflation may endure and may aspire to "keystone" status (as, perhaps, it enjoys in modern Germany), but I suspect it is too early to say.

A more durable finding, which endorses Almond and Verba's research of more than a generation ago, is Mexican distrust of the police.[45] This benefits from being an apparently long-standing attitude; it contrasts with the Chilean data (Chileans seem to rate their police about twice as highly as Mexicans); and it offers a suggestive comparison with other Mexican institutions. Where the gap is wide—compare the police's 33 percent with the Church's 77 percent—the message seems clear. It is not a very surprising or counterintuitive message (the only surprising or counterintuitive thing is that the police score as high as 33 percent: previous surveys have put the police as low as 12 percent).[46] Furthermore, as I shall mention shortly, the connection of both this finding and the fear of inflation to democratic culture seems moot. After all, one can fear inflation, or distrust the police, whether one is a dedicated democrat or an extreme authoritarian, of right or left. So while the finding may be valid, it is somewhat tangential to the main issue. I think it is also relevant to consider why this finding—like fear of inflation—seems to hold. The police, again, are a recognizable—and increasingly ubiquitous—presence. They are not ethereal values or vague intentions. Many respondents no doubt have some personal experience on which to draw. Vox populi readily discusses the police (certainly it does in the DF). As an historian with some (rather indirect) familiarity with oral inquiry, I would place greater faith in responses concerning the police than, say, general answers concerning levels and definitions of democracy. And this outcome is clearly related to the role of the police in society: they occupy a recognizable niche, they elicit certain clear, patterned responses, and respondents know what they are talking about, sometimes from bitter experience.

III

Let me now turn to those more general questions and answers, which are at the heart of the inquiry. What conclusions can be drawn from questions relating to democracy and elections? Do they entitle us to construct a "Mexican political culture"? And would such a construction help us to understand Mexico's recent political past—and, perhaps, Mexico's immediate political future? I should like to raise five related questions, some of which have already been anticipated. These can be summed up as indexicality; veracity; rote responses (or the "public transcript"); explanatory categories (a large catch-all of queries); and political context.

(1) First, there is the tricky question of "indexicality."[47] Can concepts be bandied about in different linguistic and cultural contexts without severe risk of distortion and misapprehension? This is not just a question of language and translation. We all know that many words do not easily translate; sometimes the lack of a straightforward translation suggests a major conceptual gap. Indeed, there is a fundamental paradox here: the notion of distinct (national) political cultures presupposes a large degree of cultural relativism. Different nations have different political cultures—even when they share a common language, more or less. British and U.S. political cultures differ, as do Mexican and Costa Rican, not to mention French and Haitian. Concepts may carry quite different connotations in different "cultures"—that is why they are different cultures. Yet cross-national polls presuppose a common conceptual currency. For example: what is "corrupt" in one time or place may not be "corrupt" elsewhere. Running a red light in Mexico may be winked at, while in Chile it is censured. (The relevance of this example to democracy seems to me to be scant, but that is a different point.) To conclude from this example that Mexicans are therefore less attached to legality—in some underlying, attitudinal way—seems to me very dubious. As Seligson rightly points out, it may just be that Chilean traffic police are more alert, numerous, or efficient, hence the sanctions for running a red light are more compelling.[48] The difference could be purely behavioral, rather than attitudinal: the right analogy would be Pavlov's dogs, rather than Rousseau's virtuous citizens.

(2) Another paradox arises if we consider the veracity of responses. As I have already suggested, when the question concerns imminent voting, the answers can to a degree be corroborated by subsequent "real" events—the actual election results. In broad attitudinal questions, there is no such check. The replies are nonfalsifiable. True, different questionnaires can be conducted and compared. If they contrast, the easy conclusion is that change has taken place over time. If they closely match one another, they seem to corroborate, and suggest an enduring cultural trait. Thus, Mexican suspicion of the police is something of a constant (as it is in "real" life; that I readily concede). But what of Mexican suspicion of pollsters? The question was not put. (Has it ever been? It would, of course, get us uncomfortably close to the paradox of the Cretan who affirmed that all Cretans are liars . . .) But if, as the data suggest, Mexicans live in a culture in which levels of mistrust are high, would that mistrust not extend to pollsters? Newspapers, it seems, are trusted even less than the police (29 percent compared to 33 percent).[49] I should add, in passing, that I have a specific query about that finding, which is interestingly counterintuitive, given the supposed growth of a more pluralist

and investigative press in Mexico. The figure may reflect the surprisingly low percentage of Mexicans who say they get their news from the press: a mere 14 percent (although other polls give a quite different—and much higher—figure).[50] Far from familiarity breeding contempt, indifference to the print media may translate into "mistrust"; or, perhaps, though less likely, "mistrust" of the press may deter potential readers. Either way, we have a large non-newspaper-reading public and a high degree of mistrust of the press. If the analogy holds at all, we might infer a high level of mistrust of polls and pollsters as well. So what grounds are there for assuming that replies are "honest"?

By questioning "honesty," I do not mean to equate Mexicans with Cretans. Misrepresentation may derive from several causes. One—"indexicality"—has been mentioned. Mexicans may understand certain terms—"corrupt," "happy," "smart," "how much"—in ways that are not commensurate, either with each other, or with other "cultures." But concepts such as "democracy" (as opposed to "inflation" or "the police") are particularly open to misinterpretation. We have seen that a large proportion of Mexicans define democracy in terms of equality or *bienestar social* (the latter being President Zedillo's electoral catchphrase, of course. Had "solidarity" been on offer during 1990–94, it, too, might have figured as a definitional component). A more subtle confusion also creeps in: Costa Ricans define democracy in terms of "liberty" (for which they get a pat on the back). But the relationship of "liberty" to "democracy" is, as already mentioned, a thorny question. Some electorally democratic regimes have infringed civil liberties (the U.S. has an interesting track record, from Jim Crow through Joe McCarthy); some not very democratic regimes have respected civil liberties (Britain, pre-1832; Austria-Hungary, c. 1900). Mexico, we have seen, seems to have become more democratic, yet possibly more illiberal, in recent years.

(3) Why do *ticos* stress liberty, while Mexicans persist in muddying the waters with equality and *bienestar social?* Because they form part of familiar discourses.[51] Respondents give answers that they have learned at home, in school, in *ejido* or *sindicato,* or from the media (radio and television rather than the press, it would seem). Does this not form part of an enduring political culture, whose existence I am questioning? Possibly, but not necessarily. It is one thing to record familiar answers spontaneously given in response to rather vague attitudinal questions; it is another to assume that these answers well up from some deep cultural source and contain real explanatory power. Some of the answers may be ephemeral catchphrases (e.g., *bienestar social*). Some may be tropes from familiar "public transcripts"—that is, the conventional discourse that

regimes habitually churn out and that petitioners (or, in this case, respondents) habitually use in their dealings with officialdom, or those in authority more generally.[52] Camp
refers to the "social desirability distortion," which may induce people to lie about their
voting intentions. If such a straightforward untruth can be elicited on the grounds of
"social desirability," should we not expect that respondents confronted with vague
questions concerning the nature or degree of democracy might not give the reply they
consider to be most appropriate, reasonable, or politically correct? (And right now
democracy is definitely politically correct.) Theoretical questions concerning, say, tolerance are much less likely to reveal real attitudes or proclivities than the sharp spur of
practical experience: it is when the Pentecostals move in next door that tolerance is
really put to the test.[53] The best test of the truth and durability of professed opinions
concerning democracy would be to rerun the questionnaire in circumstances of revolutionary upheaval, coup, or regime change (a point I mention below). For example, how
would Chilean attitudes to democracy have scored in 1970, 1973, and at points thereafter? Is the 50 percent preferability of democracy registered by Chileans—the same
figure, incidentally, as the Mexicans, despite the very different political histories of the
two countries—a bedrock democratic constituency, or a fluctuating mass of "floating"
respondents? Without knowing that, it is difficult to evaluate the explanatory power of
the finding.

(4) A fourth issue concerns the framing of the questions. This issue spans a wide
area, from nitpicking specificities to grand unspoken assumptions. For want of expertise, I shall not dwell on technical—but nevertheless important and tricky—questions
of semantic ambiguity. The red-light-jumping question asks whether those who
infringe rules are *listo* or *tonto*—"smart" or "stupid."[54] Since the question is trying to
get at respect for rules, it would seem more plausible to frame it in normative terms:
are the perpetrators "right" or "wrong"? After all, a queue-jumper or white-liar may be
quite "smart," but at the same time "wrong." Respecting rules is a matter of obeying
norms, not displaying intelligence.

The same question throws up a broader consideration: the relation of specific questions to general formulations about democratic "culture." As Seligson points out, three
of the hypothesized cases—queue-jumping, white-lying, and failing to hand back
"extra change"—are not obviously illegal, so they tell us nothing about respect for the
law.[55] Nor, I think, do they tell us much about democracy or democratic propensities.
To assume that an individual who tells white lies (which is legal) or even jumps red
lights (which is illegal) is somehow displaying a democratic deficit strikes me as uncon-

vincing, for two main reasons. First, it assumes some kind of across-the-board respect for norms that applies to all social activities. Yet individuals and groups construct quite different norms according to social context. A white lie may be considered entirely right—and "smart"—in one context, yet not in another. Stealing office paper clips is condoned; stealing paper clips from a shop is shoplifting. Governments have a great capacity for bringing the law into disrepute (e.g., Prohibition, or the current U.K. policy in regard to cannabis). The significance of rule-breaking can only be interpreted in specific contexts, and—save in rare cases of social breakdown and anomie—cannot be generalized to indicate a generalized democratic deficit.

Indeed—and this is my second argument—a certain amount of rule-breaking, even law-breaking, may be the sign of a "healthy," vigorous civil society. If every American had ceased drinking with the onset of Prohibition, would that have made the United States more democratic? Does the fact that British people queue—say, for buses—like docile sheep, while Mexicans often do not, indicate that British democracy is more sound and mature? If broad political culture is to be inferred from particular examples of rule-breaking and dissent (which I doubt it should), it is not at all clear what the "correct" correlation might be. A Prussian deference to laws and ruling norms can lead to the plea "I was only following orders," hence to political quietism and enhanced authoritarianism.[56] An attempt can be made to salvage the argument by postulating a just mean: "radical individualism"—which "cannot sustain democracy"—must be offset by "public spirit" and "unifying sentiment(s)."[57] So it would seem that yet more calibration is called for: of "public spirit," "unifying sentiments," and, of course, the just mean itself, which lies somewhere in the foggy zone amid all these proliferating quiddities.

Let me add another quiddity: "(interpersonal) trust," a concept much in vogue as a bedrock explanation of everything from political democracy to economic development.[58] I have already questioned how much faith we can place in respondents who display high levels of mistrust (the Cretan paradox). But there are sociological as well as methodological problems attached to "trust" and its calibration. "Trust" is a notoriously diffuse notion, inseparable from specific situations and, I would judge, highly resistant to quantitative assessment. Trust in one individual, group, or institution is likely to be offset by suspicion of others. Those who defer to the Catholic parish priest are likely to spurn the local liberal schoolmaster and vice versa: this, at least, was a common state of affairs in Mexico 60 years ago. More recently, those who believed Carlos Salinas disbelieved Cuauhtémoc Cárdenas, and vice versa. Maybe low levels of "trust"—measured (?) across the whole spectrum of political and social institutions—basically indicate a polarized society, which in turn may be a poor foundation for democracy (or, indeed, any other regime: the argument is not confined to democracies); but, in this case, "trust" reflects political polarization, rather than some enduring cultural attribute. (Political polarization can sometimes emerge—and fade—quite quickly, as it did in Mexico between roughly 1930 and 1945; it may be best analyzed in terms of political narrative and institutional organizations, not individual or collective psychology.)

Finally, a high level of trust—can one speak of "excessive" trust, even gullibility?—is presumably inimical to democracy, since it breeds dumb citizens and arrogant politicians. The price of freedom is, perhaps, eternal vigilance, domestically as well as internationally. In this light, what may seem a serious empirical problem, from the "orthodox," trust-favors-democracy perspective, may in fact corroborate my supposition: namely, that Costa Ricans, while "notably committed to democracy," are also "notoriously distrustful" of each other.[59] (In fact, the supposed consolidation of democracy in Latin America in the late 1990s seems to be accompanied by widespread disillusionment with and distrust of politicians and political parties, so maybe Costa Rica has blazed a pioneering trail. We might also recall that the suspicious, mistrustful, "amoral familist" Italian south, analyzed by Banfield in the 1950s, formed part of a relatively stable democracy.[60] Are *ticos* democratic because—or despite the fact that—they are distrustful? And is contemporary Latin American distrust a worrying sign of shallow democracy or, on the contrary, a healthy indicator of skeptical mood and modest expectations? Perhaps we need another "just mean," between naive gullibility on the one hand and rampant suspicion on the other; a cross between the Oceania of 1984 and Hobbes's state of nature.)

Similar problems arise in respect of "social norm" questions dealing with family decision-making or attitudes to potential neighbors. While the conclusions may be of some intrinsic interest (supposedly, macho Mexicans are more tolerant of gays than Chileans or Costa Ricans),[61] the political implication of these conclusions is another matter. Consider, for example, not wanting to have evangelical neighbors. This could reflect religious bigotry; but democracies can and do live with religious bigotry. (Again, the United States, a highly stable democracy, harbors a good deal of religious bigotry, as does India, whose democratic record, though imperfect, is better than many.) What is more, the preference not to have evangelical neighbors may be a rational, and non-bigoted, response to reality: one may prefer neighbors with whom one can easily get along; one may legitimately fear tensions and even violence (note the sectarian conflict in Chiapas); one may anticipate loud hymn-singing sessions next door. In short: the search for a pervasive "democratic culture" that necessarily underpins stable democracy is both empirically difficult (how can such a "culture" be defined and evaluated?)

and theoretically questionable (stable democracies may in fact live with large "undemocratic" components within them). Thus, whether the quiddity in question is adherence to rules, trust, or tolerance, we find that these concepts are elusive, and that their relationship to democracy is moot. And trying to salvage the argument by postulating an equally elusive "just mean"—just the right amount of adherence to rules, trust, or tolerance, but not too much—can seem like rather desperate, ad hoc, repair work.

Even more broadly, the framing of questions displays a set of underlying assumptions. I have already noted that the presumption that democracy connotes "equality" or "bienestar social" is, from the standpoint of mainstream political science, misleading. However, while we may "blame" some 54 percent of Mexicans for falling into this error,[62] the fact is they were offered this alternative. Why? Was there a prior presumption that some respondents would wish to answer in these terms? Or that these connotations of democracy were—in theoretical or conceptual terms—the obvious "frontrunners"? While the first presumption was correct, the second was questionable. Furthermore, how do we know that Mexicans, or others, might not wish to opt for other connotations: democracy offers, say, solidarity, social tranquillity, modernity, workers' control of the shopfloor? The Hewlett poll asks an empirical question concerning the organization of the workplace, but the survey does not offer opportunities for normative comment on the democratic organization of firms, factories, or *ejidos*.[63]

Specific sins of commission aside, we might note that quite different approaches to political culture could be pursued. Kahl, in his comparison of Mexico and Brazil, relied on a conventional traditional/modern dichotomy.[64] Almond and Verba conceived of distinct categories of political actor—citizen, subject, parochial—defined according to their supposed relationship to government.[65] While these approaches persist (the Hewlett survey is not explicit in regard to its theoretical foundations, but it would seem to stand in this tradition), they are not the only ones. Mary Douglas's fivefold typology, for example, has been developed by Wildavsky and others: though I am in no position to endorse or critique it, I would suggest that it has the advantages of *(a)* greater flexibility (it does not shoehorn society into a simple tradition/modernity dichotomy); and *(b)* an avoidance of teleology—that is, it does not come with built-in suppositions about progress, advance, and backwardness.[66] Such suppositions are not only arbitrary and theoretically questionable; they also tend to skew analysis—for example, when they create expectations of "advance" or "progress" that fail to materialize. Mexicans, it seems, have not advanced steadily in terms of political awareness since the early 1980s; interest in politics seems to fluctuate according to conjunctural events (such as major elections) rather than marching onward and upward, as a modernization thesis might seem to require.[67]

(5) This leads me logically to my final point, which relates to context. Several of the survey's conclusions can be readily understood and appreciated in terms of particular political or economic contexts, irrespective of "culture"—which I take to denote a degree of long-term durability—or of any ongoing march of modernization. Mexicans, we have seen, fear inflation. Chileans fear a divided government (president and congress of different parties). The reasons are obvious and historical—quite recently historical, indeed. Such recent historical reasons, I have suggested, should not be readily elevated to become cultural keystones. (The process whereby "contingent" aspects of a political system congeal into something more permanent—perhaps into a durable "cultural" attribute—clearly needs further investigation.)[68] A consideration of context also leads to conclusions about democratization that need no cultural underpinnings. In much of Latin America, democracy is now—in Przeworksi's much-quoted phrase—the "only game in town."[69] (It may be a somewhat corrupt game, whose players are held in low esteem, but that is not the point.) Even in Mexico, the threat of praetorian takeover, radical revolution, or even a reversion to old-style PRI-monopoly government, seems unlikely. The fact that only 31 percent of Mexicans are "satisfied" with democracy, as against 55 percent who are not, is of interest; even more interesting, perhaps, are the respective Chilean figures (37 percent and 55 percent). But I would hesitate to draw any major conclusions about the durability of democracy, not least because the Mexican count is vitiated by the incomplete nature of Mexican democracy. As a result, when 55 percent of respondents declare their dissatisfaction, we may reasonably ask whether they are authoritarians who dislike democracy and would welcome its replacement, or rather democrats who are disillusioned with Mexico's democratic deficit (especially the PRI's ancient monopoly of the presidency) and who are looking to perfect rather than to abolish democratic practices.[70]

We may also note that Mexican attitudes to democracy suggest a distinctly contingent causality: responses to the (authoritarian) statement that "a few strong leaders would do more for Mexico than all the laws and talk" reveal that university-educated Mexicans had, between 1959 and 1988–91, become significantly more authoritarian, hence less democratic.[71] The reason for this—counterintuitive?—shift seems clear: in 1988–91, "strong leadership" was represented by Carlos Salinas, a modernizing, neoliberal, technocratic, *primermundista* president, whose program appealed to—and in general benefited—the well-educated urban middle and upper class. We could compare the (1989) responses of Nicaraguans, who displayed "surprisingly" high levels of support for political participation, protest, and dissent—higher, indeed, than Costa Rican levels. "Nicaraguans of all ideological stripes remained more libertarian than Costa Ricans," notwithstanding Nicaragua's supposedly authoritarian cultural legacy.[72]

Again, the outcome reflected the political conjuncture: the Nicaraguan opposition was mobilizing for the upcoming 1990 elections. Once these were won and lost, and the Sandinistas had been removed from power, "a dramatic reversal of support for civil liberties" occurred; supporters of UNO—the newly incumbent anti-Sandinista coalition—now expressed "much lower support for civil liberties than FSLN (Sandinista) supporters."[73] Both the Mexican and the Nicaraguan examples cast doubt on the notion of durable "democratic" cultures linked to specific social groups. Preferences may well be contingent and conjunctural, hence capable of shifts and reverses. For this reason, we should take a skeptical view of the old chestnut of "working-class authoritarianism," which is often seen as the reverse side of supposed middle-class (or "bourgeois") liberalism. Domínguez and McCann feel they can "affirm with confidence that [their] data provide no support for a 'working-class authoritarianism' argument."[74]

Furthermore, estimating Mexican participation in politics (broadly defined) is highly ambiguous. The assumption—an old one—is that democracy depends on a culture of democratic participation. Hence we encounter questions concerning decision-making in the home or at work, and attempts to calibrate rates of political involvement—in strikes, demonstrations, and protests. I have already suggested that it is probably misleading to expect "democratic" values and behavior to correlate across a wide range of activities, public and private, economic and political. The United States has an active electoral system when it comes to public office (turnout, of course, is another matter); but electoral principles do not extend to corporations or the Federal Reserve. In all democratic systems there are reserve domains, beyond the reach of direct democratic decision-making.[75] In addition, increased resort to "direct action" (demonstrations, strikes, factory occupations), while it may indicate levels of political participation, also connotes a failure of the "normal" democratic process to accommodate discontent, and may presage a repressive, even authoritarian, reaction on the part of those who feel threatened. Hence Brazil 1964 or Chile 1973. It may be in the interest of "democracy"—defined, again, in liberal procedural terms—to maintain certain reserve domains, to limit ("direct") popular protest, and thus to reassure threatened vested interests. Thus, in Europe, in the nineteenth century and again in recent years, "democracy was stabilized by limiting its claims."[76] The same phenomenon is evident in Latin America today, where, given the levels of inequality and poverty, the dilemma of whether to redistribute (at the risk of causing a reaction) or to eschew reform in order to conciliate vested interests is especially acute.[77] Eighty years ago Woodrow Wilson wanted to "make the world safe for democracy," but, as Charles Maier observes, the real history of democracy is one of "making democracy safe for the world."[78]

Such an analysis tends to switch the focus away from deeply rooted "cultural" factors in the direction of class and sectoral interests, historical conjunctures, and even game-theoretic models. For, if I am right, commitments for and against "democracy" (which may not be conceived in such stark ideological terms by the actors themselves anyway) are likely to be generated by immediate pressures: wars, recessions, political and economic crises. It would be particularly interesting, therefore, to plot the "democratic" commitment of Chileans—as opposed to Mexicans or Costa Ricans—over time: pre-1973, as well as post-1989. Did polls prior to 1973 reveal a marked deterioration of the Chilean commitment to "democracy"? Did the *golpistas* of 1973 even conceive of their actions as antidemocratic (recall Jeanne Kirkpatrick's Jesuitical defense of "authoritarian," as opposed to "totalitarian," regimes)?[79] The ultimate—I do not say the only—test of a political science model, or thesis, is its predictive power. If democratic breakdowns have been psephologically signaled in advance, so much the better for psephology. If not, how much weight can we give to recent polls that indicate levels of support for—or opposition to—the new democratic status quo? Maybe we are carefully taking the temperature of a body politic whose demise is usually due less to long-incubating bacilli than to runaway trucks.

IV

In conclusion: polls in general, and the Hewlett poll in particular, can provide useful information in respect of certain specific situations and attitudes (such as voting intentions or attitudes toward the police). In such situations, the questions are relatively straightforward and unambiguous, questioners and respondents can assume a degree of mutual comprehension, and results are unlikely to be vitiated by pervasive "dishonesty." Polls will no doubt prove invaluable—and contentious—during Mexico's millennial election year of 2000. However, these sorts of questions may tell us little about underlying political values. When the latter are probed, serious problems arise. Abstract concepts do not travel well, hence cross-national surveys are inevitably compromised by the problem of "indexicality." "Veracity" may be harder to attain (especially in societies that are said to be endemically "mistrustful"?) and corroboration is elusive, for such conclusions tend to be frustratingly nonfalsifiable. They may also reflect a rote "public transcript" that is no sure guide to actual behavior. (I have elsewhere discussed the "schizoid" character of Mexican political behavior.)[80] At a deeper level, we may even question whether any profound cultural attributes, relevant and useful for our understanding of democracy, can be genuinely discerned, let alone measured. Adherence to rules, trust, and tolerance do not pervade a society in the way that, say, blood groups do. Rather, they are characteristics that crop up in specific circum-stances—specific by both time and place. They come and go, they vary in intensity, they cannot be confidently generalized (e.g., "Mexicans are more/less trusting than Costa Ricans"). Nor can they be measured with confidence: the subtleties involved in, say, "trust" are not amenable to calibration, least of all to cross-national calibration (here indexicality rears its ugly head again). Furthermore, their relationship to democ-racy is often ambiguous. How much "trust" as against "mistrust" is conducive to democracy? Here we encounter the slightly desperate search for the "just mean," which adds another vague and incalculable concept to the growing pile. In addition, both (respondents') supposed attitudes and (pollsters') chosen categories represent some-what arbitrary choices from a huge universe of possibilities; it is not clear why some are chosen at the expense of others; the philosophical bases of the inquiry remain opaque. Finally, there is the danger that surveys of "political culture" elevate transient, even superficial findings (findings subject to the failings already mentioned) to the level of enduring cultural keystones, which are supposed to have explanatory power. Passing moods are turned into permanent markers of political culture. Perhaps, over time (a "habituation phase"), "contingent and instrumental choices . . . acquire a deeper com-mitment, rooted in values and beliefs."[81] Fragile, faute de mieux democracies thus con-solidate; values acquire a relative autonomy, we might say, of the contingencies that brought them to life; such values thereby become durably affective, rather than contin-gently instrumental. Democracy really does become the only game in town. Or, we could say, the institutional supports of democracy (which may include some substan-tial "reserve domains") eventually prove strong enough to resist new, challenging con-tingencies—as British and U.S. democracy did during the interwar period, at a time when Italian and German democracy did not. Or as Costa Rican democracy did at a time when, for example, the democratic bastion of Uruguay fell to the military. Polls may usefully tell us—in June 2000—who is likely to win in July 2000; but they cannot, it seems to me, weigh the autonomy of "democratic" values, or the severity of conjunc-tural challenges to democracy that may arise. Yet, if the concept of "political culture" is to have genuine explanatory power, it is the trade-off between these two factors—autonomous values and conjunctural challenges—that should determine whether, when push comes to shove, democracy survives or succumbs.

Reference Materials

Appendix 1: *Methodological Note*

The objective of this study was to explore Latin Americans' views of democracy—specifically, how they conceptualized the term and their expectations from a functioning democracy—in three countries: Chile, Costa Rica, and Mexico. In addition, the survey included questions that tested citizens' level of satisfaction with national and state government and their knowledge about political institutions and political practices.

The universe for the survey consisted of 3,396 personal interviews, which took place in the home of the respondent. Respondents constituted a representative sample of adults (over 18 years of age). In Mexico and Chile, other locales of the same size and similar characteristics were substituted for residents living in the rain forests, on islands, or in very isolated regions, whose inclusion would have excessively raised the cost of the survey.

The margin of error for the total sample is plus or minus 2.5 percent, with a confidence level of 95 percent. For Mexico and Chile, with 1,200 and 1,194 cases, respectively, the margin of error is plus or minus 3 percent. Costa Rica, with 1,002 cases, has a margin of error of plus or minus 3.5 percent. In all three countries, the same pre-codified questionnaire was used in the home of the selected respondent. The interviews were completed during July 1998 in the three countries: July 2–9 in Mexico, July 13–19 in Costa Rica, and July 18–30 in Chile. MORI of Mexico and Dichter & Neira and MORI of Chile were in charge of the individual surveys. All data were verified through ASCII matrices, and the global data were analyzed through SPSS. MORI International in Princeton, New Jersey, coordinated the overall survey.

At the time of the survey in midsummer 1998, Costa Rica continued to enjoy a working democracy. Unlike in Chile or Mexico, political power is more evenly divided among its three branches of government (judicial, legislative, and executive). In recent years, the separation of powers has led to a certain level of disgruntlement with the decision-making process, similar to the gridlock between Congress and the presidency in the second term of the Clinton administration. The most important political change that Costa Ricans witnessed during 1998 was the implementation of new local electoral laws. For the first time, the citizens elected mayors rather than appointing city managers to administer local governments. This change in institutional structure at the local level undoubtedly highlighted Costa Ricans' traditional emphasis on pluralism in government and electoral politics. Two major parties dominate the national political scene in Costa Rica: the Partido Liberación Nacional (PLN) and the Partido Unidad Social Cristiana (PUSC). The PUSC, a party that combines a heritage of social reform with neoliberal economic policies, controlled the executive branch at the time of the poll.

In the summer of 1998, Mexico had recently emerged from a severe economic recession that began abruptly in early 1995. Politically, it was at one of its most divided points in recent history. The dominant party, the Institutional Revolutionary Party (PRI), in 1997 lost control of the lower chamber of congress to a coalition of opposition parties whose members came primarily from the National Action Party (PAN) and the Party of the Democratic Revolution (PRD). Mexicans, therefore, were experiencing firsthand the typical conflicts that occur when executive and legislative branches are controlled by opposing parties. Mexicans were also anticipating considerable future political changes, as the three leading parties contemplated additional electoral reforms—including implementing new primaries for electing presidential candidates within their own organizations, in anticipation of the presidential nomination process in 1999 and the actual race in 2000.

Chile in 1998 represented an excellent test case of the challenge between democratic and authoritarian influences, of a generation sharing two extreme political experiences, and of the degree to which democratic or authoritarian preferences might persist in an altered political environment. At the time of the survey, Chile was characterized by an electorate in which the centrists, ideologically speaking, accounted for nearly half the population, compared to only a fourth in 1973, at the time of the military coup. The Chileans were governed in 1998 by Eduardo Frei, a Christian Democrat boasting a long political history in Chile and their second elected president since General Pinochet was rejected in 1988. Nevertheless, the armed forces remained deeply entrenched in the governing process and, through conservative allies, continued to thwart constitutional reforms. The legacies of militarism and authoritarianism remain institutionalized and visible despite Chile's important democratic achievements immediately prior to 1998. The electorate also remains polarized on significant issues, including whether or not Pinochet himself should be tried in Spain for alleged crimes against humanity.

The general characteristics of the respondents were classified according to the follow categories: *Education:* primary = up to 6 grades of schooling, secondary = 7th through 12th grades, and higher = more than 12 grades. *Age:* 18–29, 30–50, and 51 and older. *Income:* 40 percent lowest income level, 25 percent lower-middle income level, 25 percent upper-middle income level, 10 percent highest income level. *Occupation:* 1 = executive, government official, professional, or business owner; 2 = white-collar worker; 3 = technician or blue-collar worker; 4 = farmer or rural worker; 5 = student; 6 = housewife; NT = unemployed, seeking work, retired, or doesn't work. *Religion:* Catholic, all other religions, no religion. *Location:* large cities = 100,000+; medium cities = 50,000–100,000; small cities = 15,000–50,000; small rural = less than 15,000. *Ethnicity:* white, light dark, deep dark.

Appendix 2: *Hewlett Poll, 1998*

COUNTRY __ __ Region: N / S / C / E / W / Folio __ __ __ __

Stating point ___ ___ ___   Interviewer No. ____ ____

Date: Month_____ day ___ ___   Starting time____ : ____

    Good morning / afternoon / evening. I am _____ from MORI International. We are conducting a survey for the University of Tulane in three Latin American countries. Your household was randomly selected. This is an anonymous interview, so we don't need your name, only your honest answers. From those who are now at home, I need to talk to the person over 18 years old, whose birthday is closer to today. Is it you? (IF S/HE IS THE PERSON, START IMMEDIATELY. IF IT IS NOT, ASK FOR THAT ONE AND START AGAIN)

    0 Gender (DON'T ASK)
    1 Male   2 Female

    1. In one word, could you tell me what democracy means to you? (DON'T READ AND MARK ONLY ONE)

1. Liberty	5. Welfare / Progress
2. Equality	6. Respect / Lawfulness
3. Vote / Elections	7. NA / DK
4. Form of Government	8. Other_____

    2. How much democracy would you say this country has: a great deal, some, little or none? (READ THE SCALE ALTERNATING THE ORDER: Nothing, little, some, a great deal . . .)

1. A great deal	4. None
2. Some	5. NS / NC
3. Little	

    3. In order for a democracy to work well, what is most important? (READ ROTATING THE ORDER OF THE ANSWERS EVERY TIME)

        1. A president who governs well
        2. Legislators that make good laws

3. Judges that make justice well

4. None (DON'T READ)

5. Other_____

6. NS / NC (DON'T READ)

4. With which of the following phrases do you agree most? (READ AND MARK *ONLY ONE ANSWER*)

1. Democracy is preferable to any other form of government.

2. I have no preference for a democratic or a non democratic regime.

3. In some circumstances, an authoritarian regime can be preferable to a democratic one.

4. Don't know (DON'T READ)

5. If you had to choose, which of the following would you say is the *main* task of democracy? (READ AND ROTATE)

1. To combat crime	4. Protect minorities
2. Elect governors	5. None (DON'T READ)
3. To distribute wealth	6. NS / NC (DON'T READ)

6. With which of the following phrases do you most agree? (READ AND MARK ONLY ONE ANSWER)

1. Authority must conform strictly to the law even at the price of not punishing a delinquent; or

2. Authority must try to punish delinquents, even at the price of not conforming strictly to the law.

3. NS / NC (DON'T READ)

7. In general, would you say you are satisfied or disatisfied with the way democracy is working in this country? (INSIST): Very or somewhat?

1. Very satisfied	4. Somewhat unsatisfied
2. Somewhat satisfied	5. Very unsatisfied
3. Neither (DON'T READ)	6. NS / NC (DON'T READ)

8. Would you be in favor or opposed to one of your children (or siblings, in case you don't have children) marrying a person of a different religion than yours? (INSIST): Very much or somewhat?

1. Very much in favor	4. Somewhat oppose
2. Somewhat in favor	5. Very much oppose
3. Neither (DON'T READ)	6. NS / NC

9. With which of the following phrases do you most agree? (READ AND MARK ONLY ONE ANSWER)

1. The media (TV, radio, newspapers, etc.) should investigate things deeply with no consideration for the private lives of people; or

2. The media should not investigate so deeply as to get into people's private lives.

3. Don't know. (DON'T READ)

10. I'm going to read to you a list of people. Tell me whom you would prefer NOT to have as a neighbor. (ROTATE)

	Mentioned	*Not mentioned*
Evangelicals	1	2
Homosexuals	1	2
Foreigners	1	2

11a. If you had to choose, which of the following things would you say is more important? (READ AND MARK ONLY ONE ANSWER)

	11a	*11b*
To keep order in the country	1	1
To give people more participation in important government decisions	2	2
To combat inflation	3	3
To protect the liberty of expression	4	4
Don't know (DON'T READ)	5	5

11b. And what would be the second most important? (MARK ABOVE IN 11B *ONLY ONE* ANSWER)

12. From what you remember, with what frequency did your parents allow the children to participate in family decisions? (WAIT FOR ANSWER)

> 1. Always
> 2. Almost always / often
> 3. Only some times / little
> 4. Never / almost never
> 5. NS / NC (DON'T READ)

13. What is more important to you: to have a government that improves democracy or that improves the economy?

> 1. That improves democracy   4. Neither (DON'T READ)
> 2. That improves the economy   5. NS / NC (DON'T READ)
> 3. Both (DON'T READ)

14. How much democracy would you say that there is in this city: a great deal, some, little or nothing?

> 1. A great deal   4. None
> 2. Some   5. NS / NC (DON'T READ)
> 3. Little

15. Do you think it's good or bad that the president of the Republic is some times from one party and some times from another? (INSIST): Very or somewhat?

> 1. Very good   4. Somewhat bad
> 2. Somewhat good   5. Very bad
> 3. Neither (DON'T READ)   6. NS / NC (DON'T READ)

16. From what you remember, with what frequency did your teachers at school allow students to participate in decisions concerning the class? (WAIT FOR ANSWER)

> 1. Always
> 2. Almost always / often
> 3. Only sometimes / little
> 4. Never / Almost never
> 5. NS / NC

17. Do you feel well or badly represented by your congressman? (INSIST): Very or somewhat?

1. Very well	4. Somewhat badly
2. Somewhat well	5. Very badly
3. Neither (DON'T READ)	6. NS / NC (DON'T READ)

18. As you may have heard, the law requires a separation between the three branches of the government. Do you remember the name of each of the three branches? (YES) What are they? (Good = name right / Average = name wrong, but concept right / bad = name and concept wrong: i.e. power of God, power of money, power of magic, etc.)

	Good	Avg.	Bad	NS
EB	1	2	3	4
LB	1	2	3	4
JB	1	2	3	4

19. Do you think it is good or bad that the president of the republic belongs to one party and the majority of the congress to another? (INSIST): Very or somewhat?

1. Very good	4. Somewhat bad
2. Somewhat good	5. Very bad
3. Neither (DON'T READ)	6. NS / NC (DON'T READ)

20. In general how often do employees participate with management in decisions concerning their jobs? (WAIT FOR ANSWER)

1. Always	4. Never / almost never
2. Almost always / very often	5. NS / NC (DON'T READ)
3. Only sometimes / little	

21. Would you personally be ready to do something to demand accountability from government officials: yes or no? (INSIST: DEFINITELY or MAYBE)

1. Definitely yes	4. Definitely not
2. Maybe yes	5. Maybe not
3. It depends (DON'T READ)	6. NS / NC (DON'T READ)

22. I'm going to read you some forms of participation in politics. Tell me about them if you . . . have done any (1), would do any (2) or would never do any (3) (NS / NC=4 DON'T READ)

	done	would	never	NS / NC
a. Sign a protest letter	1	2	3	4
b. Attend a demonstration	1	2	3	4
c. Participate in a forbidden strike	1	2	3	4
d. Take over a building or a factory	1	2	3	4
e. Participate in a boycott	1	2	3	4

23. In your opinion what is the most important political right for the functioning of democracy? (DON'T READ AND MARK ONLY ONE)

1. Liberty
2. Equality
3. Vote / Elections
4. Respect / Lawfulness

5. Welfare / Progress
6. NS / NC
7. Other_____

24. With which phrase do you most agree: the president of the republic should be more powerful than the congress or the congress should be more powerful than the president?

1. The president more powerful
2. The congress more powerful
3. Both equal (DON'T READ)

4. Either
5. NS / NC

25. Tell me which activities should be government owned and which private? (READ AND ROTATE)

	Gov't	Private	Both	NS / NC
1. Airlines	1	2	3	4
2. Schools	1	2	3	4
3. Water	1	2	3	4
4. Television	1	2	3	4

26. In your opinion how many government officials are corrupt? (DON'T READ)

1. Almost no one
2. Few
3. Many

4. Almost everyone
5. NS / NC

27. In politics, one generally speaks of "left" and "right." Within a scale from 1 to 10, where "1" means left and "10" means right, where would you put yourself?

01	02	03	04	05	06	07	08	09	10	NS=11
Left										Right

28. With which phrase do you most agree: the government should look after the individual's well-being; or each individual should look after his own well-being?

    1. The government   4. Neither

    2. Each individual   5. NS / NC

    3. Both (DON'T READ)

29. Generally speaking would you say that people are trustworthy or not trustworthy?

    1. Yes, people are trustworthy.

    2. No, people are not trustworthy.

    3. NS / NC (DON'T READ)

30. I'm going to read to you a list of different things that people do. For each one of them tell me if you believe that people in general think that those who do them are (1) very stupid, (2) somewhat stupid, (3) somewhat smart, or (4) very smart (IF HE DOESN'T KNOW, MARK 5)

	VS	SS	SS	VS	NS
a. Cutting in line	1	2	3	4	5
b. Not saying anything if they get extra change	1	2	3	4	5
c. Not paying the subway or bus fare	1	2	3	4	5
d. Run a traffic light at midnight when there is no traffic	1	2	3	4	5
e. Making up a false excuse	1	2	3	4	5

31. With which political party do you most sympathize?

    (INSIST: Very much or somewhat?)

    1. Very much (1st party in the national congress)

    2. Somewhat (1st party in the national congress)

    3. Very much (2nd party in the national congress)

    4. Somewhat (2nd party in the national congress)

    5. Very much (3rd party in the national congress)

    6. Somewhat (3rd party in the national congress)

    7. Very much other parties _____

    8. Somewhat other parties _____

    9. None

    10. NS / NC

32. In your opinion what has been the major obstacle to democracy in this country? (ONLY ONE: DON'T READ)

    1. Corruption   5. People's passivity

    2. The government   6. Lack of education

    3. Political parties   7. Other

    4. Poverty   8. NS / NC

33. How important would you say politics are: very, somewhat, little or not at all?

    1. Very   4. Not at all

    2. Somewhat   5. NS / NC

    3. Little

34. Would you say that elections are regularly "clean" or fraudulent?

    1 Clean

    2 Fraudulent

    3 NS / NC (DON'T READ)

35. If elections were tomorrow, what political party would you vote for?

    1. (1st party in the national congress)

    2. (2nd party in the national congress)

    3. (3rd party in the national congress)

    4. Other parties _____

    5. None / Doesn't usually vote

    6. NS / NC

36. How much confidence do you have in . . . ? A lot, some, little or nothing? (READ EACH QUESTION AND REPEAT THE SCALE EVERY 3–4 QUESTIONS AS A REMINDER)

	L / S / L / N / NS
1. Churches	1 / 2 / 3 / 4 / 5
2. Police	1 / 2 / 3 / 4 / 5
3. Schools	1 / 2 / 3 / 4 / 5
4. Government	1 / 2 / 3 / 4 / 5
5. The press	1 / 2 / 3 / 4 / 5
6. The courts (judges)	1 / 2 / 3 / 4 / 5
7. Unions	1 / 2 / 3 / 4 / 5
8. The Congress	1 / 2 / 3 / 4 / 5
9. Television	1 / 2 / 3 / 4 / 5
10. Political parties	1 / 2 / 3 / 4 / 5
11. Small firms	1 / 2 / 3 / 4 / 5
12. The army (armed forces)	1 / 2 / 3 / 4 / 5
13. The family	1 / 2 / 3 / 4 / 5

37. In one word could you tell me what you expect from democracy? (DON'T READ AND MARK ONLY ONE)

    1. Liberty   5. Welfare / Progress

    2. Equality   6. NS / NC

    3. Vote / Elections   7. Other _____

    4. Respect / Lawfulness

Finally,

38. Generally speaking would you say that you are very happy, somewhat happy, somewhat unhappy, or very unhappy? (READ THE SCALE ALTERNATING THE ORDER EVERY TIME)

1. Very happy	4. Somewhat unhappy
2. Somewhat happy	5. Very unhappy
3. Neither (DON'T READ)	6. NS / NC (DON'T READ)

39. Generally how do you get informed about the news? (DON'T READ)

1. Press	5. School / job
2. Radio	6. NS / NC
3. TV	7. Other _____
4. Family / friends	

40. More or less how often do you get informed about the news? (DON'T READ)

1. Daily	4. 2–3 times a month
2. 2–3 times per week	5. Almost never
3. Once per week	6. NS / NC

41. What is your opinion of the president (NAME): good or bad? (INSIST: VERY or SOMEWHAT)

1. Very good	4. Somewhat bad
2. Somewhat good	5. Very bad
3. Neither (DON'T READ)	6. NS / NC (DON'T READ)

42. How do you rate your current personal financial situation: good or bad? (INSIST: VERY or SOMEWHAT)

1. Very good	4. Somewhat bad
2. Somewhat good	5. Very bad
3. Neither (DON'T READ)	6. NS / NC (DON'T READ)

43. In the next twelve months, do you think your personal financial situation will be better or worse that it is today? (INSIST: VERY MUCH or SOMEWHAT)

1. Much better	4. Somewhat worse
2. Somewhat better	5. Much worse
3. The same (DON'T READ)	6. NS / NC (DON'T READ)

Now to end,

S1. What was the last year of school that you attended?

01. 1 year	07. 7 years	13. University incomplete
02. 2 years	08. 8 years	14. University complete
03. 3 years	09. 9 years	15. Graduate st. incomplete
04. 4 years	10. 10 years	16. Graduate st. complete
05. 5 years	11. 11 years	17. No formal education
06. 6 years	12. 12 years	18. NS / NC

S2. Could you tell me your age? ___ ___ (WRITE DOWN THE YEARS)

S3. In each country ask in the most appropriate way to determine the income level: 1 - alto (10% highest); 2 - middle high (next 20%); 3- middle and middle low (next 30%); and 4 - low (lowest 40%)

S4. More or less how many light bulbs do you have at home?

    1. WRITE DOWN _____

    2. NS / NC

S5. What do you currently do for a living? _____
(WRITE DOWN THE EXACT ANSWER AND CODIFY ACCORDING TO THE COUNTRY)

    1. Manager / Government official / Private executive

    2. Independent professional / own business

    3. Mid-level employee of firm or government

    4. Technician / blue collar

    5. Agriculture / farmer

    6. Student

    7. Housewife

    8. Unemployed / Seeking a job

    9. Retired

    10. Other _____

    11. NS / NC

S6. What is your religion? (DON'T READ)

    1. Catholic   4. None

    2. Evangelic   5. NS / NC

    3. Other (WRITE DOWN) _____

S7. Type of place (WRITE DOWN WITHOUT ASKING)

    1. Metropolis (1 million people or more)

    2. Large city (100,000 to 1 million people)

    3. Middle size city (50,000 to 100,000 people)

    4. Small city (15,000 to 50,000 people)

    5. Rural zone (Fewer than 15,000 people)

S8. Ethnicity (WRITE DOWN WITHOUT ASKING)

    1. White   4. Indian

    2. Light colored   5. Black

    3. Dark colored   6. Other _____

For verification only, could you please give me your phone number or address where a supervisor could ask you if I interviewed you correctly?

_____

Can I take your name? _____ Time of interview ending _____ _____

That's all. Many thanks for your time
June 16, 1998

Appendix 3: Wall Street Journal *Poll, 1999*

WSJ-LB (USA) March 2, 1999

Hello, my name is _____ and I'm calling from MORI for The Wall Street Journal. We're conducting a confidential poll of public opinion. The interview is anonymous. In order to get a fair representation of Americans nationwide, I am supposed to speak to the person who has had the most recent birthday. Of the people living in your household who are at least eighteen years old, including those who are not home right now, can you tell me who has had the most recent birthday? (IF PERSON DOESN'T KNOW ALL THE BIRTHDAYS, SAY:) Well, of the ones you do know, who has had the last birthday? May I speak to that person please? (IF PERSON WITH MOST RECENT BIRTHDAY IS NOT HOME, FIND OUT WHEN HE/SHE WILL RETURN AND MAKE AN APPOINTMENT TO CALL BACK.)

(IF RESPONDENT INDICATES THAT HE/SHE IS NOT THE PERSON WHO HAS HAD THE MOST RECENT BIRTHDAY, ASK TO SPEAK TO THE PERSON WHO DID AND START AGAIN. IF RESPONDENT INDICATES THAT HE/SHE IS THE ONE WITH THE MOST RECENT BIRTHDAY, SAY:) Here is my first question. (PROCEED IMMEDIATELY TO QUESTION #1 - DO NOT PAUSE)

1. Could you please tell me if you think the government should spend more money or less money on each of the following. (READ ONE BY ONE, ACCEPT ONLY ONE ANSWER PER CATEGORY)

	Spend more	Spend less	DK	RF
A. Public works	1	2	8	0
B. Health Care	1	2	8	0
C. Police forces	1	2	8	0
D. Education	1	2	8	0
E. Defense	1	2	8	0
F. Unemployment Insurance	1	2	8	0
G. Social security	1	2	8	0

2. Do you strongly agree, agree somewhat, disagree somewhat, or strongly disagree with each of the following phrases that I am going to read. (READ ONE BY ONE, ACCEPT ONLY ONE ANSWER PER CATEGORY)

	Stngly agree	SW agree	SW disgr	Stngly disgr	DK	RF
A. The government should leave economic activity to the private sector	1	2	3	4	8	0
B. Prices should be set by free competition	1	2	3	4	8	0
C. Free enterprise is best for the country	1	2	3	4	8	0
D. Foreign investment in the U.S. should be encouraged	1	2	3	4	8	0
E. Private enterprise is beneficial for the country	1	2	3	4	8	0

3. Which of the following two statements corresponds more closely to your own view:

1. The U.S. usually plays a constructive role in world affairs or
2. The U.S. is trying to dominate the world.
3. DK/REF (DO NOT READ)

4. We would like to hear your opinion regarding the efforts that the US government is making to reduce illegal drug use in this country. Would you say that these efforts are very good, good, poor or very poor, or have you not heard enough about it to give an opinion?

1. Very good
2. Good
3. Poor
4. Very poor
5. Have not heard enough
6. DK/REF

5. Which Latin American country is the best friend of the US? (DO NOT READ - ACCEPT ONLY ONE)

1. Mexico
2. Brazil
3. Colombia
4. Argentina
5. Venezuela
6. Chile
7. Other (SPECIFY)_____
8. DK/REF

6. And which country in the World do you think is the best friend of the US? (DO NOT READ - ACCEPT ONE)

1. Canada
2. England
3. Mexico
4. Brazil
5. France
6. Germany
7. Japan
8. Other (SPECIFY)_____
9. DK/REF

7. Which political party, the Democratic or the Republican, do you think . . . ?

	Democ Party	Repub Party	Other Party	Neither None
A. Best represents your interests	1	2	8	0
B. Best represents your values	1	2	8	0
C. Is more sympathetic to minorities	1	2	8	0

8. I am going to read you a list of some concerns in this country. Please tell me which one is of greatest concern to you (READ LIST - MARK ONLY ONE - ROTATE)

     1. Crime and violence

     2. Weakening of family values

     3. Better and safer schools

     4. Finding good jobs and opportunities

     5. High taxes and government spending

     6. Racism

     7. Immigration

     8. The need for a cleaner environment

9. When it comes to abortion, do you think the government should use legislation to prevent abortions, or do you consider an abortion a decision that should be left to a woman and her doctor?

     1. Govt should use legislation   3. Other_____

     2. Left to woman & doctor   4. Neither/none

10. Do you consider yourself more a Republican or more a Democrat?

     1. Democrat   3. Other _____

     2. Republican   4. None / DK

11. If the presidential elections were held today, who would you vote for: Al Gore (the Vice President) or George Bush (the Governor of Texas)?

     1. Al Gore   3. Other _____

     2. George Bush   4. None / DK

12. In one word, could you tell me what democracy means to you? (DON'T READ / MARK ONLY ONE)

     1. Liberty / Freedom   5. Progress / Welfare

     2. Equality   6. Legality / Respect

     3. Vote / Elections   7. NA / DK

     4. Form of Government   8. Other_____

13. If you had to choose, which of the following would you say is the main task of democracy? (READ 1-4 AND ROTATE)

     1. Combat crime   5. OTHER_____ (DON'T READ)

     2. Elect politicians   6. NONE (DON'T READ)

     3. Distribute wealth   7. DK / NA (DON'T READ)

     4. Protect minorities

14. From what you remember, how frequently did your parents allow their children to partic-ipate in family decisions? (DO NOT READ)

1. Always	4. Never/ almost never
2. Almost always / often	5. NS/NC (DON'T READ)
3. Only some times/ little	

15. Of all the rights that people have in this country - Which plays the biggest part in the suc-cess of democracy? (DON'T READ / MARK ONLY ONE)

1. Liberty / Freedom	5. Progress / Welfare
2. Equality	6. NS / NC
3. Vote / Elections	7. Other_____
4. Legality / Respect	

16. In politics, one generally speaks of "Left" and "Right." Within a scale from 1 to 10, where "1" means Left and "10" means Right, where would you put yourself?

01 02 03 04 05 06 07 08 09 10 DK/REF= 11
Left   Right

17. In your opinion what has been the major obstacle to democracy in this country? (ONLY ONE: DON'T READ)

1. Corruption	5. People's apathy
2. Government	6. Lack of education
3. Political parties	7. Other _____
4. Poverty	8. NS/NC

18. In one word please tell me what do you expect most from democracy? (DON'T READ / MARK ONLY ONE)

1. Liberty / Freedom	5. Progress / Welfare
2. Equality	6. NS / NC
3. Vote / Elections	7. Other_____
4. Legality / Respect	

SOCIO-DEMOGRAPHICS

S1. Gender
S2. Age
S3. Education
S4. Employment & Occupation
S5. Income
S6. Religion
S7. (IF HISPANIC) country of family origin
S8. Where were you born
S9. (IF FOREIGN BORN) time in country
S10. Married

Notes

Chapter 1: Democracy through Latin American Lenses

1. Bilateral Commission on the Future of United States–Mexican Relations, *The Challenge of Interdependence: Mexico and the United States* (Lanham, Md.: University Press of America, 1989), 237.

2. The exception to this, and an attempt to address many of the values thought to be associated with democracy, is the work of Richard S. Hillman in Venezuela. See his "Political Culture and Democracy: Attitudes, Values, and Beliefs in Venezuela" (paper presented at the Latin American Studies Association Meeting, Guadalajara, Mexico, April 1997).

3. Terry Karl has addressed these issues, including her own conceptualization of democracy, for Latin America. See her "Dilemmas of Democratization in Latin America," *Comparative Politics* 23 (October 1990): 1–21. See also Kenneth A. Bollen and Robert W. Jackman, "Economic and Noneconomic Determinants of Political Democracy," *Research in Political Sociology* 1 (1985): 27–48.

4. The working group consisted of Miguel Basáñez, MORI-USA; Mary Clark, Tulane University; Kenneth Coleman; Jorge Domínguez, Harvard University; Ronald Inglehart, University of Michigan; Matthew Kenney, Tulane University; Marta Lagos, MORI-Chile; Kevin Middlebrook, University of California, San Diego; Yemille Mizrahi, Center for Economic Research and Teaching, Mexico City; Alejandro Moreno, Autonomous Technological Institute of Mexico; Pablo Parás, MORI-Mexico; and Frederick Turner, University of Connecticut.

5. "Democracy through Latin American Lenses: Views of the Citizenry" (proposal to the Hewlett Foundation, September 1997), appendixes 1 and 2, "Survey on Popular Conceptions of Democracy."

6. See, for example, the image survey among experts by Kenneth F. Johnson, "The 1980 Image-Index Survey of Latin American Political Democracy," *Latin American Research Review* 19 (1982): 193–201.

7. For background on Mexico, see Roderic Ai Camp, *Politics in Mexico: The Decline of Authoritarianism*, 3rd ed. (New York: Oxford University Press, 1999).

8. These controversies are presented in Ronald Inglehart, "The Renaissance of Political Culture," *American Political Science Review* 82, no. 4 (1988): 1203–30.

9. Larry Diamond, ed., *Political Culture and Democracy in Developing Countries* (Boulder, Colo.: Lynne Rienner, 1994), 7.

10. Camp, *Politics in Mexico*, 53.

11. Edward N. Muller and Mitchell A. Seligson, "Civic Culture and Democracy: The Question of Causal Relationships," *American Political Science Review* 88, no. 3 (1994): 636.

12. Larry Diamond, "Causes and Effects," in Diamond, *Political Culture*, 411–35.

13. Gabriel A. Almond and Sidney Verba, *The Civic Culture: Political Attitudes and Democracy in Five Nations* (Boston: Little, Brown, 1965).

14. Richard Dawson and Kenneth Prewitt, *Political Socialization* (Boston: Little, Brown, 1969).

15. These arguments are nicely summarized by Ruth Lane in "Political Culture: Residual Category or General Theory?" *Comparative Political Studies* 25, no. 4 (1992): 362–87.

16. Gabriel Almond, one of the initial contributors to the survey research on civic culture, suggests that it definitely affects governmental performance and structure but that it does not determine those patterns. "Foreword: A Return to Political Culture," in Diamond, *Political Culture*, ix.

17. Kenneth A. Bollen, "Political Democracy: Conceptual and Measurement Traps," in *On Measuring Democracy*, ed. Alex Inkeles (New Brunswick, N.J.: Transaction Publishers, 1991), 8; Paul Cammack, "Democratization and Citizenship in Latin America," in *Democracy and Democratization*, ed. Geraint Perry and Michael Moran (New York: Routledge, 1994), 177.

18. See, for example, Mehran Kamrava, "Political Culture and a New Definition of the Third World," *Third World Quarterly* 16, no. 4 (1995): 698–99.

19. For a brief discussion of these principles, see Shannan Mattiace and Roderic Ai Camp, "Democracy and Development: An Overview," in *Democracy in Latin America: Patterns and Cycles*, ed. Roderic Ai Camp (Wilmington, Del.: Scholarly Resources, 1996), 3–19.

20. Samuel P. Huntington, "Democracy's Third Wave," in *The Global Resurgence of Democracy*, ed. Larry Diamond and Marc F. Plattner (Baltimore: Johns Hopkins University Press, 1993), 3–25.

21. Robert H. Dix, "History and Democracy Revisited," *Comparative Politics* 27 (October 1994): 94. An excellent assessment of the possible causal relationships between economic and political liberalism is presented by Peter H. Smith, "The Political Impact of Free Trade on Mexico," *Journal of Interamerican Studies and World Affairs* 34, no. 1 (spring 1992): 1–25.

22. For detailed survey information on this issue in the United States, see Herbert McClosky and John Zaller, *The American Ethos: Public Attitudes toward Capitalism and Democracy* (Cambridge: Harvard University Press, 1984).

23. Marta Lagos, "Actitudes económicos y democracia en Latinoamérica," *Este País*, January 1997, 2–9.

24. Ronald Inglehart and Marita Carballo, "Does Latin America Exist? (And Is There a Confucian Culture?): A Global Analysis of Cross-Cultural Differences," *PS: Political Science and Politics* 29 (March 1997): 46.

25. Arend Lijphart, "The Structure of Inference," in *The Civic Culture Revisited*, ed. Gabriel A. Almond and Sidney Verba (Boston: Little, Brown, 1980), 37–102.

26. For background on Costa Rica, see Bruce M. Wilson, *Costa Rica: Politics, Economics, and Democracy* (Boulder, Colo.: Lynne Rienner, 1998).

27. Gabriel Almond, "The Intellectual History of the Civic Culture Concept," in Almond and Verba, *The Civic Culture Revisited*, 26ff.

28. See Rafael Segovia's classic study, *La politización del niño mexicano* (Mexico City: El Colegio de México, 1975), 152.

29. For example, Muller and Seligson suggest on the basis of survey research that democratic politics contributes to trust. "Civic Culture and Democracy," 645–52. The opposing argument, that democratic politics does not produce trust, has been offered by Robert D. Putnam with Robert Leonardi and Raffaella Y. Nanetti, *Making Democracy Work: Civic Traditions in Modern Italy* (Princeton: Princeton University Press, 1993).

30. Ronald Inglehart, *Culture Shift in Advanced Industrial Society* (Princeton: Princeton University Press, 1990).

31. Putnam, *Making Democracy Work*.

32. Robert D. Putnam, "Tuning in, Tuning Out: The Strange Disappearance of Social Capital in America," *PS: Political Science and Politics* 27, no. 4 (December 1995): 664–83.

33. Carlos B. Gil, *Hope and Frustration: Interviews with Leaders of Mexico's Political Opposition* (Wilmington, Del.: Scholarly Resources, 1992), 48–57.

34. Sheldon Annis, "Giving Voice to the Poor," *Foreign Policy*, no. 84 (fall 1991): 100.

35. Jack Dennis, "Major Problems of Political Socialization Research," in *Socialization to Politics*, ed. Jack Dennis (New York: Wiley, 1973), 24.

36. Theodore Newcomb, "Persistence and Regression of Changed Attitudes: Long-Range Studies," in Dennis, *Socialization to Politics*, 422.

37. Allen H. Barton, "Background, Attitudes, and Activities of American Elites," in *Studies of the Structure of National Elites*, vol. 1, ed. Gwen Moore (Greenwich, Conn.: JAI, 1985), 213.

38. Roderic Ai Camp, "Mexico's Mandarins: Crafting a Power Elite for the Twenty-first Century" (manuscript, 2000).

39. For additional background on democratic features in Mexico, see Guy Poitras, "Mexico's Problematic Transition to Democracy," in *Assessing Democracy in Latin America*, ed. Philip Kelly (Boulder, Colo.: Westview Press, 1998), 63–75.

40. John Booth and Mitchell Seligson, "The Political Culture of Authoritarianism in Mexico: A Reexamination," *Latin American Research Review* 19, no. 1 (1984): 106–24.

41. For background on this issue, see Timothy Scully, *Rethinking the Center: Party Politics in Nineteenth and Twentieth Century Chile* (Stanford: Stanford University Press, 1992).

42. Kenneth Wald, Dennis E. Owen, and Samuel S. Hills, "Political Cohesion in Churches," *Journal of Politics* 52 (February 1990): 197–215; idem, "Churches as Political Communities," *American Political Science Review* 82 (June 1988): 531–48.

Chapter 2: Democracy and Mass Belief Systems in Latin America

1. Ronald Inglehart, *Modernization and Postmodernization: Cultural, Economic, and Political Change in 43 Societies* (Princeton: Princeton University Press, 1997).

2. Gabriel A. Almond and Sidney Verba, *The Civic Culture: Political Attitudes and Democracy in Five Nations* (Boston: Little, Brown, 1965).

3. Neil Nevitte, *The Decline of Deference: Canadian Value Change in Comparative Perspective* (Peterborough, Ont.: Broadview Press, 1996); Ronald Inglehart, *Culture Shift in Advanced Industrial Society* (Princeton: Princeton University Press, 1990).

4. W. Lance Bennett, "The UnCivic Culture: Communication, Identity, and the Rise of Lifestyle Politics," *PS: Political Science and Politics* 31, no. 4 (1998): 741–61.

5. Giuseppe Di Palma, *To Craft Democracies: An Essay on Democratic Transitions* (Berkeley: University of California Press, 1990), 27.

6. Robert Dahl, *Polyarchy: Participation and Opposition* (New Haven: Yale University Press, 1971).

7. Philip E. Converse, "The Nature of Belief Systems in Mass Publics," in *Ideology and Discontent*, ed. David Apter (New York: Free Press, 1964), 207.

8. Ibid.

9. See, for example, John Zaller, *The Nature and Origins of Mass Opinion* (Cambridge: Cambridge University Press, 1992).

10. See, for example, the discussion in Edward N. Muller and Mitchell A. Seligson, "Civic Culture and Democracy: The Question of Causal Relationships," *American Political Science Review* 88, no. 3 (1994): 635–52; and Inglehart, *Modernization and Postmodernization*.

11. Seymour M. Lipset, *Political Man* (New York: Doubleday, 1960); Almond and Verba, *The Civic Culture;* Inglehart, *Modernization and Postmodernization*.

12. Adam Przeworski, *Democracy and the Market: Political and Economic Reforms in Eastern Europe and Latin America* (Cambridge: Cambridge University Press, 1991).

13. Robert D. Putnam with Robert Leonardi and Raffaella Y. Nanetti, *Making Democracy Work: Civic Traditions in Modern Italy* (Princeton: Princeton University Press, 1993).

14. Juan J. Linz and Alfred Stepan, *Problems of Democratic Transition and Consolidation: Southern Europe, South America, and Post-Communist Europe* (Baltimore: Johns Hopkins University Press, 1996).

15. Marta Lagos, "Latin America's Smiling Mask," *Journal of Democracy* 8, no. 3 (July 1997): 125–38.

16. Inglehart, *Modernization and Postmodernization*, 163.

17. Linz and Stepan, *Problems of Democratic Transition*.

18. The index of democratic and nondemocratic attitudes was constructed by using principal component factor analysis of individual-level data from 48 societies. The data come from the 1995–97 World Values Survey and included 45,011 individual cases after missing data. Question wording may be consulted in the appendix to this chapter. The countries from the data set are listed in order according to their code number in the ICPSR (Inter-university Consortium for Political and Social Research) archives; sample sizes are shown in parentheses: 3 West Germany (1,017); 8 Spain (1,211); 11 USA (1,542); 13 Japan (1,054); 14 Mexico (1,510); 15 South Africa (2,935); 17 Australia (2,048); 18 Norway (1,127); 19 Sweden (1,009); 20 Tambov (500); 22 Argentina (1,079); 23 Finland (987); 24 South Korea (1,249); 25 Poland (1,153); 26 Switzerland (1,212); 27 Puerto Rico (1,164); 28 Brazil (1,149); 29 Nigeria (2,769); 30 Chile (1,000); 31 Belarus (2,092); 32 India (2,040); 34 East Germany (1,009); 35 Slovenia (1,007); 39 China (1,500); 40 Taiwan (1,452); 44 Turkey (1,906); 46 Lithuania (1,009); 47 Latvia (1,200); 48 Estonia (1,021); 49 Ukraine (2,811); 50 Russia (2,040); 51 Peru (1,211); 53 Venezuela (1,200); 54 Uruguay (1,000); 56 Ghana (96); 58 Philippines (1,200); 61 Moldova (984); 62 Georgia (2,593); 63 Armenia (2,000); 64 Azerbaijan (2,002); 68 Dominican Republic (417); 75 Basque (2,205); 78 Andalusia (1,803); 79 Galicia (1,200); 80 Valencia (501); 81 Serbia (1,280); 82 Montenegro (240); 84 Croatia (1,196).

19. Some of the early comments on my chapter asked me to take the variable about democracy and economic performance out of the index, given that it would threaten its validity and make it dependent upon each society's current economy. However, I preferred to include such a variable, because fears about economic crises such as those in Venezuela or Russia in the 1990s, or even the Weimar Republic in the early 1930s, may be conducive to the erosion of support for democratic rule. I do consider the seven-item index as a relatively complete and reliable measure if we want to assess support for democracy in a cross-national perspective.

20. Almond and Verba, *The Civic Culture*.

21. Support for democracy seems higher in Argentina and Uruguay than in other Latin American societies, even though neither one of them was considered a consolidated democracy by the time of the survey. See Linz and Stepan, *Problems of Democratic Transition*.

22. Alejandro Moreno, *Political Cleavages: Issues, Parties, and the Consolidation of Democracy* (Boulder, Colo.: Westview Press, 1999).

23. Lagos, "Latin America's Smiling Mask."

24. The 1996 Latinobarómetro shows that support for democracy (percentage of respondents who agree with the statement "Democracy is preferable to any other kind of government") is 81% in Spain; 80% in Costa Rica; 80% in Uruguay; 75% in Panama; 71% in Argentina; 64% in Bolivia; 63% in Peru; 62% in Venezuela; 60% in Colombia; 59% in Nicaragua; 59% in Paraguay; 56% in El Salvador; 54% in Chile; 53% in Mexico; 52% in Ecuador; 51% in Guatemala; 50% in Brazil; and 42% in Honduras. Lagos, "Latin America's Smiling Mask."

25. Herbert Kitschelt, *The Radical Right in Western Europe: A Comparative Analysis* (Ann Arbor: University of Michigan Press, 1995).

26. Jorge I. Domínguez and James A. McCann, *Democratizing Mexico: Public Opinion and Electoral Choices* (Baltimore: Johns Hopkins University Press, 1996), 28.

27. John A. Booth and Mitchell A. Seligson, "Paths to Democracy and the Political Culture of Costa Rica, Mexico, and Nicaragua," in *Political Culture and Democracy in Developing Countries,* ed. Larry Diamond (Boulder, Colo.: Lynne Rienner, 1994).

28. Edgardo Catterberg, *Los Argentinos frente a la política: Cultura política y opinión pública en la transición Argentina a la democracia* (Buenos Aires: Planeta, 1989).

29. Inglehart, *Modernization and Postmodernization.*

30. Terry Nichols Clark and Ronald Inglehart, "The New Political Culture: Changing Dynamics of Support for the Welfare State and Other Policies in Postindustrial Societies," in *The New Political Culture,* ed. Terry Nichols Clark and Vincent Hoffmann-Martinot (Boulder, Colo.: Westview Press, 1998).

Chapter 3: Does Trust Matter?

1. Ronald Inglehart, "The Renaissance of Political Culture," *American Political Science Review* 82, no. 4 (December 1988): 1203–30.

2. For these and other criticisms of political culture theory, see David J. Elkins and Richard E. B. Simeon, "A Cause in Search of Its Effect, or What Does Political Culture Explain?" *Comparative Politics* 11 (January 1979): 127–45; and Ruth Lane, "Political Culture: Residual Category or General Theory?" *Comparative Political Studies* 25, no. 4 (October 1992): 362–87.

3. A vigorous critique of such deterministic ethnocentrism is found in Lars Schoultz, *Beneath the United States: A History of U.S. Policy toward Latin America* (Cambridge: Harvard University Press, 1998), especially pp. 380–86.

4. For classic modernizationist approaches to political culture, see Gabriel A. Almond and Sidney Verba, *The Civic Culture: Political Attitudes and Democracy in Five Nations* (Princeton: Princeton University Press, 1963); and Alex Inkeles and David Smith, *Becoming Modern: Individual Change in Six Developing Countries* (Cambridge: Harvard University Press, 1974). A critical symposium on the original civic culture thesis is found in Gabriel Almond and Sidney Verba, eds., *The Civic Culture Revisited* (Boston: Little, Brown, 1980). For important works that helped foment the revival of political culture in the 1990s, see Ronald Inglehart, *Culture Shift in Advanced Industrial Society* (Princeton: Princeton University Press, 1990); Inglehart, *Modernization and Postmodernization: Cultural, Economic, and Political Change in 43 Societies* (Princeton: Princeton University Press, 1997); and Robert D. Putnam with Robert Leonardi and Raffaella Y. Nanetti, *Making Democracy Work: Civic Traditions in Modern Italy* (Princeton: Princeton University Press, 1993).

5. Inglehart, *Modernization and Postmodernization,* 174.

6. Edward N. Muller and Mitchell A. Seligson, "Civic Culture and Democracy: The Question of Causal Relationships," *American Political Science Review* 88, no. 3 (September 1994): 645–52.

7. Putnam, *Making Democracy Work.*

8. Inglehart, *Modernization and Postmodernization,* 174.

9. Adam Przeworski, *Democracy and the Market: Political and Economic Reforms in Eastern Europe and Latin America* (New York: Cambridge University Press, 1991), 10.

10. Inglehart, *Modernization and Postmodernization,* 172.

11. Larry Diamond, *Developing Democracy: Toward Consolidation* (Baltimore: Johns Hopkins University Press, 1999), 207–8.

12. Robert D. Putnam, "Tuning In, Tuning Out: The Strange Disappearance of Social Capital in America," *PS: Political Science and Politics* 27, no 4 (December 1995): 665.

13. See Putnam, *Making Democracy Work*, 86–91; see also Robert D. Putnam, "Bowling Alone: America's Declining Social Capital," *Journal of Democracy* 6, no. 1 (January 1995): 65–78; and Putnam, "Tuning In, Tuning Out."

14. Diamond, *Developing Democracy*, 208.

15. For a persuasive theoretical discussion of why institution building is critical for young democracies, see Guillermo O'Donnell, "Delegative Democracy," *Journal of Democracy* 5, no. 1 (January 1994): 55–69.

16. See Howard Wiarda, "Social Change, Political Development, and the Latin American Tradition," and Glen Dealy, "Pipe Dreams: The Pluralistic Latins," both reprinted in *Politics and Social Change in Latin America*, 3rd ed., ed. Howard Wiarda (Boulder, Colo.: Westview Press, 1992).

17. Lawrence Harrison, *Underdevelopment Is a State of Mind: The Latin American Case* (Lanham, Md.: University Press of America, 1985). For extensions of his arguments, see also Lawrence Harrison, *Who Prospers? How Cultural Values Shape Economic and Political Success* (New York: Basic Books, 1992); and Harrison, *The Pan-American Dream: Do Latin America's Cultural Values Discourage True Partnership with the United States and Canada?* (New York: Basic Books, 1997).

18. Two important exceptions in the 1980s were John Booth and Mitchell Seligson, "The Political Culture of Authoritarianism in Mexico: A Reexamination," *Latin American Research Review* 19, no. 1 (1984): 106–24; and Susan Tiano, "Authoritarianism and Political Culture in Argentina and Chile in the Mid-1960s," *Latin American Research Review* 21, no. 1 (1986): 71–98.

19. Marta Lagos, "Latin America's Smiling Mask," *Journal of Democracy* 8, no. 3 (July 1997): 125–26.

20. Guillermo O'Donnell, "Situaciones: Micro-escenas de la privatización de lo público en São Paulo," Working Paper No. 121, Helen Kellogg Institute for International Studies, University of Notre Dame, 1989. See also his essays "Democracy in Argentina: Micro and Macro," and "'And Why Should I Give a Shit?' Notes on Sociability and Politics in Argentina and Brazil," both reprinted in O'Donnell, *Counterpoints: Selected Essays on Authoritarianism and Democratization* (Notre Dame: University of Notre Dame Press, 1999).

21. Frederick C. Turner, "Reassessing Political Culture," in *Latin America in Comparative Perspective: New Approaches to Methods and Analysis,* ed. Peter H. Smith (Boulder, Colo.: Westview Press, 1995), 195–224.

22. Cited in Inglehart, *Modernization and Postmodernization*, 359.

23. See Lagos, "Latin America's Smiling Mask."

24. Ibid., 133.

25. Here follow some notes on the coding of basic demographic variables. For urbanization, a value of 1 is a rural area; a value of 2 is a community of 15,000 to 50,000; a value of 3 is a community of 50,000 to 100,000; 4 is for cities of 100,000 to 1 million; and 5 refers to metropolises with more than 1 million inhabitants. Education was recoded in the following way: values 0 to 12 are actual years of formal education; the value of 13 is some university; and the value of 14 combines college graduates and those who have attended postgraduate programs. For income, 1 is the bottom 40% of income distribution, 2 is the next 30%, 3 is the next 20%, and 4 is the top 10%. As for age: 1 is for 18–29 years, 2 is for 30–49 years, and 3 is for respondents 50 and over.

26. See Lagos, "Latin America's Smiling Mask."

27. Putnam, "Tuning In, Tuning Out," 667 (italics in original).

28. O'Donnell, "Situaciones."

Chapter 4: Costa Rica

1. In his excellent review of the political culture literature, Larry Diamond finds that the values and orientations most often associated with democratic political culture include participation, tolerance, restraint, and civility. See his "Introduction: Political Culture and Democracy," in *Political Culture and Democracy in Developing Countries*, ed. Larry Diamond (Boulder, Colo.: Lynne Rienner, 1993), 1–21.

2. For descriptions of political violence prior to 1948, see Fabrice Edouard Lehoucq, "The Institutional Foundations of Democratic Cooperation in Costa Rica," *Journal of Latin American Studies* 28, no. 1 (May 1996): 330; and Cynthia Chalker, "Elections and Democracy in Costa Rica," in *Elections and Democracy in Central America, Revisited*, ed. Mitchell A. Seligson and John A. Booth (Chapel Hill: University of North Carolina Press, 1995). Some authors do not see the events of 1948 as having created an abrupt change in political development. Rather, they emphasize the way that democratic practices evolved from previous eras toward the mid-twentieth century. In its original version, this argument held that the privations of the colonial period produced an unusually egalitarian society from which democracy naturally evolved. The classic statement of this thesis is Carlos Monge Alfaro, *Historia de Costa Rica*, 16th ed. (San José: Libreria Trejos, 1980). In English, see Charles Ameringer, *Democracy in Costa Rica* (New York: Praeger, 1982); and James L. Busey, *Notes on Costa Rican Democracy* (Boulder, Colo.: University of Colorado Press, 1962). Another version credits the interdependence of large and small coffee growers during the nineteenth and twentieth centuries with the gradual development of a national ideology valuing participation, equality, and consensus in political matters. See José Luis Carballo, *Poder político y democracia en Costa Rica* (San José: Editorial Porvenir, 1982).

3. For thorough descriptions of the alliances involved in the 1948 war and of José Figueres's background, see Deborah J. Yashar, "Civil War and Social Welfare: The Origins of Costa Rica's Competitive Party System," in *Building Democratic Institutions: Party Systems in Latin America*, ed. Scott Mainwaring and Timothy R. Scully (Stanford: Stanford University Press, 1995); and John Patrick Bell, *Crisis in Costa Rica: The 1948 Revolution* (Austin: University of Texas Press, 1971).

4. While living in exile in Mexico during 1942–44, Figueres had helped to found the Caribbean Legion, a group that planned to overthrow regional dictators such as Somoza in Nicaragua and Trujillo in the Dominican Republic. After Figueres returned home, the Legion helped him stockpile arms on his farm south of the capital.

5. A loophole allowed Figueres to serve two terms as president.

6. Andrew R. Nickson, *Local Government in Latin America* (Boulder, Colo.: Lynne Rienner, 1995), 58.

7. Unless otherwise noted, all of the data reported here come from a public opinion survey commissioned by Roderic Ai Camp with the support of the Hewlett Foundation. MORI International conducted the survey in Mexico, Costa Rica, and Chile during July 1998. The Costa Rican survey was national and included 1,002 respondents, approximately half of whom resided in small towns and rural areas. The Costa Rican survey had a ±3.5 percent margin of error.

8. Reported in Marta Lagos, "Latin America's Smiling Mask," *Journal of Democracy* 8, no. 3 (1997), table 3.

9. Ibid. The index includes three questions gauging citizens' support for democracy, satisfaction with democracy, and willingness to defend democracy.

10. Party identification was determined by asking, "If the election were today, who would you vote for?" Thirty-three percent chose the Partido Unidad Social Cristiana (United Social Christian Party, or PUSC), 29 percent chose the Partido Liberación Nacional (National Liberation Party, or

PLN), and 24 percent said "none" or that they did not usually vote. The remainder named another party or refused to answer.

11. Mary A. Clark, *Gradual Economic Reform in Latin America: The Costa Rican Experience* (Albany: SUNY Press, forthcoming), table 2.1.

12. Yashar, "Civil War and Social Welfare," 88.

13. Ibid., 89.

14. A host of small right-wing paramilitary organizations operated in Costa Rica during the 1980s and 1990s. Most had relationships with or were inspired by the Nicaraguan *contras,* including the Movimiento Costa Rica Libre. For more information, see John A. Booth, *Costa Rica: Quest for Democracy* (Boulder, Colo.: Westview Press, 1998), 120–21; and Martha Honey, *Hostile Acts: U.S. Policy in Costa Rica in the 1980s* (Gainesville: University Press of Florida, 1994).

15. Chalker, "Elections and Democracy in Costa Rica," 112.

16. Three came from the Fuerza Democrática (Democratic Force) party and one from the Partido Agrícola Laboral Auténtico (Authentic Agricultural Labor Party).

17. I am grateful to Carlos Sojo, who clarified the development of postwar labor organizations for me. Personal communication, September 30, 1999.

18. Bruce M. Wilson, *Costa Rica: Politics, Economics, and Democracy* (Boulder, Colo.: Lynne Rienner, 1998), 70.

19. Booth, *Costa Rica,* 70.

20. See Inter-American Development Bank, *Economic and Social Progress in Latin America: 1997 Report* (Washington, D.C., 1997), 96.

21. This is the argument put forth in the conclusions of John A. Booth and Mitchell A. Seligson in "Paths to Democracy and the Political Culture of Costa Rica, Mexico, and Nicaragua," in Diamond, *Political Culture,* 107–38.

22. Gabriel A. Almond and Sidney Verba, *The Civic Culture: Political Attitudes and Democracy in Five Nations* (Princeton: Princeton University Press, 1963). The authors relate citizen culture to democracy and relate its opposite, subject culture, to political passivity and authoritarianism.

23. Booth, *Costa Rica,* 103–10.

24. Ibid., 104.

25. Alex Inkeles defines the authoritarian personality syndrome in "National Character and Modern Political Systems," in *Psychological Anthropology: Approaches to Culture and Personality,* ed. Francis L. K. Hsu (Homewood, Ill.: Dorsey Press, 1961), 193–99.

26. Florisabel Rodríguez, Silvia Castro, and Rowland Espinosa found that Costa Ricans reported liking homosexuals less than extremists of the right or left, atheists, Nicaraguans, or military personnel. *El sentir democrático: Estudios sobre la cultura política centroamericana* (San José: Editorial Fundación UNA, 1998).

27. In two descriptive essays, Guillermo O'Donnell argues that microlevel, everyday behavior reflecting citizens' concern for civicness (by, say, not illegally occupying a handicapped parking space) has an important impact on the prospects for democratic consolidation. See Guillermo O'Donnell, "Y a mí que mierda me importa? Notas sobre sociabilidad y política en Argentina y Brasil," Working Paper No. 9, Helen Kellogg Institute for International Studies, University of Notre Dame, January 1984; and O'Donnell, "Situaciones: Micro-escenas de la privatización de lo público en São Paulo," Working Paper No. 121, Helen Kellogg Institute for International Studies, University of Notre Dame, 1989.

28. Ronald Inglehart, *Culture Shift in Advanced Industrial Society* (Princeton: Princeton University Press, 1990).

29. Diamond, "Introduction," 11.

30. Mavis Hiltunen Biesanz, Richard Biesanz, and Karen Zubris Biesanz, *The Ticos: Culture and Social Change in Costa Rica* (Boulder, Colo.: Lynne Rienner, 1999), 76–77.

31. Ibid., 83.

32. San José's leading daily, *La Nación,* has recently taken to publishing headlines drawing attention to the growing fear of crime. See, for example, Ronald Moya and Irene Vizcaíno, "País enfermo de violencia," *La Nación,* October 18, 1998; and "Ticos marcados por inseguridad," *La Nación,* November 10, 1998. To the extent that news sources sensationalize crime and corruption issues, Costa Ricans' exposure to the news may afflict them with something like the "mean world effect" discussed by Robert D. Putnam. In "Tuning In, Tuning Out," *PS: Political Science and Politics* 28, no. 4 (December 1995): 679, Putnam describes the mean world effect as one in which heavy television watchers become unusually pessimistic about human nature and tend to overestimate crime rates. It is possible that in Costa Rica, news coverage of corruption and crime issues is having a similar effect.

33. United Nations Development Program, *Estado de la Nación, 1996* (San José, 1997), statistics taken from the electronic version, <http://www.estadonacion.or.cr/>.

34. Criminologists have yet to specify the roots of the problem in Costa Rica. But possible explanations include frustration among those on the margins of the economic model, the growing number of tourists in the country who are easy marks for thieves, an infiltration of criminals and arms from neighboring countries, and spillover effects from local narcotics trafficking.

35. In this survey, Chileans and Mexicans were also more intolerant of homosexuals than of evangelicals or foreigners. In the 1997 six-country Central American survey that forms the basis of Rodríguez, Castro, and Espinosa, *El sentir democrático,* people in every country were more intolerant of homosexuals than any other group. As for interpersonal trust, in "Latin America's Smiling Mask," Lagos finds low trust throughout Latin America.

Chapter 5: Costa Rican Exceptionalism

I would like to thank Roderic Ai Camp for sharing the data set with me, Cynthia Chalker Franklin for her comments on the draft version, and the Hewlett Foundation for providing the financial support to collect the data.

1. The World Bank reports a 1997 per capita income for Costa Rica of $2,640, compared to the United States with $28,740. See World Bank, *World Development Report, 1998/99* (Washington, D.C.: Oxford University Press, 1999); Mitchell A. Seligson, Juliana Martínez, and Juan Diego Trejos, *Reducción de la pobreza en Costa Rica: El impacto de las políticas públicas,* Serie Divulgación Económica No. 51 (San José: Instituto de Investigaciones en Ciencias Económicas Universidad de Costa Rica, 1996); and Mitchell A. Seligson, Juliana Martínez F., and Juan Diego Trejos, "Reducción de la pobreza en Costa Rica: El impacto de las políticas públicas," in *Estrategias para reducir la pobreza en América Latina y el Caribe,* ed. José Vicente Zevallos (New York: United Nations Development Program, 1997).

2. Costa Rica's real GDP per capita rank minus its Human Development Index (HDI) rank is a +27. Zaire, with a score of 31, actually exceeds Costa Rica, but it ranks at 142 out of 175 countries on the HDI measure, compared to Costa Rica's 33. The real GDP for Zaire is only a rough estimate ($429 per capita), compared to the reliable figure of $5,919 obtained for Costa Rica. Note that these are *real* GDP figures. See World Bank, *World Development Report, 1998/99,* 192–93; and United Nations Development Program, *Human Development Report* (New York: Oxford University Press, 1997), 45.

3. Former president Oscar Arias Sánchez won the Nobel Peace Prize in 1987 for his successful efforts to bring an end to the fighting in El Salvador and Nicaragua.

4. See Raymond D. Gastil, *Freedom in the World: Political Rights and Civil Liberties* (New York: Freedom House, 1980).

5. In Costa Rica, and to a lesser extent in Chile, the final sample overrepresented females, so MORI introduced a weighting factor to adjust for this difficulty. The sample analyzed here uses that weighting factor.

6. Of course, a "don't know" response was permitted, and 4.5 percent of the respondents in the three countries did not respond on this item. Those individuals are excluded from further analysis.

7. In the regression analysis presented at the end of this chapter, the full three-choice format is utilized.

8. There seems to be no dispute about the last 50 years, but some argue that the period prior to the Civil War of 1948 was not democratic. See Deborah J. Yashar, *Demanding Democracy: Reform and Reaction in Costa Rica and Guatemala, 1870s–1950s* (Stanford: Stanford University Press, 1997); and John A. Booth, *Costa Rica: Quest for Democracy* (Boulder, Colo.: Westview Press, 1998).

9. In most countries the samples hovered around 1,000 respondents, except in Venezuela, where the number was 1,500, and in Bolivia and Paraguay, where the samples were smaller. In the published summary of the Central American cases, a slight variation of 2–3 cases was found for Costa Rica, Nicaragua, and Panama from the data set reported on here. The variation is a result of ambiguous coding of the country location for a total of eight interviews out of the more than 18,000 in the database. The data from the 1996 Latinobarómetro were made available by the Inter-American Development Bank. See PNUD (Programa de las Naciones Unidas para el Desarrollo), Desarrollo Humano Sostenible, *Informe Latinobarómetro: Consolidado de Centroamérica*, Proyecto CAM.96.001 (San José, 1996); and Marta Lagos, "Latin America's Smiling Mask," *Journal of Democracy* 8, no. 3 (July 1997): 125–38.

10. See Edward N. Muller, "Democracy, Economic Development, and Income Inequality," *American Sociological Review* 53 (February 1988): 50–68; Adam Przeworski and Fernando Limongi, "Political Regimes and Economic Growth," *Journal of Economic Perspectives* 7, no. 3 (summer 1993): 51–69; and Erich Weede, "Political Regime Type and Variation in Economic Growth Rates," *Constitutional Political Economy* 7 (1996): 167–76.

11. See Robert A. Dahl, *Polyarchy: Participation and Opposition* (New Haven: Yale University Press, 1971).

12. According to the 1996 Latinobarómetro data, Catholics represent 82 percent of Costa Ricans, 83 percent of Mexicans, and 73 percent of Chileans. The remainder are largely various Protestant groups.

13. A test of the other two social tolerance measures revealed that only in one case, tolerance toward foreigners in Mexico and Chile, is the difference statistically significant, but in absolute terms the differences are very small—77 versus 82 percent in Mexico, and 87 versus 91 percent in Chile. Thus, for this measure, only 5 percentage points at most separate those who prefer democracy from those who do not.

14. See Robert D. Putnam with Robert Leonardi and Raffaella Y. Nanetti, *Making Democracy Work: Civic Traditions in Modern Italy* (Princeton: Princeton University Press, 1993); and Ronald Inglehart, *Modernization and Postmodernization: Cultural, Economic, and Political Change in 43 Societies* (Princeton: Princeton University Press, 1997).

15. See Francis Fukuyama, *Trust: The Social Virtues and the Creation of Prosperity* (New York: Free Press, 1995).

16. See Gabriel A. Almond and Sidney Verba, *The Civic Culture: Political Attitudes and Democracy in Five Nations* (Princeton: Princeton University Press, 1963).

17. See Mitchell A. Seligson, "A Problem-Solving Approach to Measuring Political Efficacy," *Social Science Quarterly* 60 (March 1980): 630–42.

18. It should be noted that there are three errors in the MORI report on this item. First, the English translation does not match the Spanish. The English translation reads: "Would you personally be ready to do something to demand accountability from government officials: yes or no?" The Spanish version that was actually used does not mention government officials but refers instead to "los gobernantes." The Spanish version also does not ask directly about willingness to do something, but whether citizens *should* demand accountability. Second, the Spanish questionnaire includes only a "yes/no" response, whereas the actual data set contains a five-point scale. Third, coding of the five-point scale is incorrect, since it codes "maybe not" as a "5" and "definitely not" as a "4." The analysis performed here is based on the version in the Spanish questionnaire—the one that was actually read to respondents—and the coding error was corrected by making the "4" into a "5" and the "5" into a "4."

19. The four-item response category, both here and for the following question on happiness, was recoded into a 0–100 scale to ease comparability with the other items.

20. It is difficult to see which variables might be used in a two-stage least squares analysis that would help us untangle the direction of causality in these data.

21. This was a summative scale. Mean scores were assigned to respondents who answered at least three of the five questions, and missing values were assigned to the remainder. This procedure produced only 147 missing cases out of the total of 3,396.

22. The item on relatives' marrying outside of one's religion was not included in the scale because it had a different format from the other three.

23. The dependent variable used is the recoded preference-for-democracy item. When this item is used in its trichotomous form, the overall results are similar, but weaker. Ordinary least squares regression is used here because of its wide familiarity to students. The more appropriate technique, logistic regression, was also employed with these same variables, but the models remain unchanged.

24. These are the variables that are significant in both model 1 and model 2.

25. Cynthia Chalker Franklin, "Riding the Wave: The Domestic and International Sources of Costa Rican Democracy" (Ph.D. diss., University of Pittsburgh, 1998).

Chapter 6: Transition to Democracy

1. See, for example, Tim Weiner, "PRI Claims Mexico State Vote but Opposition Cries Fraud," *New York Times*, October 24, 2000, A5.

2. Dankwart A. Rustow, "Transitions to Democracy: Toward a Dynamic Model," *Comparative Politics* 2 (April 1970): 361.

3. Ibid., 355.

4. See, for example, Jesús Rodríguez Zepeda, "Toward a Politics of Consensus in Mexico," *Voices of Mexico* 48 (July–September 1999): 7–10. Rodríguez Zepeda argues (on p. 10) that while there has been consensus regarding electoral competition, "what marks the institutional weakness of Mexico's public space is the lack of consensus at the level of joint promotion of state policies."

5. The low level of interpersonal trust reported by Costa Rican respondents (only 22 percent) is puzzling, given the country's relatively long tradition of democracy. Pablo Parás suggested at a Tulane University conference in January 1999 that part of the reason may be the wording of the question (¿se puede confiar en la gente?), as Costa Ricans typically refer to poor immigrants (who are frequently blamed for crime and other social ills), particularly to Nicaraguans, as *la gente*.

6. For an excellent account of election observers in Mexico and their importance in its transition to democracy, see Sergio Aguayo Quezada, "Electoral Observation and Democracy in Mexico," in *Electoral Observation and Democratic Transitions in Latin America*, ed. Kevin J. Middlebrook (La Jolla, Calif.: Center for U.S.-Mexican Studies, 1998). On the impact of the 1994 elections, see Wayne

A. Cornelius, *Mexican Politics in Transition: The Breakdown of a One-Party-Dominant Regime* (La Jolla, Calif.: Center for U.S.-Mexican Studies, 1996), 98; and Roderic Ai Camp, *Politics in Mexico: The Decline of Authoritarianism*, 3d ed. (New York: Oxford University Press, 1999), 187–89, 243–44.

7. In 1987, Cornelius wrote that in Mexico, "[m]ost citizens who participate in the electoral process do so with little or no expectation that their votes will influence the outcome of the election: the winner has been determined by the selection process within the PRI." Wayne A. Cornelius, "Political Liberalization in an Authoritarian Regime: Mexico, 1976–1985," in *Mexican Politics in Transition*, ed. Judith Gentlemen (Boulder, Colo.: Westview Press, 1987), 17. For many Mexicans, the national elections in 1988 marked a turning point away from such inconsequential participation—a process that has continued to the present, as seen in the federal elections of 1997 and 2000.

8. Camp, *Politics in Mexico*, 237.

9. For a brief summary of Salinas's political strategies and successes, see Camp, *Politics in Mexico*, 237–39.

10. For the most thorough treatment of corruption and fraud in Mexico, see Stephen D. Morris, *Corruption and Politics in Contemporary Mexico* (Tuscaloosa: University of Alabama Press, 1991).

11. Among the best analyses of twentieth-century Mexican presidentialism is Luis Javier Garrido, "The Crisis of *Presidencialismo*," in *Mexico's Alternative Political Futures*, ed. Judith Gentleman and Peter H. Smith (La Jolla, Calif.: Center for U.S.-Mexican Studies, 1989), 421. Lorenzo Meyer's penetrating essay shows the linkages between pre- and postrevolutionary presidentialism. Meyer, "Historical Roots of the Authoritarian State in Mexico," in *Authoritarianism in Mexico*, ed. José Luis Reyna and Richard S. Weinert (Philadelphia: Institute for the Study of Human Issues, 1977), 3–22. An excellent recent review of presidential powers in Mexico, including their evolution under Zedillo, is Jeffrey Weldon, "The Political Sources of *Presidencialismo* in Mexico," in *Presidentialism and Democracy in Latin America*, ed. Scott Mainwaring and Matthew Soberg Shugart (New York: Cambridge University Press, 1997), 225–58.

12. On the political role of Solidarity and other heavy-handed political reforms in the Salinas administration, see Stephen D. Morris, "Political Reformism in Mexico: Salinas at the Brink," *Journal of Interamerican Studies and World Affairs* 34, no. 1 (1992): 27–57.

13. Judith Teichman, "Neoliberalism and the Transformation of Mexican Authoritarianism," *Mexican Studies/Estudios Mexicanos* 13 (winter 1997):122–23.

14. Surprisingly, the 1998 survey on democracy indicates that ordinary Mexicans have largely accepted some of the broader social implications of a less interventionist state. When asked whether the state or the individual should look after the well-being of the latter, Mexicans were significantly less likely than Chileans or Costa Ricans to look to the state. These findings are discussed in greater detail below.

15. For more on the rise of the technocrats, see Miguel Angel Centeno, *Democracy within Reason: Technocratic Revolution in Mexico* (University Park: Pennsylvania State University Press, 1994).

16. Samuel P. Huntington, *The Third Wave: Democratization in the Late Twentieth Century* (Norman: University of Oklahoma Press, 1991), 6.

17. Rodríguez Zepeda, "Toward a Politics of Consensus in Mexico," 10.

18. Ronald Inglehart, Neil Nevitte, and Miguel Basáñez, *The North American Trajectory: Cultural, Economic, and Political Ties among the United States, Canada, and Mexico* (New York: Aldine de Gruyter, 1996), 85.

19. Ronald Inglehart, *Modernization and Postmodernization: Cultural, Economic, and Political Change in 43 Societies* (Princeton: Princeton University Press, 1997), 215. See also p. 164.

20. John Stuart Mill, *Considerations on Representative Government* (Chicago: Henry Regnery, 1962), 34.

21. For a discussion of the 1997 elections, see Luis Rubio, "Coping with Political Change," in *Mexico Under Zedillo*, ed. Susan Kaufman Purcell and Luis Rubio (Boulder, Colo.: Lynne Rienner, 1998), 34–35.

22. Miguel Basáñez et al., *Reporte 1995: Encuesta Latino Barómetro* (Mexico City, 1996), cuadro 23.

23. John Bailey and Arturo Valenzuela, "The Shape of the Future," *Journal of Democracy* 8, no. 4 (1997): 44.

24. "The no-reelection clause, the one feature of the Mexican system that could be seen as contributing to a democratic regime, is also partly responsible for the failure to develop more democratic mechanisms." Miguel Angel Centeno, "The Failure of Presidential Authoritarianism: Transition in Mexico," in *Politics, Society, and Democracy*, ed. Scott Mainwaring and Arturo Valenzuela (Boulder, Colo.: Westview Press, 1998), 39. Along these lines, see also Rubio, "Coping with Political Change," 26; and Bailey and Valenzuela, "The Shape of the Future," 52.

25. Civilian control over the military figures prominently in many empirical definitions of democracy. See, for example, Terry Lynn Karl, "Dilemmas of Democratization in Latin America," *Comparative Politics* 23 (October 1990): 2. Although it is sometimes overlooked, Dahl was also keenly aware of the need for civilian control of the military in democratic systems. See Robert A. Dahl, *Polyarchy: Participation and Opposition* (New Haven: Yale University Press, 1971), 50, 60; and Dahl, *Democracy and Its Critics* (New Haven: Yale University Press, 1989), chap. 18.

26. For a useful and concise overview of the Salinas *sexenio*, see Cornelius, *Mexican Politics in Transition*.

27. Ernesto Zedillo, "Presidential Candor about Mexico's Crisis," *Miami Herald*, April 16, 1995, reprinted in *Information Services in Latin America* 50 (April 1995): 55–56. For an assessment of Zedillo's performance with regard to electoral reform and other measures to solidify Mexico's democracy, see Rubio, "Coping with Political Change."

28. Ernesto Zedillo Ponce de León, *Plan nacional de desarrollo, 1995–2000* (Mexico City, 1995), sección 3.3.

29. Camp, *Politics in Mexico*, 175. Still, as Camp notes (p. 163), Zedillo's approval ratings generally rose while he was in office.

30. Sergio Muñoz, "Tackling Economic Crises, Corruption and Political Violence in Mexico," *Los Angeles Times*, September 15, 1996, M3.

31. *1996 Current Biography Yearbook* (New York: H. W. Wilson Company, 1996), 646.

32. Quoted in Ricardo Alemán, "Político, el problema de México: Zedillo," *La Jornada*, June 24, 1996, sección El País, 1.

33. Ronald Inglehart et al., *World Values Surveys and European Values Surveys*, 1981–84, 1990–93, and 1995–97, computer file, ICPSR version (Ann Arbor, Mich.: Inter-university Consortium for Political and Social Research, 2000).

34. Dahl, *Polyarchy*, 151.

35. Gabriel A. Almond and Sidney Verba, *The Civic Culture: Political Attitudes and Democracy in Five Nations* (Newbury Park, Calif.: Sage Publications, 1989), 356–57.

36. Inglehart, *Modernization and Postmodernization*, 173. A similar finding was reported in an earlier article by Inglehart, "The Renaissance of Political Culture," *American Political Science Review* 82, no. 4 (December 1988): 1214.

37. To date, Costa Rica has not been included in the World Values Survey.

38. On the theoretical implications of such a view, see Karl, "Dilemmas of Democratization in Latin America," 5.

39. Almond and Verba, *The Civic Culture*, 39, 61, 84, 158, 185, 350–51, 364.

40. Inglehart, Nevitte, and Basáñez, *The North American Trajectory*.

Chapter 7: Legacies of Authoritarianism

1. Here I follow Robert Dahl's argument in *Polyarchy: Participation and Opposition* (New Haven: Yale University Press, 1971), 124ff.

2. Gabriel A. Almond and Sidney Verba, *The Civic Culture: Political Attitudes and Democracy in Five Nations* (Princeton: Princeton University Press, 1963), 13.

3. Ibid., 14–15.

4. Joseph L. Klesner, "Economic Integration and Regional Electoral Dynamics in Mexico," in *NAFTA at the Grassroots: Local Impacts of Trade and Integration in Mexico and the United States*, ed. John Bailey (Austin, Tex.: L.B.J. School of Public Affairs, 2000).

5. Juan J. Linz, "An Authoritarian Regime: Spain," in *Mass Politics: Studies in Political Sociology*, ed. Erik Allardt and Stein Rokkan (New York: Free Press, 1970), 255.

6. For descriptions of the character of Pinochet's rule, see J. Samuel Valenzuela and Arturo Valenzuela, eds., *Military Rule in Chile: Dictatorship and Oppositions* (Baltimore: Johns Hopkins University Press, 1986); Karen L. Remmer, *Military Rule in Latin America* (Boston: Unwin Hyman, 1989); and idem, "Neopatrimonialism: The Politics of Military Rule in Chile, 1973–1987," *Comparative Politics* 21 (January 1989): 149–70.

7. Early exponents of a view of Mexican politics that stressed the authoritarian nature of the political system, especially focusing on the electoral hegemony of the Institutional Revolutionary Party (Partido Revolucionario Institucional, or PRI), included Frank Brandenburg, *The Making of Modern Mexico* (Englewood Cliffs, N.J.: Prentice-Hall, 1964); and Pablo González Casanova, *Democracy in Mexico* (New York: Oxford University Press, 1970 [1965]). Stronger statements about the authoritarian nature of the Mexican regime came after the 1968 massacre of students at Tlatelolco; see especially Roger D. Hansen, *The Politics of Mexican Development* (Baltimore: Johns Hopkins University Press, 1971); Evelyn P. Stevens, *Protest and Response in Mexico* (Cambridge: MIT Press, 1974); José Luis Reyna and Richard S. Weinert, eds., *Authoritarianism in Mexico* (Philadelphia: Institute for the Study of Human Issues, 1977); and Peter H. Smith, *Labyrinths of Power: Political Recruitment in Twentieth-Century Mexico* (Princeton: Princeton University Press, 1979).

8. Pamela Constable and Arturo Valenzuela, *A Nation of Enemies: Chile under Pinochet* (New York: Norton, 1991).

9. Paul Sigmund, *The Overthrow of Allende and the Politics of Chile, 1964–1976* (Pittsburgh: University of Pittsburgh Press, 1977); Arturo Valenzuela, *The Breakdown of Democratic Regimes: Chile* (Baltimore: Johns Hopkins University Press, 1978).

10. Constable and Valenzuela, *A Nation of Enemies*, 20, 94.

11. Ibid., 267–70; Tina Rosenberg, *Children of Cain: Violence and the Violent in Latin America* (New York: Morrow, 1991).

12. A useful description of the response of the regime in the 1970s is Judith Adler Hellman, *Mexico in Crisis*, 2d ed. (New York: Holmes and Meier, 1983).

13. Alan Riding, *Distant Neighbors: A Portrait of the Mexicans* (New York: Knopf, 1985).

14. For the continuing challenges of overcoming clientelism, see Jonathan Fox, "The Difficult Transition from Clientelism to Citizenship: Lessons from Mexico," *World Politics* 46, no. 2 (January 1994): 151–84.

15. Javier Martínez and Alvaro Díaz, *Chile: The Great Transformation* (Washington, D.C.: Brookings Institution, 1996). For a contrary view stressing the distributive consequences of neoliberal-

ism, see Joseph Collins and John Lear, *Chile's Free Market Miracle: A Second Look* (Oakland, Calif.: Food First, 1995).

16. The specific responses (in percentages):

With which of the following phrases do you agree most?	Mexico	Chile	Costa Rica
Democracy is preferable to any other form of government	50	50	80
We are indifferent to a democratic or a nondemocratic regime	26	28	9
In some circumstances, an authoritarian regime can be preferable to a democratic one	20	17	6
Don't know	3	5	5

17. Almond and Verba, *The Civic Culture*, 284–88.

18. Ann L. Craig and Wayne A. Cornelius, "Political Culture in Mexico: Continuities and Revisionist Interpretations," in *The Civic Culture Revisited*, ed. Gabriel A. Almond and Sidney Verba (Boston: Little, Brown, 1980), 372–73.

19. Ibid.

20. Almond and Verba, *The Civic Culture*, 268–69.

21. Of Chileans under age 30, 39 percent responded to the question "If elections were tomorrow, what political party would you vote for?" with the "none/doesn't usually vote" answer, compared to 23 percent of those 30–49 and 29 percent of those 50 and older.

22. Alan Angell and Benny Pollack, "The Chilean Elections of 1993: From Polarisation to Consensus," *Bulletin of Latin American Research* 14, no. 2 (1995): 116–17.

23. John Booth and Mitchell Seligson, "The Political Culture of Authoritarianism in Mexico: A Reexamination," *Latin American Research Review* 19, no. 1 (1984): 106–24.

24. Guillermo O'Donnell and Philippe Schmitter, *Transitions from Authoritarian Rule: Tentative Conclusions about Uncertain Democracies* (Baltimore: Johns Hopkins University Press, 1986); Terry Lynn Karl, "Dilemmas of Democratization in Latin America," *Comparative Politics* 23 (October 1990).

Chapter 8: Color and Democracy in Latin America

Special thanks for their help and comments to Sergio Aguayo, Tatiana Beltrán, Carlos Elordi, Brian Gibbs, Carlos López, Marcia Margolis, Alejandro Moreno, Lourdes Rébora, and Francisco Sarmiento.

1. *New York Times*, November 9, 1998, A20.

2. See Samuel Ramos, *El perfil del hombre y la cultura en Mexico* (Mexico: UNAM, 1979); Octavio Paz, *Laberinto de la soledad* (Mexico: FCE, 1972); Glen Dealy, *The Public Man* (University of Massachusetts Press, 1977); and Lawrence Harrison, *Underdevelopment Is a State of Mind: The Latin American Case* (Cambridge: Harvard University Press, 1985).

3. See Roderic Camp, *Intellectuals and the State in Twentieth-Century Mexico* (Austin: University of Texas Press, 1985); and Ronald Inglehart, *Modernization and Postmodernization: Cultural, Econom-*

ic, and Political Change in 43 Societies (Princeton: Princeton University Press, 1997).

4. See Donald R. Kinder and Lynn M. Sanders, *Divided by Color* (Chicago: University of Chicago Press, 1996).

5. Roderic Camp, personal communication referring to conversations with Daniel Cosío Villegas, January 29, 1999.

6. María Teresa Ruiz, *Racismo, algo mas que discriminación* (Costa Rica, Colección Análisis, Departamento Ecuménico de Investigaciones, 1988).

7. John A. Booth and Mitchell A. Seligson, "The Political Culture of Authoritarianism in Mexico: A Reexamination," *Latin American Research Review* 19, no. 1 (1984): 106–24.

8. Silvia Del Cid, "Ethnicity, Political Culture, and the Future of Guatemalan Democracy" (Ph.D. diss., University of Pittsburgh, 1997), 260.

9. Ronald Inglehart, "The Renaissance of Political Culture: Central Values, Political Economy, and Stable Democracy," *American Political Science Review* 82, no. 4 (1988); also in *Modernization and Postmodernization.*

10. Robert D. Putnam with Robert Leonardi and Raffaella Y. Nanetti, *Making Democracy Work: Civic Traditions in Modern Italy* (Princeton: Princeton University Press, 1993).

11. Frederick C. Turner, "Reassessing Political Culture," in *Latin America in Comparative Perspective: New Approaches to Methods and Analysis,* ed. Peter H. Smith (Boulder, Colo.: Westview Press, 1995).

12. Mitchell Seligson, "Political Culture and Democratization in Latin America," in *Democracy in Latin America: Patterns and Cycles,* ed. Roderic Ai Camp (Wilmington, Del.: SR Books, 1996).

13. Peter Smith, "The Changing Agenda for Social Science Research on Latin America," in Smith, *Latin America in Comparative Perspective.*

14. The table below (color orientation, controlled by education) shows the number of cases for each cell.

Education	Mexico	Costa Rica	Chile
White			
Basic	52	323	176
Higher	79	107	92
Total	200	613	457
Moreno			
Basic	449	249	322
Higher	179	34	91
Total	968	359	722

Chapter 9: Mexico and the United States

1. Gabriel A. Almond and Sidney Verba, *The Civic Culture: Political Attitudes and Democracy in Five Nations* (Princeton: Princeton University Press, 1963), 6–9, 31–32.

2. Ibid., 498.

3. Discussion with Lourdes Arizpe, Palma de Mallorca, Spain, November 28, 1990. Dr. Arizpe is Professor of Anthropology at the Universidad Nacional Autónoma de México, a former president of the International Union of Anthropological and Ethnological Sciences, and Vice President of the International Social Science Council. During the 1990s, she was also the Assistant Director General for Culture of the United Nations Educational, Scientific, and Cultural Organization (UNESCO).

4. Samuel P. Huntington, *American Politics: The Promise of Disharmony* (Cambridge: Harvard University Press, 1981), 51.

5. Jorge I. Domínguez and James A. McCann, *Democratizing Mexico: Public Opinion and Electoral Choice* (Baltimore: Johns Hopkins University Press, 1996), 2.

6. Tom W. Smith, "Is There Real Opinion Change?" *International Journal of Public Opinion Research* 6, no. 2 (summer 1994): 200.

7. Harry Eckstein, "A Culturalist Theory of Political Change," *American Political Science Review* 82, no. 3 (September 1988): 794.

8. Adam Przeworski, "Culture and Democracy," in *World Culture Report*, ed. Lourdes Arizpe et al. (Paris: UNESCO Publishing, 1998), 143.

9. Alex Inkeles, *National Character: A Psycho-Social Perspective* (New Brunswick, N.J.: Transaction Publishers, 1997), 239–40.

10. Almond and Verba, *The Civic Culture*, 496–97.

11. James A. McCann, "The Mexican Electorate in a North American Context: Assessing Patterns of Political Engagement," in *Polling for Democracy: Public Opinion and Political Liberalization in Mexico*, ed. Roderic Ai Camp (Wilmington, Del.: SR Books, 1996), 88.

12. Miguel Basáñez, *El pulso de los sexenios: 20 años de crisis en México*, 2d ed. (Mexico City: Siglo Veintiuno Editores, 1991), 325–28.

13. John A. Booth and Mitchell A. Seligson, "The Political Culture of Authoritarianism in Mexico: A Reexamination," *Latin American Research Review* 19, no. 1 (1984): 112–17; John A. Booth and Mitchell A. Seligson, "Paths to Democracy and the Political Culture of Costa Rica, Mexico, and Nicaragua," in *Political Culture and Democracy in Developing Countries*, ed. Larry Diamond (Boulder, Colo.: Lynne Rienner, 1994), 102–4, 123.

14. Booth and Seligson, "Political Culture of Authoritarianism," 118.

15. Robert R. Kaufman and Leo Zuckermann, "Attitudes toward Economic Reform in Mexico: The Role of Political Orientations," *American Political Science Review* 92, no. 2 (June 1998): 366–70.

16. Ronald Inglehart, *Culture Shift in Advanced Industrial Society* (Princeton: Princeton University Press, 1990), 45, 428–29.

17. See Alan Knight, "Mexico and Latin America in Comparative Perspective," in *Elites, Crises, and the Origins of Regimes*, ed. Mattei Dogan and John Higley (Lanham, Md.: Rowman and Littlefield, 1998).

18. Almond and Verba, *The Civic Culture*, 13, 15.

19. Seymour Martin Lipset, Robert M. Worcester, and Frederick C. Turner, "Survey Research and the Growth of Democracy," in *World Social Science Report*, ed. Ali Kazancigil and David Makinson (Paris: UNESCO Publishing/Elsevier, 1999), 260.

20. Enrique Alduncin Abitia, *Los valores de los mexicanos; México: Entre la tradición y la modernidad* (Mexico City: Fomento Cultural Banamex, A.C., 1989), 35.

21. Ronald Inglehart, *Modernization and Postmodernization: Cultural, Economic, and Political Change in 43 Countries* (Princeton: Princeton University Press, 1997), 137.

22. Harold D. Lasswell, *Democratic Character*, reprinted in *The Political Writings of Harold D. Lasswell* (Glencoe: Free Press, 1951), 502. Lasswell's italics.

23. Inkeles, *National Character*, 319.

24. One of the most helpful criticisms that we received after the Tulane conference in 1998 related directly to this point, asking how, if we used this question to gauge interpersonal trust, and if we defined values as highly resistant to change, we could explain the variations in interpersonal trust in the two countries during these years. This question made us rethink our interpretations, being more mindful of the limitations of the survey instruments in question. In the process, this criticism

indicated how important it is to argue about one's conclusions with colleagues before they are published, underlining the importance of the process by which Rod Camp put this volume together.

25. Edward N. Muller and Mitchell A. Seligson, "Civic Culture and Democracy: The Question of Causal Relationships," *American Political Science Review* 88, no. 3 (September 1994): 645–47.

26. Ibid., 646.

27. See Seymour Martin Lipset, Robert M. Worcester, and Frederick C. Turner, "Opening the Mexican Political System: Public Opinion and the Elections of 1994 and 1997," *Studies in Comparative International Development* 33, no. 3 (fall 1998): 70–89.

28. Ronald Inglehart, "The Renaissance of Political Culture," *American Political Science Review* 82, no. 4 (December 1988): 1215.

29. Muller and Seligson, "Civic Culture and Democracy," 647.

30. Knight, "Mexico and Latin America in Comparative Perspective," 82.

31. Kenneth A. Bollen, "Political Democracy: Conceptual and Measurement Traps," in *On Measuring Democracy: Its Consequences and Concomitants*, ed. Alex Inkeles (New Brunswick, N.J.: Transaction Publishers, 1991), 5.

32. Ann L. Craig and Wayne A. Cornelius, "Political Culture in Mexico: Continuities and Revisionist Interpretations," in *The Civic Culture Revisited*, ed. Gabriel A. Almond and Sidney Verba (Boston: Little, Brown, 1980), 337–38.

33. The coding of region was done by two different organizations with slightly different codes.

34. In the coding of the World Values Survey, 13 occupational groups were established. Therefore, in order to have enough respondents in each occupational group to make valid comparisons, data from the 1990 and 1995–97 waves of the World Values Survey are combined in the analysis here. This provides reasonable cell sizes in tables 3 and 4, except in the case of agricultural workers in the United States, where the tables reflect the views of only 20 agricultural workers.

35. Lorenzo Meyer, "Desarrollo político y dependencia externa: México en el siglo XX," in *Críticas constructivas del sistema político mexicano*, ed. William P. Glade and Stanley R. Ross (Austin: Institute of Latin American Studies, University of Texas at Austin, 1973), 12–24.

36. Linda S. Stevenson and Mitchell A. Seligson, "Fading Memories of the Revolution: Is Stability Eroding in Mexico?" in Camp, *Polling for Democracy*, 60–61, 74–77.

37. Almond and Verba, *The Civic Culture*, 79.

38. See Miguel Basáñez, "Problems of Interpreting Electoral Polls in Authoritarian Countries: Lessons from the 1994 Mexican Election," *International Social Science Journal*, no. 146 (December 1995): 645–48.

39. See Mattei Dogan, ed., "When People Lose Confidence," special issue of *Studies in Comparative International Development*, 32, no. 3 (fall 1997).

40. Frederick C. Turner and John D. Martz, "Institutional Confidence and Democratic Consolidation in Latin America," *Studies in Comparative International Development* 32, no. 3 (fall 1997): 69.

41. Inglehart, *Modernization and Postmodernization*, 323.

42. Ronald Inglehart, Neil Nevitte, and Miguel Basáñez, *The North American Trajectory: Cultural, Economic, and Political Ties among the United States, Canada, and Mexico* (New York: Aldine de Gruyter, 1996), 24.

43. William M. Reisinger, "The Renaissance of a Rubric: Political Culture as Concept and Theory," *International Journal of Public Opinion Research* 7, no. 4 (winter 1995): 334–36.

Chapter 10: Politics and Markets in Latin America

Thanks are extended to Robert L. Ayres, Miguel Basáñez, John A. Booth, Roderic Ai Camp, Charles L. Davis, Alan Knight, Daniel C. Levy, Alejandro Moreno, Rita Palacio, Pablo Parás, Margaret Wells, and an anonymous reviewer for suggestions that proved helpful to this work.

1. A summary of the emergent agreement on 10 policy instruments that became the core of the Washington Consensus among international financial agencies can be found in John Williamson, ed., *Latin American Adjustment: How Much Has Happened?* (Washington, D.C.: Institute for International Economics, 1990), 7–20. On the evolution of subsequent thinking, see Shavid Burki et al., *Beyond the Washington Consensus: Institutions Matter* (Washington, D.C.: World Bank, 1998).

2. One of the 10 points of the Washington Consensus was that among reduced public expenditures, priority should be placed on health and education (an area considered below). What remained open to discussion was how best the public monies should be spent—*on public institutions as providers* or via *subventions to private providers*.

3. For an illustrative treatment of this point, see Howard Wiarda, "Corporative Origins of the Iberian and Latin American Labor Relations Systems," *Studies in Comparative International Development* 8, no. 1 (1978): 1.

4. Anderson argued that an essential problem of governance was that the most important arena for human interaction in much of Latin America was not the nation-state, but rather subnational or supranational communities. Hence, the state was often irrelevant to the world in which citizens lived. Indeed, until well into the twentieth century, the sense of citizenship was often "not national," but sub- or supranational, if it existed at all.

5. Anderson surely assumes that the United States exhibits such a "cultural consensus" against a major role for the state in mobilizing economic resources or providing services.

6. Charles W. Anderson, *Politics and Economics in Latin America: The Governing of Restless Nations* (New York: Van Nostrand, 1967), 71–72.

7. Adam Przeworski and Henry Teune, *The Logic of Comparative Social Inquiry* (New York: Wiley-Interscience, 1970).

8. The fourth column under each service represents the average of the three country samples. It should not be taken as a precise estimate of the average view of citizens of these countries, because the country samples have *not* been weighted in accord with their relative populations.

9. These data are reported excluding cases where no opinion was rendered. "No opinion" answers reached 5 percent on the airline item, 4.1 percent on the television item, 2.7 percent on the water item, and 2.3 percent on the schools item.

10. One irony is that Mexico, which for 70 years had one of the more nationalist governments of the area, would appear to have in 1998 a citizenry less statist than that of neighboring states, which speaks strongly to the extent of the neoliberal reordering of the Mexican economy since 1982. (But see note 9.) A contrasting irony is that Chile, which had one of the strongest experiments with privatization of education via the use of educational vouchers under Augusto Pinochet, dictator from 1973 to 1990, exhibits in 1998 a citizenry that remains strongly supportive of public education.

11. In Mexico there appear to be two distinct types of services in the minds of respondents, so the concept of an "average service" is merely a heuristic to illustrate the point that Mexicans in mid-1998 seem to be less enamored of public-sector service provision than are Costa Ricans and Chileans. A *Wall Street Journal Americas* survey conducted in 1998 reports data for Mexico on identical items that are much more in accord with the Latin American averages. This would suggest that Mexico might not differ and that there might be only one dimension of attitudes about service provision. However, that data set underweights urban respondents, which may produce a more statist orientation. For a full exposition of the differences between the two data sets (Hewlett versus *Wall Street Journal Americas*) and why the Hewlett data set is to be preferred, see appendix D to this chapter.

12. The 14 countries surveyed encompass 95 percent of the population of Latin America.

13. Such an "average" is a hypothetical construct, which would be influenced by the particular service areas one chooses to ask about and the particular countries one samples as part of Latin

America. Given that the *Wall Street Journal Americas* sample covered 95 percent of the population of the region, an alternate choice of countries would not have influenced the results. An alternative array of services to be provided publicly or privately might have influenced the outcomes reported.

14. I can report only summaries of the *Wall Street Journal Americas* data, as all I have access to are published reports. No additional analyses are possible.

15. The preference of Chileans for public provision of services is a striking finding, given the dramatic process of privatization that occurred during the Pinochet years. In education, for example, Chile pursued experiments with vouchers for the purchase of private education that went far beyond those experienced elsewhere in the hemisphere. Partially as a consequence, private secondary-school enrollment increased from 24 percent to 42 percent between 1980 and 1990. Yet 68 percent of Chileans, in this survey, still claim to prefer the public provision of education. On the larger issue of reforming education in the Americas, see Burki et al., *Beyond the Washington Consensus*, chap. 5; and Daniel C. Levy and Claudio de Maura Castro, "Higher Education in Latin America and the Caribbean," Strategy Paper No. EDU-101, Education Unit, Sustainable Development Department, Interamerican Development Bank (Washington, D.C., 1997).

16. The scales are labeled *pubserve* (wherein the provision of water and schooling are the dominant items) and *priserve* (wherein air travel and television service are the dominant items). See appendix B.

17. While this proposition is empirically derived from preliminary analyses, it is consistent with the theoretical proposition, long advanced by students of inter-American relations, that U.S. influence in the hemisphere diminishes as proximity to the United States decreases. That is, U.S. influence (in this case, the well-known U.S. preference for the private provision of services) should be strongest in Mexico, next strongest in Central America and the Caribbean, considerably weaker in the northern Andean states, and weakest in Southern Cone countries. Such a hypothesis was seemingly contradicted over decades by Mexico's studied resistance to U.S. hegemony. But the Salinas de Gortari presidency seemed to capitulate to these long-term forces.

18. See, for example, Charles L. Davis and Kenneth M. Coleman, "Who Abstains? The Situational Meaning of Non-voting," *Social Science Quarterly* 64, no. 4 (1983): 764–76.

19. A common surrogate income scale, based on the number of light bulbs in the house of the respondent, was developed by Miguel Basáñez at MORI-Mexico, but it can be, and has been, applied productively across countries in this study. See item S4 in the Hewlett questionnaire (in appendix 2 to this book). However, only one dummy variable can be devised pertaining to employment; that item identifies those who are privately employed as independent professionals or business owners. That is from response category 02 to item S5.

20. See Levy and de Maura Castro, "Higher Education," 45; and Daniel C. Levy, *Higher Education and the State in Latin America: Private Challenges to Public Dominance* (Chicago: University of Chicago Press, 1986), 329.

21. See Timothy J. Steigenga and Kenneth M. Coleman, "Protestant Political Orientations and the Structure of Political Opportunity," *Polity* 27, no. 3 (1995): 465–82; and Timothy J. Steigenga, "Religion and Politics in Central America: The Religious Determinants of Political Activities and Beliefs in Costa Rica and Guatemala" (Ph.D. diss., University of North Carolina, Chapel Hill, 1996).

22. Beta weights are measured in terms of standard deviation units on a normalized variable. Since the normal curve has a mean of 0 and a standard deviation of ±1.0, variables transformed into normal curves can be compared in terms of standard deviation units from the mean.

23. Again, see appendix D.

24. See Anthony King, "Ideas, Institutions, and the Policies of Government: A Comparative Analysis," *British Journal of Political Science* 3, no. 4 (1973–74): 291, 409–23.

25. See Frederick C. Turner, *The Dynamic of Mexican Nationalism* (Chapel Hill: University of North Carolina Press, 1968).

26. See *Wall Street Journal Americas*, Mirror on the Americas Poll report, January 1998, 5.

27. However, the proximity explanation is only a partial one. Costa Rica, while closer to the United States physically, remains ideologically more distant from it than Chile would appear to be.

28. See Carlos Huneeus, *Los chilenos y la política: Cambio y continuidad en el autoritarismo* (Santiago: Centro de Estudios de la Realidad Contemporanea, Academia de Humanismo Cristiano, 1987), 120. Huneeus reports that in 1966, 32 percent of Chileans favored an economy based principally on private property, 21 percent an economy based principally on state property, and 40 percent a mixed economy, whereas in 1986 the preferences had shifted toward a mixed economy: 15 percent favored principally private property, 7 percent principally state property, and 54 percent mixed, the percentage of "don't knows" increasing from 7 to 24. The 1986 survey data, from late in the Pinochet era, may reflect some "social undesirability avoidance behavior" in the higher percentage of "don't knows": those Chileans who preferred statist solutions might have been answering "don't know" because of a context in which their preference was not approved by the state. Whatever the case, Chileans' answers are clearly biased toward a continuing role for the state in the economy— more so than one might expect in the United States. On a similar item in a 1999 *Wall Street Journal Americas* survey, 65 percent of U.S. respondents agreed strongly or agreed that "the government should leave economic activity to the private sector," whereas 53 percent of Chileans took such a position; 32 percent of the U.S. respondents agreed strongly with such a posture, but only 14 percent of Chileans agreed strongly.

29. Jorge Domínguez, "Free Politics and Free Markets in Latin America," *Journal of Democracy* 9, no. 4 (1998): 70–84.

30. Indicative of change in the thinking of the IFIs is Burki et al., *Beyond the Washington Consensus.* The IFIs now appear to be coming around to the view that in some respects, "strong states" are necessary to provide complements to market reforms.

31. See *Wall Street Journal Americas*, Mirror on the Americas Poll report, January 1998, 1.

32. The Venezuelan case is illustrative. Although the country has the second-longest run of elected civilian government in Latin America (after Costa Rica), the 1998 *Wall Street Journal Americas* survey showed Venezuelans to exhibit the third-lowest frequency of positive responses to an item regarding "how democratic our country is." Only Paraguayans and Guatemalans were more negative. The Venezuelans were also third least positive about their legislative body and fourth least positive about their police, but fourth most positive (58 percent giving positive answers) about their armed forces, which have made two unsuccessful coup attempts in the 1990s. The inability of Venezuelan democracy after four decades (1958–98) to deliver palpable economic benefits and to address economic inequality eroded public support to the point that Hugo Chavez, a former coup plotter, was elected president on December 6, 1998, with 56 percent of the vote. However, that same inability contributed to the reelection of President Rafael Caldera, once a Christian Democratic president (1958–63), who ran in 1993 as a populist and nationalist against the IFIs. Venezuelan citizens, frustrated with four decades of democracy, appear tempted in the 1990s to abandon either markets or democracy for those who promise visible economic "results."

33. The differences that exist within Latin American nations on privatization issues are profound, representing the kind of dissensus of which Charles Anderson wrote. The *Wall Street Journal Americas* report asked identical questions about 11 dimensions of service provision. In Latin America, the mean percentage (across 14 countries and 11 services) favoring public ownership was 48 percent, while in the United States the comparable mean was 26 percent. Clearly, the "average" distribution of public opinion on public versus private ownership issues in Latin America closely

approximates absolute dissensus (a 50 percent–50 percent split). In the United States it falls about halfway between consensus (100 percent versus 0 percent) and dissensus.

34. The phrase is that of Denis Goulet. The implication, following Maslovian psychology, is that until the material needs of human beings are fulfilled, their needs for self-actualization are not given full expression. The participatory opportunities that democracy affords may be secondary for the poor, but they may prove to be valued more highly once basic material needs are fulfilled.

Elsewhere in this volume, chapters by Clark and Seligson indicate that when democratic institutions appear to be focused on attaining widespread human welfare, as in Costa Rica, levels of support for democracy can be remarkably high, even among less-than-affluent populations.

Chapter 11: Chilean Citizens and Chilean Democracy

1. See Jack C. Plano and Milton Greenberg, *The American Political Dictionary* (Fort Worth, Tex.: Harcourt, Brace, Jovanovich, 1993), 9.

2. Robert A. Dahl, *Democracy and Its Critics* (New Haven: Yale University Press, 1989), 221.

3. Larry Diamond, Juan J. Linz, and Seymour Martin Lipset, eds., *Democracy in Developing Countries*, vol. 2, *Africa* (Boulder, Colo.: Lynne Rienner, 1988), xvi.

4. Francis Fukuyama, *The Great Disruption: Human Nature and the Reconstruction of Social Order* (New York: Free Press, 1999).

5. See Quintin Hoare and Geoffrey Nowell Smith, *Selections from the Prison Notebooks of Antonio Gramsci* (New York: International Publishers, 1971).

6. Arturo Valenzuela, *Political Brokers in Chile* (Durham, N.C.: Duke University Press, 1977), 171–74.

7. Seymour Martin Lipset and Stein Rokkan, "Cleavage Structure, Party Systems, and Voter Alignments: An Introduction," in *Party Systems and Voter Alignments: Cross-National Perspectives*, ed. Seymour Martin Lipset and Stein Rokkan (New York: Free Press, 1967). In this pathbreaking work, the authors explain the emergence of different political party alignments in western Europe, focusing on "cleavages" resulting from fundamental social and political conflicts associated with the national and industrial revolutions. They argued, in 1967, that European political party systems became "crystallized" around divisions such as center/periphery, church/state, agriculture/industry, and owners/workers.

8. This term and the resulting periodization of Chilean politics are developed by Timothy R. Scully in his *Rethinking the Center: Party Politics in Nineteenth and Twentieth Century Chile* (Stanford: Stanford University Press, 1992).

9. Carlos Huneeus, *Los chilenos y la política* (Santiago: CERC, 1987), 163, reported in Scully, *Rethinking the Center*, 200.

10. The 1998 data are the Chilean answers to question 27 of the questionnaire in appendix 2.

11. Reported in Arturo Valenzuela, *The Breakdown of Democratic Regimes: Chile* (Baltimore: Johns Hopkins University Press, 1978), 35.

12. Isabel Allende, "Pinochet without Hatred," *New York Times Magazine*, January 17, 1998, 27.

13. Ibid.

14. The causes of, experiences with, and reactions to cultures of political fear in Latin America are discussed in Juan E. Corradi, Patricia Weiss Fagen, and Manuel Antonio Garreton, eds., *Fear at the Edge: State Terror and Resistance in Latin America* (Berkeley: University of California Press, 1992).

15. Scully, *Rethinking the Center*, 185.

16. Ibid., 201.

17. The following argument is taken from Arturo Valenzuela, "Party Politics and the Crisis of

Presidentialism in Chile," in *The Failure of Presidential Democracy*, ed. Juan J. Linz and Arturo Valenzuela (Baltimore: Johns Hopkins University Press, 1994), 165–244.

18. Ibid., 221.

Chapter 12: Polls, Political Culture, and Democracy

1. Alan Knight, "México bronco, México manso: Una reflexión sobre la cultura cívica mexicana," *Política y Gobierno* 3, no. 1 (1996): 5–30.

2. Octavio Paz, *The Labyrinth of Solitude: Life and Thought in Mexico* (New York: Grove Press, 1961); Carlos Fuentes, *A New Time for Mexico* (London: Bloomsbury, 1997); Samuel Ramos, *Profile of Man and Culture in Mexico* (Austin: University of Texas Press, 1962); Joseph A. Kahl, *The Measurement of Modernism: A Study of Values in Brazil and Mexico* (Austin: University of Texas Press, 1974), 116.

3. Paz, *Labyrinth of Solitude*, 23, 78.

4. Glen C. Dealy, *The Public Man: An Interpretation of Latin American and Other Catholic Countries* (Amherst: University of Massachusetts Press, 1977); Howard J. Wiarda, "Toward a Framework for the Study of Political Change in the Iberic-Latin Tradition: The Corporative Model," *World Politics* 25, no. 2 (1973): 206–35. Needless to say, such stereotypes have influenced the foreign policy of the great powers (especially the United States) toward Latin America: Lars Schoultz, *Beneath the United States: A History of U.S. Policy toward Latin America* (Cambridge: Harvard University Press, 1998), 378–79.

5. As Paz notes; *Labyrinth of Solitude*, 122.

6. Deborah J. Yashar, *Demanding Democracy: Reform and Reaction in Costa Rica and Guatemala, 1870s–1950s* (Stanford: Stanford University Press, 1997), 5; John Booth and Mitchell A. Seligson, "Paths to Democracy and the Political Culture of Costa Rica, Mexico, and Nicaragua," in *Political Culture and Democracy in Developing Countries*, ed. Larry Diamond (Boulder, Colo.: Lynne Rienner, 1993), 113.

7. Seligson, "Costa Rican Exceptionalism," this volume, citing the 1996 Latinobarómetro survey.

8. Fuentes, *A New Time for Mexico*, 13.

9. For a sensible application of the "colonial legacy" argument, see Nils Jacobsen, *Mirages of Transition: The Peruvian Altiplano, 1780–1930* (Berkeley: University of California Press, 1993), 3–4.

10. Coleman, "Politics and Markets in Latin America," this volume.

11. Seligson, "Costa Rican Exceptionalism."

12. Aviva Chomsky, *West Indian Workers and the United Fruit Company in Costa Rica, 1870–1940* (Baton Rouge: Louisiana State University Press, 1996), 2–5, 259–60. Nicaragua's discursive "ladinización" similarly glossed over the republic's Indian population: Jeffrey L. Gould, *To Die in This Way: Nicaraguan Indians and the Myth of Mestizaje, 1880–1965* (Durham, N.C.: Duke University Press, 1998).

13. Alexander von Humboldt, *Political Essay on the Kingdom of New Spain*, ed. Mary Maples Dunn (Norman: University of Oklahoma Press, 1988), 64, 234. Humboldt's essay also contains (p. 58) a percipient warning against "pronouncing on the moral or intellectual dispositions of nations from which we are separated by . . . difference[s] in language, manners and customs."

14. Alan Knight, "Popular Culture and the Revolutionary State in Mexico, 1910–40," *Hispanic American Historical Review* 74, no. 3 (1994): 434–38.

15. Jeffrey W. Rubin, *Decentering the Regime: Ethnicity, Radicalism, and Democracy in Juchitán, Mexico* (Durham, N.C.: Duke University Press, 1997); Luis González, *San José de Gracia* (Austin: University of Texas Press, 1972); Paul Friedrich, *The Princes of Naranja: An Essay in Anthrohistorical Method* (Austin: University of Texas Press, 1986).

16. D. A. Brading, *The Origins of Mexican Nationalism* (Cambridge: Centre of Latin American Studies, 1985), 96.

17. Laura Nader, *Harmony Ideology: Justice and Control in a Zapotec Mountain Village* (Stanford: Stanford University Press, 1990), 275.

18. See, for example, the excellent analysis by Jennie Purnell, *Popular Movements and State Formation in Revolutionary Mexico: The Agraristas and Cristeros of Michoacán* (Durham, N.C.: Duke University Press, 1999).

19. Clifford Geertz, *The Interpretation of Cultures* (London: Fontana, 1973), 21.

20. Enrique Krauze, *Por una democraciá sin adjetivos* (Mexico City: Joaquín Mortiz, 1986).

21. Robert A. Dahl, *Polyarchy: Participation and Opposition* (New Haven: Yale University Press, 1971).

22. Samuel P. Huntington, *The Third Wave: Democratization in the Late Twentieth Century* (Norman: University of Oklahoma Press, 1991), 59–72.

23. Joe Foweraker and Todd Landman, *Citizenship Rights and Social Movements* (Oxford: Oxford University Press, 1997), 95–97.

24. Ibid., 111–15.

25. Charles Maier, "Democracy since the French Revolution," in *Democracy, The Unfinished Journey,* ed. John Dunn (Oxford: Oxford University Press, 1993), 130–32.

26. See Foweraker and Landman, *Citizenship Rights,* 95–96.

27. Daniel Dennet, *Darwin's Dangerous Idea* (London: Penguin, 1995), 338.

28. Geertz, *Interpretation of Cultures,* 4.

29. Neil J. Smelser, "Culture: Coherent or Incoherent," in *The Theory of Culture,* ed. Richard Münch and Neil J. Smelser (Berkeley: University of California Press, 1992), 4.

30. Ernest Barker, *National Character* (London: Methuen, 1948).

31. Larry Diamond, "Introduction: Political Culture and Democracy," in Diamond, *Political Culture and Democracy,* 8–9.

32. Ernest Gellner, *Anthropology and Politics* (Oxford: Blackwell, 1995), 21.

33. Stephen Welch, *The Concept of Political Culture* (Basingstoke: Macmillan, 1999), 69, citing Alfred Meyer.

34. Roderic Ai Camp, *Politics in Mexico* (New York: Oxford University Press, 1993), 62; Wayne Cornelius, "The Fear Vote Gives Way to the Punishment Vote," *Los Angeles Times,* July 9, 1997, B7.

35. Alan Knight, "Caciquismo and Political Culture in Mexico" (paper presented at the conference on Mexican political culture, Center for U.S.-Mexican Studies, University of California, San Diego, April 1998) (publication forthcoming).

36. Diamond, "Introduction," 8.

37. Eric J. Hobsbawm, *On History* (New York: The New Press, 1997), 207.

38. Camp, *Politics in Mexico,* 7.

39. *Visión latinoamericana de la democracia: Encuestas de opinión pública en México, Chile, y Costa Rica: Reporte final* (Hewlett/MORI, October 1998), section A, p. 38.

40. Jorge I. Domínguez and James A. McCann, *Democratizing Mexico: Public Opinion and Electoral Choices* (Baltimore: Johns Hopkins University Press, 1996), 67.

41. *Visión latinoamericana,* section A, p. 11.

42. Linda S. Stevenson and Mitchell A. Seligson, "Fading Memories of the Revolution: Is Stability Eroding in Mexico?" in *Polling For Democracy: Public Opinion and Political Liberalization in Mexico,* ed. Roderic Ai Camp (Wilmington, Del.: SR Books, 1996), 59–80.

43. Edwin Kemmerer, *Inflation and Revolution: Mexico's Experience of 1912–17* (Princeton: Princeton University Press, 1940).

44. The parallel was briefly revived in the 1980s, when Spain's transition to democracy was seen (by some) as a possible model for Mexico.

45. Gabriel A. Almond and Sidney Verba, *The Civic Culture: Political Attitudes and Democracy in Five Nations* (Boston: Little, Brown, 1965), 68–78; *Visión latinoamericana*, section A, p. 54.

46. Cf. Camp, *Mexican Politics*, 57.

47. Welch, *The Concept of Political Culture*, 76–77; a similar point is made by W. G. Runciman, *The Social Animal* (London: HarperCollins, 1998), 22.

48. Seligson, "Costa Rican Exceptionalism."

49. *Visión latinoamericana*, section A, p. 57.

50. Ibid., p. 69; cf. Domínguez and McCann, *Democratizing Mexico*, 29.

51. Seligson, "Costa Rican Exceptionalism."

52. James C. Scott, *Domination and the Arts of Resistance: Hidden Transcripts* (New Haven: Yale University Press, 1990).

53. *Visión latinoamericana*, section A, p. 10.

54. *Visión latinoamericana*, section A, p. 41.

55. Seligson, "Costa Rican Exceptionalism."

56. As demonstrated by the famous Milgram experiments: Barrington Moore, Jr., *Injustice: The Social Bases of Obedience and Revolt* (London: Macmillan, 1979), 94–96.

57. Diamond, "Introduction," 13.

58. Ronald Inglehart, *Culture Shift in Advanced Industrial Society* (Princeton: Princeton University Press, 1990); Francis Fukuyama, *Trust: The Social Virtues and the Creation of Prosperity* (London: Penguin, 1995).

59. Clark, "Costa Rica," this volume.

60. Edward C. Banfield, *The Moral Basis of a Backward Society* (New York: Free Press, 1958).

61. *Visión latinoamericana*, section A, p. 10.

62. Ibid., 66.

63. Ibid., 22.

64. Kahl, *Measurement of Modernism.*

65. Almond and Verba, *The Civic Culture.*

66. Aaron Wildavsky, *Culture and Social Theory* (New Brunswick, N.J.: Transaction, 1998).

67. Domínguez and McCann, *Democratizing Mexico*, 29.

68. Diamond, "Introduction," 11.

69. Adam Przeworski, *Democracy and the Market: Political and Economic Reforms in Eastern Europe and Latin America* (Cambridge: Cambridge University Press, 1991).

70. *Visión latinoamericana*, section A, p. 7.

71. Domínguez and McCann, *Democratizing Mexico*, 40.

72. Booth and Seligson, "Paths to Democracy," 115–22, 124.

73. Ibid., 128.

74. Domínguez and McCann, *Democratizing Mexico*, 43; compare Moreno, "Democracy and Mass Belief Systems in Latin America," this volume.

75. J. Samuel Valenzuela, "Democratic Consolidation in Post-transitional Settings: Notion, Process, and Facilitating Conditions," in *Issues in Democratic Consolidation: The New South American Democracies in Comparative Perspective*, ed. Scott Mainwaring, Guillermo O'Donnell, and J. Samuel Valenzuela (Notre Dame: University of Notre Dame Press, 1992).

76. Maier, "Democracy since the French Revolution," 146.

77. Yashar, *Demanding Democracy*, 20.

78. Maier, "Democracy since the French Revolution," 126.

79. Jeanne Kirkpatrick, "Dictators and Double Standards," *Commentary* 68 (November 1979): 34–45.

80. Knight, "México bronco."

81. Diamond, "Introduction," 3.

Contributors

Miguel Basáñez is president of Global Quality Research, Princeton, New Jersey, and MORI of Mexico. He has taught for many years at the Autonomous Technological Institute of Mexico. He is the author of numerous articles and essays on public opinion research in Mexico, and he coauthored, based on the World Values Survey, *Convergence in North America* (1995).

Roderic Ai Camp is the Philip M. McKenna Professor of the Pacific Rim at Claremont McKenna College. He has authored more than 20 books on Mexican politics, including a work on public opinion and democracy. He currently directs the Hewlett project Democracy through Mexican Lenses: Influential Trends through the Millennium.

Mary A. Clark is associate professor of political science and Latin American studies at the Roger Thayer Stone Center for Latin American Studies at Tulane University. She is the author of several articles and a forthcoming book on Latin America. She received her Ph.D. from the University of Wisconsin, and has engaged in field research in Costa Rican politics.

Kenneth M. Coleman has been a student of public opinion in Latin America for more than 30 years. He and colleague Charles Davis, who together have published numerous articles on Mexico, pioneered the analysis of survey research there. Coleman earned his Ph.D. at the University of North Carolina at Chapel Hill under the tutelage of the late John D. Martz.

Carlos Elordi is a Ph.D. candidate in political science at the University of Connecticut and a research assistant at MORI, London. His research interests center on methodology, applied statistics, and public opinion in Latin America.

Louis W. Goodman is professor and dean of the School of International Service at American University in Washington, D.C. He has written widely on prospects for development and on democracy-building in Latin America. He formerly directed the Latin America Program of the Woodrow Wilson Center for International Scholars, Smithsonian Institution.

Matthew T. Kenney is a Ph.D. candidate in political science at Tulane University. He has taught in Mexico City and Guadalajara, and he served as an election observer in the July 2000 presidential elections in Mexico. His dissertation is a comparative study of liberal values in Latin America and Western Europe.

Joseph L. Klesner is professor of political science at Kenyon College. His research has focused on Mexico's political transition and electoral politics in Mexico. His articles have appeared in *Comparative Politics, Mexican Studies/Estudios Mexicanos, Electoral Studies,* and the Center for Strategic and International Studies Mexican election series.

Alan Knight is professor of history of Latin America, director of the Latin American Center, and fellow of St. Anthony's College, Oxford. He formerly taught at the University of Texas, Austin. He is the author of numerous articles and essays on Mexican history and politics, as well as *US-Mexican Relations, 1910–40* (1987) and *The Mexican Revolution* (1986).

Alejandro Moreno received his Ph.D. in political science from the University of Michigan. He is professor of political science at the Autonomous Technological Institute of Mexico and director of public opinion research at *Reforma* in Mexico City. His book *Political Cleavages: Issues, Parties, and the Consolidation of Democracy* was published in 1999.

Pablo Parás is Director General of the Center of Public Opinion Studies and Associate Director of MORI of Mexico. He has been involved in survey research projects since 1991. He studied business administration and marketing at the Autonomous Technological Institute of Mexico, and received an M.A. in Latin American studies from Georgetown University.

Timothy J. Power is assistant professor and Director of the Graduate Program in Political Science at Florida International University. He is the author of *Elites, Institutions, and Democratization: The Political Right in Post-authoritarian Brazil* (2000) and is a contributing editor to the Library of Congress's *Handbook of Latin American Studies.*

Mitchell A. Seligson holds the Daniel H. Wallace Chair in Political Science at the University of Pittsburgh. He has conducted research on mass politics in Central America since his service there as a Peace Corps volunteer. His most recent book is *Development and Underdevelopment: The Political Economy of Global Inequality* (1998), coedited with John Pasé Smith.

Frederick C. Turner is professor of political science at the University of San Andrés in Victoria, Argentina. A former president of the World Association for Public Opinion Research, he has also served as vice president of the International Social Science Council in Paris. His most recent book is *Opinión pública y elecciones en América* (2000), coedited with Friedrich Welsch.
Accountability, political, 98–100, 104

Index

Instructions for Using CD-ROM

To install, open the window for your CD-ROM drive and double-click the "Setup" icon.

You will see a window that says "Welcome." Click "OK".

At the next window, click on the button which has a picture of a computer on it.

After successful installation, you will see a C:\window (C:\Windows\StartMenu\Programs\Democracy\SurveyProgram). Close this window, and you will see a message telling you that installation ended correctly.

Return to the window for the CD-ROM drive and open the folder called "Survey," then choose the "JDS" logo. This will open instructions for using the data set. When you click "OK," the data will automatically open.